Mick Jagger

Also by DAVIN SEAY

San Francisco Nights: The Psychedelic Music Trip 1965–1968
(with Gene Sculatti)
Stairway to Heaven: The Spiritual Roots of Rock 'n' Roll
The Wanderer: Dion's Story

MICK JAGGER

The Story Behind the Rolling Stone

by Davin Seay

A Birch Lane Press Book
Published by Carol Publishing Group

A Birch Lane Press Book
Published by Carol Publishing Group
Birch Lane Press is a registered trademark of Carol Communications, Inc.
Editorial Offices: 600 Madison Avenue, New York, N.Y. 10022
Sales and Distribution Offices: 120 Enterprise Avenue, Secaucus, N.J. 07094
In Canada: Canadian Manda Group, P.O. Box 920, Station U, Toronto, Ontario M8Z 5P9
Queries regarding rights and permissions should be addressed to Carol Publishing Group,
600 Madison Avenue, New York, N.Y. 10022

Carol Publishing Group books are available at a special discounts for bulk purchases, for
sales promotions, fund-raising, or educational purposes. Special editions can be created to
specifications. For details, contact Special Sales Department, Carol Publishing Group, 120
Enterprise Avenue, Secaucus, N.J. 07094

Manufactured in the United States of America
10 9 8 7 6 5 4 3 2 1

Library of Congress Cataloging-in-Publication Data

Seay, Davin.
    Mick Jagger : the story behind the Rolling Stone / by Davin Seay.
        p.   cm.
    "A Birch Lane Press book."
    ISBN 1-55972-192-8
    1. Jagger, Mick. 2. Rock musicians—England—Biography.
I. Title.
ML420.J22S4   1993
782.42166'092—dc20   93-23070
    [B]   CIP
                                                             MN

To Isaiah
Because heroes are hard to find

Contents

The Captain on the Burning Deck

Whether it's the instant global reach of their music, the astonishing sums of money they generate, or the millions of fans coming together for the rock-'n'-roll ritual, nothing matches the size, splendor, and surfeit of a Rolling Stones tour. The supergroup's 1990 Steel Wheels international extravaganza was no exception. The tour marshaled an array of high-tech hardware, supply trains, and support personnel that came together in a musical assault across three continents for 150 stadium-packing performances.

Steel Wheels was a crusade, dedicated to presenting the World's Greatest Rock 'n' Roll Band in the manner which their fans had come to expect. Listed on the Stones' payroll for this portable epiphany was a staff of over 150 specialists, technicians, grunts, and hangers-on. Included in the roll call: twenty-two caterers, ten carpenters, a credentials coordinator, an inflatables expert, a merchandising administrator, and fifty-five drivers to transport the troops in plushly appointed tour buses. Also on hand, should the excitement become simply overwhelming: a staff psychotherapist.

Steel Wheels advance men would arrive at concert sites months before a performance to determine, as the tour's official chroniclers put it, "the impact on the local infrastructure." Ten days before zero hour, a second, larger wave would deploy, erecting tents, installing phones, office trailers, food and medical facilities. At eight days and counting, eleven truckloads of scaffolding would arrive along with a crew of seventy-five scaffolders. By this time locally recruited labor and security guards would swell the ranks of workers to well over four hundred.

More often than not, the Stones' invasion would establish several beachheads at once, with the capacity to erect and dismantle up to four separate, thirty-ton stage sets in different cities at the same time, as the group leapfrogged from one concert to the next. As show time drew near, so too did thirty-eight lumbering, forty-five-foot Scania, Volvo, and Def rigs, disgorging the raw materials from which the Stones would forge their blazing spectacle.

The tools of their trade—guitars, drums, keyboards, microphones—accounted for a relatively small percentage of all that gross tonnage. The bulk consisted of the means to convey a sense of event: the miles of cable humming with 550,000 volts; the 270 bulkhead stage lights; the forty-foot inflatable sex dolls, held down against head winds by a gang of roadies; the ton of flash powder ignited each night to open the show and the 50,000 fireworks and 100,000 pounds of aerial shells that closed it in a dazzling display of pyrotechnics.

The Steel Wheels stage was wider than a football field, with a 130-foot tower topped by a federally mandated aircraft collision warning light. It was the largest transportable structure ever built.

At the center of this extraordinary setting was the main attraction, the five Rolling Stones. "On any given night," according to Keith Richards, "any rock-'n'-roll band can be the greatest in the world." And while that may be true, it's a fact that his band had more than their share of "given nights" on that sprawling stage as Steels Wheels rolled on. The fans, in short, went home happy. And the Stones went home immensely enriched.

"Satisfaction," "Ruby Tuesday," "Honky Tonk Woman," "Midnight Rambler," "Sympathy for the Devil," "Let's Spend the Night Together," "Jumpin' Jack Flash"—that's rock'n' roll. But more than a collection of jukebox staples, the music of the Rolling Stones has comprised a universal language, with riffs and refrains familiar around the world, for over thirty years. In a business where only the strongest, only the most ruthless and determined cling to their celebrity, the Rolling Stones have won their stardom at harrowing cost.

And it was the most famous Stone of all who took center stage. Mick Jagger's face is still among the most familiar of our time. His voice, with its salacious undertones, is instantly recognizable to millions. His persona is a model for countless aspiring rock 'n' rollers. And his history is an object lesson in audacity.

Yet behind it all, Jagger remains a private, profoundly secretive individual. "He's a chameleon," a friend has noted. "I think people find it difficult to accept multifaceted people," Jagger has disingenuously declared. "That you can be a person who has children, but yet you can go out and get wild and crazy and mad and drunk, and go on the road and be completely sober because that's what you have to be. . . . I don't find life quite so simple, that everyone's got these tiny personalities and that they can only behave in one kind of way."

Who, then, is Mick Jagger? Beyond his revolving repertoire of identities, you will find a personal history that is simple, telling, and often touching. Rooted in the restless aspirations of wartime England, Jagger's fiscal canniness and pragmatism are not only lifelong character traits: they are revealing clues to a middle-class London lad's career goals.

By the same token, his relentless quest for respectability sharply accents the same class barriers that early on defined his horizons. When eventually given the chance, he would cultivate liaisons with European nobility, such as his longtime financial advisor Prince Rupert Lowenstein, and trend-jumping jet-setters—most notably his first wife, Bianca Pérez Moreno de Macías.

Yet Jagger is anything but contrived in his craft. Rhythm and blues and the pinball lunacy of early rock 'n' roll called forth an astonishing gift in this quite conventional teenager. Because Mick Jagger possessed a natural affinity for black music, he had the ability to translate its spirit and substance to a whole new generation.

"We did the blues to turn people on," he remarked in a 1968 interview. "But why they should be turned on by us is unbelievably stupid. I mean, what's the point in listening to us do 'I'm a King Bee' when you can listen to Slim Harpo do it?"

The reason, of course, is that Mick and the Stones were polar opposites of their black blues heroes. White, English, astutely attuned to the ironies of the age, the Stones were positioned to reconnect rock 'n' roll to its roots. To say that the band reinterpreted the blues is to miss the point. The group *decoded* the music, primarily through Mick's infinitely malleable voice.

Underpinning Mick's artistry has also been a spirit of generosity and affability—a spirit too often lost in his gallery of poses and postures. It's a quality personified, fittingly enough, by his smile. When caught off guard, his lips, so often expressing arrogance or disdain, reveal a boyish enthusiasm. For a brief moment another Mick Jagger emerges—a youngster ardent over some blues treasure or taking his ease on the Brighton boardwalk.

Finally, the most intriguing question remains: What happens when an average guy becomes an icon of his era? It's in the answer to that question that one can understand the central theme of Mick's life. Fame is rarely kind, and rock-'n'-roll stardom, predicated on bad attitudes and the cult of eternal youth, is especially cruel. Given the choice of flaming out or facing old age, most rockers delay the decision until it simply overtakes them. The sagas of Jim Morrison, Janis Joplin, and Jimi Hendrix may seem tragic and truncated, but by the logic of the rock lifestyle, they were the lucky ones. "Hope I die before I get old," howled the Who, underscoring the *real* sin: not leaving behind a good-looking corpse.

No one is more aware of that ruinous paradox than the Rolling Stones. So famous, so fast, the advance of years has seemed, on them, particularly unseemly. Wrinkles and receding hairlines not only beg the question of how long can they keep it up but diminish the chances for a graceful exit. After years of insisting that there was no point in continuing to make the music past age thirty, Keith Richards has lately been heard to ask what's wrong with fifty-year-old men playing the game.

It's the special grace, the cool genius of Mick Jagger that he has, more than most, dodged the alternatives of his profession. Where others have failed he has, to a remarkable degree, preserved both his relevance and his dignity.

Which is hardly the same as saying that Mick is unfamiliar with the whims of fame. "High and dry," he sang in the 1967 ditty of the same name, "well, I'm up here with no warning." Jagger has indeed been up there, on more than one occasion: under the lights of Altamont, mouthing hippie platitudes while Hell's Angels beat bystanders with pool cues; solemnly intoning Shelley at a Hyde Park concert to explain away the death of his drug-addled bandmate Brian Jones; insisting, at one of the group's periodic nadirs, that "it's only rock 'n' roll but I like it," when it was neither rock nor the least bit likeable.

But if being caught out is the price of prestige, then surviving must certainly be the best revenge. Jagger has survived, and one need look no further than his lifelong partner and occasional bête noir, Keith Richards, to appreciate the accomplishment.

Richards's early image of jug-eared exuberance, exemplified in his overamped guitar riffs, was an appealing counterpoint to Jagger's own sexuality. But over the years, Richards's face has become a road map of the band's tortuous journey to stardom. By the time Steel Wheels rolled around, Richards's visage was shocking in its total collapse. His stumbling stance and no-one-home stare makes it clear that Keith isn't coming back. Rock has made him old before his time.

Jagger, by comparison, presents the persona of vigorous late middle age. He takes great pains to maintain peak fitness, echoing his upbringing as the son of a physical education instructor. Anyone who, at nearly fifty, could prance, strut, and often sprint across the vast Steel Wheels stage for the better part of two hours is obviously fueled by something more than the regular rock diet of Benzedrine and Jack Daniels. Far too practical, too vain, to succumb to the fate of his partner, Jagger has turned the corner on growing old. It is, perhaps, his most impressive feat of self-invention.

Today, after thirty years in the grip of celebrity, Mick Jagger is more than ever firmly in control of his personal and professional destiny. His early incarnation as a dissolute dandy has been replaced by the rock-'n'-roll equivalent of the self-starting entrepreneur. "Let's work!" he cheerfully urged in a song of the same name from his failed 1985 debut solo album.

Jagger remains dedicated to the quality of his output. While his recent solo effort, 1993's *Wandering Spirit*, may be familiar in its studied decadence and casual pilfering of black idioms, it is still a showcase for his unique brand of showmanship, as sly and subversive as ever. "It means a lot to me," he insists, "playing and singing. . . . I write all the time. And you have to sing every day too, so you can build up to being, you know, Amazingly Brilliant in the end."

Critical to his appeal, of course, is the desire of ordinary folk to live his life, specifically his love life. Yet Jagger's romantic entanglements expose a man as entranced by his own images and illusions as any of his fans. Chrissie Shrimpton, the canny waif of Carnaby Street; Marianne Faithfull, the dewy convent candidate; Bianca, Jagger's icy alter ego; and Jerry Hall, the long-legged Lone Star gold digger who would raise his family—all played parts in Jagger's narcissistic passion play. And all, finally, would fall short in fulfilling the role of consort to the prince.

For all its trappings of bedroom farce and centerfold fantasy, Jagger's search for a woman worthy of his fame has left a trail of broken hearts, and none more battered than his own. Insularity breeds isolation, leaving the luster of his legend as Mick's singular comfort.

His legend now takes a variety of forms: his globe-trotting lifestyle, his fabulous riches, his strategies against old age and obsolescence. But the near-seamless merging of man and myth was perhaps most dazzlingly displayed in a unique documentary film of the Steel Wheels tour.

Rolling Stones at the Max was shot in the futuristic IMAX format, with film twice the size of ordinary celluloid and a resulting image a full five stories high. But it isn't the technical specs, the scope and stunning detail of the IMAX process that makes *Rolling Stones at the Max* so revealing. It's the undeniable fact that the image of Mick Jagger towering a hundred feet high seems perfectly proportioned to the man. Larger than life, Jagger pulls off a feat of high-tech showmanship with the consummate ego and innate good nature that have always been part of him, leaving far below that middle-class kid of middling prospects from the dreary fringes of London.

O N E

The Star of Fame

Bill Wyman remembers. The golem-faced bassist for the Rolling Stones remembers *everything*: singles charted, gates tallied, groupies groped, rooms ransacked—the numbing minutiae of the whole super-star routine. For Bill Wyman, the rise of the Rolling Stones is measured in statistics and session sheets, itineraries and collected clippings.

One of the things Bill Wyman well remembers is the freezing London winter of 1962. Three teenagers had taken a flat together that dreary year, a trio of pasty layabouts pooling their poverty, playing the occasional pub date, and dreaming of nothing that could have prepared them for the eventual reality. Wyman can see their faces still, unseamed and eager.

Mick Jagger, Keith Richards, and Brian Jones were calling them-selves the Rollin' Stones. It seemed a dicey proposition to Wyman. After all, he was married and had a real job, clerking at Dupont's on Penge High Street, along with weekend gigs for his band, the Cliftons, playing youth clubs and church halls in Greenwich and Lower Sydenham for two quid a night. If not respectable, at least he was presentable and not given to hand-to-mouth living and bohemian excess.

But it was the music that brought him back—that collection of scratchy sides the roommates played over and over until something in Wyman's stolid soul rose up and rattled at the signifying moans of Jimmy Reed, Howlin' Wolf, and Elmore James. He took to hanging around the Edith Grove dive, soaking up the sounds and watching with an impassive stare.

He can still feel the chill of those frigid nights they sat round the kitchen table, bored and broke, with Muddy Waters muttering his Delta incantations on the hi-fi. Someone would fry up the last of the potatoes, stolen fresh that morning from the corner store, and the smell of rancid fat would hang in the air on wreaths of stale cigarette smoke.

And it was on such a mildewed evening, just before Christmas 1962, that Judy had first peered into the future. Judy Credland was the druggist who lived downstairs from the boys' walk-up and who occasionally slipped them a jar of instant coffee and sometimes something more.

She fancied herself a palm reader. For a lark that night she took Mick's hand in her own and traced the lines etched in his palm. She stared and blinked and looked up. "You've got the Star of Fame," she whispered, as if she could really see the end from the beginning. "It's all there."

And Mick with a frightened flutter grabbed back his hand, while the others laughed and scrounged through the ashtray for serviceable butts.

The circumstances of Mick Jagger's birth and breeding suggest a life predestined to pedestrian unraveling. He was born on a Monday, July 26, 1943. On that date, half a world away, General Douglas MacArthur launched the long-awaited Allied offensive in the Pacific. The Eighth Army entered Palermo, and the Russians had gained the upper hand over Hitler's hordes at the Battle of Kursk. The outcome of World War II now seemed certain.

It was a sense of cautious optimism that found its way onto the hit parade. Earlier that year, Kay Kyser had rallied the troops with his rousing rendition of "Praise the Lord and Pass the Ammunition," while springtime had bloomed a little brighter with Vaughn Monroe's poignant "When the Lights Go On Again (All Over the World)." By the summer of Mick's uneventful arrival, the number-one song in the free world was "As Time Goes By" intoned by Rudy Vallee.

Joe and Eva Jagger were a trim, tidy couple and from all outward appearances, contentedly conventional. Basil Fanshawe "Joe" Jagger had married Eva Mary Scutts three years before in a modest ceremony followed by a reception at Coneybeare Hall in the town of Dartford. The couple had set up house among the precise semi-detached rows of Denver Street, just across from a laundry in Dartford, where orchards and fields had only recently been swallowed up in London's suburban sprawl. There were, in fact, still apple trees in the Jagger family's small, walled backyard. This was County Kent, "The Garden of England," a place now given over to the uniform unfolding of middle-class prosperity and the nation's desire for order.

A pinched and dour Northerner from the fens of Lancashire, Joe Jagger had a self-sufficiency that found expression in his careful grooming. Slight and wiry, balding and bantam-weight, he was a physical education instructor at a local secondary school, a scholar of athletics, in fact, and a pioneer of British basketball. His was a solid (grounding in that tenet) of empire-building—an unshakable faith in the benefit of sports. The crisp white shorts and deep knee bends, the whistle, clipboard, and frosty breath on a winter playing field—the little man embraced the beloved traditions and all their attendant rectitude.

It's an odd boy that doesn't like sports, so the old English expression goes. And young Michael Jagger was by no means an odd boy. The earliest photos show an earnest, robust child—happy, guileless, safe in the embrace of hearth and home. He wears gym clothes, at age eight, in a photo of the Dartford Grammar School basketball club, his body gangly, his head too large, his features unfinished. Traces of the face we know can be seen in the mouth and lips parted in that wide and winning smile.

Joe and Eva's memories of their firstborn are also locked in simpler times. "He could have been a great athlete," muses a wistful Joe. "He was excellent at basketball and cricket, but he didn't want to be tied down with all the practice. He rebelled against that kind of prestige." It's a telling turn of phrase, that precocious kicking at convention and its attendant rewards.

"Once," remembers Eva, "we were walking down the beach, when he knocked down every single sand castle we came across." She laughs, as much for remembering herself, the nervous young mother, as for the faded image of her firstborn.

"We called him Mike," says his brother, Chris Jagger, born four years later. "He hated the name Mick. I only used it when I was teasing him."

Taken together, the family memories make up a scant scrapbook, faded by fond handling, casting back to a life captured in holiday postcards and washed-out snapshots. They are the recollections of people at a loss to explain the extraordinary events that soon overtook them.

Mick's own memories reflect the unperturbed indolence of a happy childhood. "My mum was very working-class," he allows, "my father bourgeois . . . so I came from somewhere in between. Neither one or the other. I don't think I was a popular kid, but then I wasn't particularly unpopular. Truthfully, I can't remember too much about those days. I was just an ordinary, rebellious, studious, hardworking kid."

He was also a kid whose ambitions were evident from a very early age. Brother Chris recalls, "As far back as I can remember, he said the thing he wanted most was to be rich."

Beyond the emotional boundaries that bordered their lives, another story can be faintly traced. It is the story of a woman tightly bound by the strictures of class and status, of her uneasy alliance with a man of rigid habits, and most importantly, the story of their son, caught between the two of them.

The currents of Eva's life ran deeper than her husband's, back to Australia, where she was born and raised, finally coming to England as a teenager. She was "a lovely girl with real golden hair, a slim figure," recalls her friend and neighbor Elsa Smith, who remembers also, "the blue eyes that smile when she talks."

Elsa and Eva shared the same boyfriends until Eva met Joe and began a resolute quest for bourgeois respectability that would, she fervently hoped, erase the lower-class stigma of her Aussie roots. The Dartford house, with its pebbled walls and French windows opening to the garden where young Mike and Chris swung from the apple trees, was immaculate. Eva's reputation for fastidiousness was matched by Joe's stiff and unyielding regimens. Neighbors recall a yard laid out with cricket pitches, dumbbells, and other sporting accoutrements. Household order was maintained by a carefully administered system of punishment and reward. "I was brought up in a very protected environment," Mick has said, and it was an equilibrium he did nothing to upset.

"I always thought he was a bit of a mother's boy," recounts John Spinks, one of Mick's earliest playmates.

"He did everything he was told at home." Others recall mandatory daily exercise routines, push-ups, weight lifting, and laps around the garden before Joe allowed the youngster out to play.

It's not hard to imagine the family's subtle, mutually reinforced taboos against unseemly displays and emotional outbursts—precisely the extravagant expressions upon which Mick would later build his career.

"You have to remember that part of the hero image is making it from the bottom," Mick asserts. "It's more of a hang-up making it if you're from the bourgeoisie, because if you're from the bottom you've got nothing to lose." It seems likely that Mick found a kindred spirit in Eva, for whom British propriety had to be carefully emulated rather than simply learned. Everyone agrees she kept a spotless home, yet something of her unruly Australian roots did survive the tidy streets of Dartford and the tyrannical dictates of her husband, and she passed that something on to her son.

Eva was "fun," her friends would say, and "lively" and "well liked," and even her determination to find a place in the British class system speaks of a spirited woman. She was unwilling to accept the implied inferiority of her colonial upbringing and set about to keep up appearances.

What she imparted to her son in the language of mother and child was a hint of life's secret possibilities. "What he had that we didn't," recounts schoolmate Peter Keir, "was a wider view of things." "He gave the idea," recalls another chum, Robert Wallis, "that he'd sooner be somewhere else than with us, doing far more glamorous things." "You couldn't help being aware of Mick," agrees Ian Harris, one of his teachers at Dartford Grammar School, "because he seemed alive, where the other kids would just sink down in their chairs."

There's a curious contradiction that runs through accounts of Mick's early years, alternating imagery of robust insubordination and a cameleonlike ability to fade into the scenery. "He was an India rubber character, really," says John Spinks. "He could bend any way to stay out of trouble." "He was so deliberately insulting," Dr. Bennett, a teacher at Dartford Grammar School, recalls of a particular incident, "that I simply knocked him down." "Mike was already looking like a useful cricketer," another teacher, Ken Llewellyn, recounts. "If I remember him at all, it's running in from the play-ground with both knees grazed and a great big smile on his face."

"I just couldn't take to games," says Mick himself. "All that running around for no real reason seemed a waste of time."

Revised recollections aside, the impression Joe and Eva's oldest boy left on his peers and superiors is fleeting and formless. Little Mike Jagger hardly cut a commanding figure as a scholar, an athlete, or even a fledgling reprobate. His infractions were minor, most often having to do with school dress codes. "He didn't wear anything really outrageous," classmate Peter Keir recounts, "just an exaggerated version of what was allowable."

The composite that emerges coheres only in the context of his family life—delicately balanced between the subconscious pull of his spirited mother with her sun-dazzled roots and the ceaseless, stead-fast self-control of his father. It's a dynamic glimpsed between all the glib quotes and guarded interviews of his public life. It's a conflict that would express itself in Jagger's ever-nimble dance between passion and pragmatism. It's a paradox that would come to define the man, his music, and his impact on a generation.

T W O

The Mimic

It's the winter of 1959 and fifteen-year-old Mike sits huddled before a battered tape recorder in the cramped back bedroom of his friend and schoolmate Dick Taylor. Watching anxiously in the late afternoon shadows as Mike hits the play switch are Bob Beckwith and Alan Etherington, two more friends in their final year at Dartford Grammar.

Together the foursome have been banging out ragged renditions of American blues, R & B, and rock 'n' roll for several months now, with Mike as the group's vocalist. Their hazy notions of forming a band are as much for the tantalizing possibility of meeting girls as for any musical ambitions, real or imagined. They've called themselves, with salacious whimsy, Little Boy Blue & the Blue Boys. No dream of stardom looms beyond these lazy afternoons, loud and fun and annoying to adults.

At this particular moment, however, the fledgling quartet's prospects are already in jeopardy. A week before, Little Boy Blue himself had been straining through a set of sweaty calisthenics at the school gym. Caught off balance in the middle of a full frontal somersault, he slipped, fell, and, catching his tongue between his front teeth, neatly snipped off its tip. Drooling blood and howling with pain, he was sent home to recover, spending several days in swollen silence.

Returning to rehearsal sessions at the Taylors' Bexleyheath home, Mike worried that the accident had ruined his singing voice. With Taylor on a secondhand drum kit inherited from his grandfather, Beckwith on a guitar plugged into a six-watt amp the size of a cigarette pack, and Etherington rattling a set of souvenir maracas, Mike sat on the bed facing the old recorder. The group belted out a version of Chuck Berry's "Around and Around."

They listen now as the song is played back, straining to catch some nuance behind the static and distortion. "Well," Mike asks tentatively after the last fuzzy notes fade, "what do you think?" There is a long pause before Beckwith allows that, yes, maybe there *is* something different about Mike's vocals, a slight slur, a sibilant stutter that wasn't there before.

Taylor agrees. There's a drawl to the lyrics now, a drawn-out diction that reminds him of, well, a Negro. "That's it," chimes in Etherington. "You've got a lazy tongue action. You can't sharpen your consonants. Your voice is . . . blacker."

After all, the mishap makes no difference to the group's professional prospects. By the end of the year Little Boy Blue & the Blue Boys have disappeared, a schoolboy lark never heard by anyone save Dick Taylor's mother.

"She dug Mick right from the start," recounts Taylor, who would later serve stints in a nascent Rolling Stones along with their early rivals, the Pretty Things. "She always told him he'd got something special."

Mrs. Taylor recalls it all a bit differently. "We used to sit in the next room and crease up with laughter. I didn't dream they were serious."

But there *was* something serious, and special, about the young white English boy's innate affinity for the blues. Almost from the beginning he had an instinctive understanding of its essence and urgency. In the years to come, Bruce Springsteen, among many, would point to the Rolling Stones as his first exposure to the rollicking rhythms of Chuck Berry. From Aerosmith to the Black Crowes to a hundred shaggy garage bands pounding out "Mona," "Down the Road Apiece," or "Little Red Rooster," the line of descent is clear: out of the Delta, the bayous, and the red-light districts of Chicago, across the ocean to Dick Taylor's bedroom, and from there, out across the planet. Little wonder the story of the blunted tongue took on such mythic proportions.

Mick's formative years were marked by a talent, charisma, and audacity glaring in their utter absence. Yet there *was* one youthful trait that unequivocally expressed his uniqueness, virtually from the cradle.

"Michael could have been a very good impersonator if he wanted to," asserts Eva. "He could probably have made a living at it. Ever since he was eleven or so, he had this knack of listening to hit songs over the wireless just a few times and then he'd stand up and sing them over just like the originals. He was so serious about it. . . . When he imitated something, it had to be got off just right."

Mick's burgeoning musical ambitions were hardly met with approval by his father. "My father was bloody awful," Mick recalls. "He was a schoolteacher. I mean, they're not known for their libertarianism. I wanted to be a musician—it was so obvious, you know—and he just didn't want me to be."

Eva was another matter. She recalls her son standing in front of the radio, singing along to "La Paloma" or "Rancho Grande," spewing a stream of nonsense Spanish. It's a picture conjured up by Taylor as well: one of the first songs aped by the Blue Boys was Richie Valens's "La Bamba."

"Mick used to come out with this stream of words that sounded just like Spanish," says Taylor with a smile. "He'd just make them up as he went along."

"I've never known a youngster with such an analytical approach to things," says Joe Jagger. "If he copied a song, he copied it slavishly, every note. He was able to capture the song exactly."

The music that young Mike was getting just right reflected a spectrum of sounds and styles that gave the British music scene in the fifties its curious catch-all feel. American crooners and white-bread rhythm-and-blues pretenders, anachronistic vestiges of the Big Band era, novelty hits from the Continent and South America, traditional jazz, ersatz country, ragtime blues: it was a varied hit parade that aptly represented England's lack of musical identity. Chris Barber, Kenny Ball, Acker Bilk—these and other actual English attractions were little more than hoked-up and watered-down versions of Dixieland minstrels, with their bowler hats, plaid waistcoats, and wah-wah trumpets.

But for Mick, all this assorted kitsch brought out that singular skill at mimicry that would become, in time, the basis for his brilliant blues interpretations. "When I was very, very young," he says, "I used to listen to everything from the BBC to Radio Luxembourg. Everyone was dreaming about America. The whole American dream was in vogue then."

Skiffle, a washboard-and-gut-bucket mix of jazz, folk, and ragtime, had swept Britain in the early fifties and brought with it the first faint savor of the blues. It was a homemade sound epitomized by Lonnie Donnegan's sprightly 1956 hit "Rock Island Line," and Mick's affinity for skiffle harked back to his membership in various jazz clubs at school. "There was traditional jazz and skiffle," he explains. "People tend to forget how enormous that was. I was in a load of skiffle groups and these groups also played rock-'n'-roll numbers. English rock 'n' roll really started with skiffle groups."

Marked by syncopated rhythms, lopsided bass lines, and rollicking, full-tilt guitar riffs, skiffle inevitably led the fledgling singer to the next step in pop music evolution—the black blues and white hillbilly racket that had recently come together in the electrifying hybrid called rock 'n' roll.

Bill Haley and the Comets were the first rockers to shake up England's scene with their 1955 string of frantic, up-tempoed hits: "Rock Around the Clock," "See You Later, Alligator," "Razzle Dazzle," and others. The group toured the UK a year later, yet Mick was left decidedly less impressed than his countrymen. "I wasn't particularly fond of Elvis or Bill Haley," he recalls. "They were very good but for some reason they didn't appeal to me."

More seductive were the raw sounds of such early rock masters as Little Richard and Jerry Lee Lewis. Haley, Presley, and their ilk were already, it seems, one step removed from the musical source Mick instinctively sought. From rock 'n' roll he proceeded directly to the reservoir of rhythm and blues, and from there, deeper still, to the fountainhead of the blues.

"I was crazy over Chuck Berry, Bo Diddley, Muddy Waters, and Fats Domino," he enthuses, not knowing, he adds, "what it meant, just that it was beautiful. My father used to call it 'jungle music' and I used to say, 'Yeah, that's right—jungle music.' That's a very good description. Every time I heard it, I just wanted to hear more. It seemed like the most real thing I had ever known. I became interested in the blues when I found out that it was much as existed. It was never played on the radio and, if it was, it was only by accident. I subsequently became aware that Big Bill Broonzy was a blues singer and Muddy Waters was also a blues singer and they were all really the same. It didn't matter. There were no divisions and I'd realized that by the time I was fifteen."

Mike and his mates focused on finding those rare recordings with the ardent determination only teens can muster. It was Taylor who had actually introduced Mike to the most exotic strains in the blues hothouse, playing him a well-worn collection of scratchy records that included Jimmy Reed, Howlin' Wolf, and Elmore James. The pair were soon making weekly pilgrimages to London and the import record shops on Charing Cross Road, rifling through the stacks for ever more obscure waxings on such exotic labels as Okeh, Chess, Roulette, and Imperial.

Taylor's rudimentary instrumental abilities and Jagger's uncanny knack for mimicry made the next step inevitable. With Etherington and Beckwith as game, if slightly bemused, recruits, Little Boy Blue & the Blue Boys were born and nurtured on renditions of "Susie Q," "Good Morning, Little School Girl," and "Shame, Shame, Shame." They were songs that celebrated appetites and experiences far beyond the scope of these virginal aficionados, a fact which hindered them not at all. They knew exactly what the music and its magnetism were really all about. "Basically the thing at that period was that you used to just try and find girls that would screw," Jagger confesses. "I was very emotional at the time . . . always overdramatizing situations."

It was an intriguing recipe: libidinous music, a penchant for the melodramatic, and the diction of an actual black. All Mike & Co. needed was a venue, an audience, and the slightest excuse to take their obsession to the next level.

That excuse would emerge sooner than the fledgling musicians believed possible. Their occasional record-hunting forays to London had brought them onto the outer fringes of what was proving to be a tiny but thriving British blues scene. It was centered around a clutch of old hands who had turned their appreciation for the music into a going concern. The catalyst was Chris Barber, whose traditional jazz band had become one of the most popular ensembles in the country. As part of the group's live show, Barber would feature a blues segment which spotlighted veteran musician and musicologist Alexis Korner on electric guitar along with Cyril Davies on harmonica. The

duo eventually formed their own aggregate, commonly acknowledged as the nation's first professional blues practitioners. Dubbed
Blues Incorporated, the group would serve as a launching pad for
many of the kingdom's premier blues and R & B performers, including Keith Richards, Brian Jones, Stones drummer Charlie Watts, and
Mick himself.

Giorgio Gomelski, pioneering promoter and the Rolling Stones'
earliest booster, remembers it this way: "The jazz people, who *should*
have been on our side, were, except for a very few, against us because
they thought we were rock 'n' roll. By the beginning of the sixties,
attendance was going down in jazz clubs because everyone had
jumped on the 'trad' bandwagon. The quality was so plastic. . . . So
we had to go back to something authentic, which is always what
happens in these things. . . . The blues were authentic. In 1959,
1960, there were twenty people in the whole of London who were
interested in the blues."

It was an interest that would soon grow with the emergence of a
cult of earnest acolytes pursuing the blues grail. Recalls Chris Barber:
"I've a feeling that to a certain extent the blues message, the way it's
presented, seemed more close to people's consciousness than the
white American rock 'n' roll which was stolen from it. Maybe it was
more direct and down to earth and they were looking for something
not tricked up with million-dollar suits."

It was, finally, a process of reaching a creative critical mass, an
aptitude and awareness that would ignite a musical revolution. For
the adolescent Mike Jagger, fresh out of primary school and well on
his way to some form of middle-class respectability, the moment had
almost arrived. All that was missing was the event that would bring
the smoldering spark to life.

T H R E E

Brian and Keith

Nowhere is the slapdash serendipity of rock 'n' roll more evident than in the accidental alignments that have produced the music's great songwriting teams. The Beatles' psychodrama-set-to-music played the quirks and penchants of Lennon and McCartney brilliantly off each other, producing a dazzling balancing act that defined their collaboration. More than a musical marriage, it was often a soundtrack for hand-to-hand combat, lovingly fought.

For the Rolling Stones, personality clashes yielded some of the most memorable music of the era. The writing partnership of Jagger and Richards was the exuberant outgrowth of an improbable friendship—a do-or-die pact between two local boys who would, in time, treat one another with the bitchy regard of an old, and overly familiar, couple.

But there was a third player in the early episodes of the Stones' hard-core soap opera. Brian Jones's influence, creative and destructive, lit a fire under the fledgling group. Drugs, genius, and narcissistic romance eventually consumed Jones and left Richards badly scorched. In the end, it was Mick who would make it through, wiser for having witnessed the harrowing descent of his partners.

"The triangular flow of energy between Brian, Mick, and myself was the thing the Stones ran on," Richards recalls. "It was this conflict and interchange of allegiances which was the basic emotional engine of the Stones."

During the heady early days of their performing career, the songs would cascade off the stage. With the grim-visaged rhythm section of Watts and Wyman looking on, Mick, Keith, and Brian fed off each other in a frenzy of invention, showmanship, and sheer nerve. It was music-making history.

It was a history that began with a music-making partnership. A photo of the 1954 class of Wentworth County Primary School captures the earliest days of that friendship. Eleven-year-old Mike and Keith are sitting cross-legged in the first row. The faces, with their famous protuberances, are instantly recognizable: Mick's malleable mouth between a cushion of baby fat cheeks, Keith's jug ears poking out beneath a jauntily angled school cap.

"Keith and I went to school together," Mick would later remember. "We lived in the same block." Keith's home was, in fact, two blocks from the Jaggers' Denver Road house. "We weren't great friends but we knew each other. He used to dress in a cowboy outfit, with holsters and a hat, and he had these big ears that stuck out. I distinctly remember this conversation I had with Keith. I asked him what he wanted to do when he grew up. He said he wanted to be like Roy Rogers and play guitar."

The fact that they had even a nodding aquaintance points to the shifting rules of class mingling that took hold in England after the war. From the upwardly mobile outlook of the Jaggers, Keith Richards came from the wrong side of the tracks.

Keith was born in the winter of 1943, at the Livingstone Hospital in East Hill. Mick had arrived here too, five months before. The hospital was located in the midst of what had become known in the waning years of the war as the Graveyard, for the near-constant German aerial bombardments that nightly rained shrapnel on the beleaguered neighborhood. Keith's birth was attended by just such a raid, the beginning of what would prove a lifetime of narrow escapes. Five months later, when mother and child had been evacuated to escape Hitler's V-1 rockets, one of the silent killers landed on their house, hurling "a great big brick through the cot" of her only child, Doris Richards recalls.

Doris and Bert Richards had brought their only son into a world verging on unconditional victory over fascism. They would face another challenge in the years to follow. The strictures of class and poverty that defined their lives would stand in marked contrast to the relative security of the sternly middle-class Jaggers, leaving, in turn, markedly different imprints on their offspring.

Hailing from a large working class family from Walthamstow in northeast London, Bert worked long hours as a foreman in a light bulb factory. Most of his meager wages went to providing his family with the strictly rationed essentials parceled out in the postwar economy. Abstemious, tightly wound, Bert struggled for simple survival, and the effort scarred both the man and his marriage: he would rise at 5 A.M. only to return, spent and sullen, at 6 P.M. to pass the evening in an exhausted silence. His wife suffered the lack of love and, by all accounts, the couple were barely on speaking terms at the time of Keith's birth. It was a rare moment of happiness in a union that would not survive his teenage years.

As with Eva and Joe Jagger, Bert and Doris each embued their son with different and conflicting characteristics. But while Joe was around to enforce Mick's innate caution and conformity, there was nothing in Keith's early years to counterbalance the unconventional influence of his mother. "My mother's father, Theodore Augustus Dupree, he was a complete freak," Richards recounts. "He used to have a dance band in the thirties, played fiddle, sax, and guitar. The coolest old coot you could ever meet. My mother's family was all very artistic, all musicians, actresses. I come from a weird mixture. Very stern on one side and very frivolous, gay, artistic on the other." Under the eccentric tutelage of his grandfather "Gus" Dupree, the youngster was introduced to bawdy British musical hall, B-grade American cinema, and life on the edge. "He was one of those cats who could always con what he wanted," Keith says.

At the age of eleven, Keith was passed by for the grammar school education that was considered the fast track for brighter and more motivated students. He was placed instead at Dartford Technical College, which would provide a career in the trades. It was a tough, unsparing place, where fistfights and physical abuse led the thin, gawky youngster to skip classes on a regular basis. Left behind to repeat a year, Keith found the only bright spot in a life preordained to grinding poverty was a stint in the school choir. Encouraged by the choirmaster, Keith became part of a trio that, as winners in various interschool competitions, would sing regularly at London's Royal

Festival Hall. On one luminous occasion they performed the "Hallelujah Chorus" for the young Queen Elizabeth II on her coronation.

But it would take more than Handel to rein in the boy. Thrown out of the choir program, rapidly losing ground in school, he would turn to what was becoming his primary obsession, rock 'n' roll.

It was his colorful grandfather Gus who encouraged the boy's nascent musical abilities, introducing him to the guitar and teaching him the basics of picking and chording. For his fifteenth birthday he was given a guitar by his mother and began to work out the rudiments of the wild new sound emanating from across the Atlantic. "The music from *The Blackboard Jungle*—'Rock Around the Clock'—hit first," he explains. "Not the movie, just the music. Everybody stood up for that music. I didn't think of playing it at first. I just wanted to go and listen to it. It took a year or so before anyone in England could make that music."

Aside from his instinctive, if hardly promising, affinity for the rhythms of Elvis, Jerry Lee, Little Richard, and, most especially Chuck Berry, Keith showed a modicum of skill as a graphic artist. After being expelled from Dartford Technical after one too many absences—this time roaming the streets on a borrowed motorcycle looking for girls—Keith was saved by the school's sympathetic headmaster. He arranged for the boy's enrollment in Sidcup Art College, located about halfway between Dartford and London. It was to Sidcup, a distinctly seedy establishment with a third-rate reputation, that Keith was going one bitter cold morning in 1961 when he again met his faintly remembered schoolmate, Mike Jagger.

Meanwhile Mike was busy pursuing his future. Singing like a black man for the Blue Boys offered no prospects for a young man of his class ambitions. Spared the draft by the postwar end of England's National Service, he worked with the kind of resentful diligence that marked the onset of his teenage years. "I found that he worked, but somewhat grudgingly," remarked one teacher. "In his fourth year his term marks for French made him thirteenth out of a class of twenty-five, while his exam mark, sixty-five percent, made him fifth."

It was a time for small acts of token rebellion, met by equal measures of mild punishment. An afternoon spent in the dank embrace of the local pub was met by a warning against tarnishing the three-century-old reputation of Dartford Grammar School, where

Mike had been enrolled. After it became clear that he would not, after all, be serving in the military, Mike participated with a handful of fellow students in a boycott of the Combined Cadet Force, the British equivalent of the ROTC. It was an act that earned him the undying enmity of the Dartford Grammar's headmaster.

On cross-country runs, Mike would take to ducking into the sand dunes of Dartford Heath to share a leisurely cigarette with his fellow delinquents Clive Robson and Tony Gorman. There they would share tales of sexual conquests before joining the others for the last lap of the run. "It was perfectly obvious to the other two that whoever was talking was telling a pack of lies," Mick recounts. "But we never said so."

Girls were, in fact, the object of distant longing. "None of us got beyond the occasional groping," Robson recalls and, for Mick, even the opportunity for a little slap and tickle was stymied by his natural shyness. One early girlfriend, two years younger than Mick's innocent fifteen, remembers no fumbling attempts at seduction but vividly recalls the box of makeup that belonged to Mick's mother, who had become an Avon lady. Such were the times.

And the times, in turn, made scant allowance for a lad unwilling to take full advantage of his social standing. In sharp contrast to Keith, Mick was afforded a full range of chances to better himself. Stolen drags on a cigarette and a boyish enchantment for American music were the extent of the wild teenage oats he would sow. It appears the young man's course had long ago been ordained and Mick would do nothing to upset that course.

A single incident from his final year at Dartford Grammar reveals a determination to succeed. An English teacher, perhaps under the influence of one too many afternoon sherries, would take to reciting large portions of *King Lear* to his befuddled charges, weeping at his own performance. Mick, questioning the instructor's stability, feared he would fail the ensuing A-level exams, the outcome of which would determine his chances of attending a respectable university. His solution was to enroll in a correspondence course in English to prepare for the all-important tests.

In July of 1961 Mick passed three A-level exams in history, English literature, and English language, failing a fourth, French. He was awarded a scholarship to the London School of Economics, with a course of study that included economics and political science. "I wanted to do art," he says, "but thought I ought to do science. Economics seemed about halfway in between. But when I went to university I thought of going into politics." It didn't much matter. Politics or economics, Mick's future was taking shape of its own accord.

The school itself boasted a number of illustrious alumni, mostly in business and law, but also an increasing cadre of creative profes-sionals—including such seminal British television personalities as Michael Peacock, Robert Mackenzie, and Bernard Levin. The Lon-don School of Ecomonics—LSE—was, in fact, something of a hotbed for bright, ambitious young turks, attentive to the opportunities a degree provided them in a postwar shake-up of class strictures.

Young Mick did his best to make an impression. His chosen A levels made him more suited to a future in English and history, but that way lay certain obscurity. Economics, with its serious emphasis on math, was not a natural choice, but he tried. "He was very bright, very determined," remembers fellow student Michael Densham, "and always very keen on business."

University life became, in fact, another of the bet-hedging maneu-vers that helped define the boy and eventually the man. The college represented freedom, an escape from the dreary environs of Dartford —but only during school hours. He would return nightly to the same room he had grown up in, eat the same dull dinner with his family, and toss the night away on the same sprung mattress of his youth. His dreams, too, consisted of the same fervid fantasies that torment teenage boys everywhere.

The eighteen-year-old's fancy seems to have fallen on an unattrac-tive local girl by the name of Bridget. She was seen hanging on his arm as he made the pub rounds that Christmas, "with a face like a pudding," as one mate remembered. Mike professed to have "found happiness" with her, leaving his friends to fill in the blanks.

But on the whole the earnest, callow student hung back. "Some-times you could almost see him mapping out the structures that operated," recalls a contemporary. "He wanted to be sure of himself before he committed to relationships that might not be useful." It was another early indicator of a key personality trait. "He would talk about sex at parties, put his arm around me and endlessly proposition me," recalls another early object of his attentions, an LSE classmate. "But whenever I was alone with him, he'd never do anything about it."

Shy, out of his depth in the faster London crowd, Mike became Mick in 1962. It was the name given to him by his new friends, who hung out at the local pub, the Three Tuns, getting sauced until last call and then heading out to catch the train to Surbiton or Dartford or begging space from one of the lucky few with a flat in the city.

It was a heady time for a tentative young man, a little unnerved by the scent of change that hung in the charged air of a new decade. "We were very much into the idea that things were about to change," recalls a Three Tuns regular, "and that we had the power to alter them." But for a lad with his foot on the first rung of the social ladder, changing things was not the game. The game was going along to get along.

So it was Mick, then. The name suited him—harder, yet with a certain dramatic flair, something to grow into, an attitude to perfect.

The expression of that attitude was naturally musical. Mick's high-spirited love of blues, rock 'n' roll, and all the rich noise in between was the spark of originality that would release him from the clockwork course he himself had set in motion. When Mick listened to the licks and moans of Muddy Waters, Howlin' Wolf, Elmore James, he felt a stirring in his own soul. The music was proof that life was a beautiful, deeply felt, and passionate affair. It was, in short, the dark opposite of the sunny optimism surrounding them. England was about the business of winning the peace. Louts with loud guitars and leisure time didn't fit. It was a very real conflict for a generation catching that scent of change and for a youngster anxiously creating his identity.

Mick and Keith had had a few glancing encounters between their Wentworth days and that day in 1961 when they met again on the platform of the Dartford train station. "I once met him selling ice cream outside the public library," Keith recounts. "I bought one. He was trying to make extra money." The vending job was one of several Mick had taken up for pocket money between semesters. At Christmas breaks, he served time as, variously, a temporary postman and a porter at the Bexley Mental Hospital.

By the time Mick and Keith reconnected, Mick's student life had become a routine whirl of long-winded lectures and casual flirtations, nights alternating between frantic cramming and bleary-eyed pub crawls. In the same way, Sidcup and its lazy rounds of drafting lessons and life studies suited Keith. With its faint air of bohemian charm, the mantle of art student fit him. "I disappointed him incredibly," Keith says, speaking of his beleaguered father. "I turned out to be a Dupree instead of a Richards."

Keith remembers the moment best: "One day I met Jagger again, man. Of all places, on the fucking train. . . . There's Jagger and under his arm he has four or five albums. . . . We hadn't hung around since we were five, six, ten years old. We recognized each other straight off." Keith recognized the records too: Little Walter, Muddy Waters, and most significant to the young guitar player, Chuck Berry's *One Dozen Berries*. " 'You're into Chuck Berry, man, really? That's a coincidence.' He said, 'Yeah, I got a few more albums.' " Mick had been sending away to Chess Records in Chicago and was building an impressive blues library.

Keith recalls, "So I invited him up to my place for a cup of tea. He started playing me these records and I really turned on to it."

It turned out the Dartford boys had more music in common than they realized. "Dick Taylor was the first guy I played with," Keith recounts. "We played together on acoustic guitars. Then I got an amplifier, like a little beat-up radio." It was, of course, the same Dick Taylor who, two years before, had jammed with Mick and the other Blue Boys.

"About four or five lads used to rehearse around my place quite a bit," Taylor recalls. He was attending Sidcup with Richards. "Keith asked me if I knew a guy named Mick Jagger."

There was something inevitable about the friendship that sprang up immediately between the two. "Mick liked Keith's laid-back quality, his tough stance, his obsession with the guitar," Taylor says. "Keith was attracted to Mick's intelligence, his dramatic flair, his streak of ambition."

Taylor, Jagger, and various sidemen had kept the Blue Boys sporadically alive since the days of Mick's clipped tongue. It was to one of the group's rehearsals, in late 1961, that Taylor invited Keith. But it was Mick who asked him to join the band. Taylor remembers best: "Mick and Keith were always the ones. Mick liked Keith's playing. As various people dropped in, were ousted, whatever, it was the combination of Keith and Mick that lasted. Mick was really behind Keith quite a lot."

The group began to play together—the eighteen-year-old Mick singing, Dick Taylor playing his hand-me-down drum set, Bob Beckwith playing guitar, and Alan Etherington holding down maracas. Music fed the friendship in those exhilarating moments when they got it right. They could sense the power of the rhythm among them. For just that time, the sheer sway of the volume was louder than anything else in their lives. Something was taking shape, and it was at that precise moment that Brian Jones stepped out of the nightclub shadows.

Whatever else they thought they were—artists, students, budding bluesmen—Mick and Keith remained at heart unreconstructed yobs, rattling around a London suburb in a complacent time. School, music, the ever-present possibility of women. It was all a lark. Real life would wait a while longer.

For Brian Jones, real life was happening, all around him. With his Cheshire cat grin, his soft eyes, and his musical gift, Brian possessed a daring ambition, a headstrong streak of independence, and a bent for self-destruction neither of the Dartford boys could have drawn from their suburban roots. Brian loved the down-and-out, hard luck truth of the blues. He did his best to live up to its calling: he raised hell.

By the spring of 1962 the twenty-year-old Brian lived harder and faster than Mick and Keith could have dreamed possible. He had come to London from the foothills of the Cotswolds and the prim Gloucestershire spa town of Cheltenham, an enclave of the old Empire, haunted by retired colonels and shy young girls from the women's college. Born February 28, 1942, Brian was the son of a Welshman, Lewis Jones, who played the church organ and presented a model of probity to his delicate, asthmatic son.

In contrast, Brian was moody and mercurial. His bruised spirit found natural expression in the blues. "I went out one morning and came back in the evening and Brian was blowing harp, man," Keith recalls of an early encounter. "He's got it together. He's standing at the top of the stairs saying, 'Listen to this.' All these blues notes comin' out. 'I've learned how to do it. I've figured it out.'"

"All of a sudden," Brian's father would lament, "he became very difficult. He started to rebel against everything—mainly me." The issue, initially, was music. Brian's natural aptitude was recognized early and encouraged by both parents. His mother, Louisa Beatrice, was a piano teacher. At age six Brian began taking lessons from her, and eventually he picked up the clarinet as well. His obvious ability prompted Lewis and Louisa to entertain the notion of a classical career for their cherubic blond prodigy, a hope that quickly died.

By his early teens, Brian had taken to American jazz, Charlie Parker in particular. Bird's energy rattled the windows of the Jones's world before Lewis forbade the music to be played. Brian paid no attention: he laid hold of an alto sax and within weeks was good enough to sit in with some local traditional jazz bands, including an occasional stand with Chris Barber.

The Lewises were right to worry. The heady flavors of hard-core bebop were becoming the soundtrack for adventures beyond Cheltenham. At sixteen, while attending the local grammar school, where he was known as "Buster," Brian got a fourteen-year-old girl named Valerie pregnant. The child was given up for adoption and the family never spoke of it again, but having survived the scandal, Brian had stepped, irretrievably, over the line.

That summer he passed his exams and abruptly decided to forgo college. He stalled his outraged father with the unlikely promise of getting into dentistry. After a brief stint in London, working at a job Lewis had landed for him as an optician's assistant, Brian took off for an impromptu vacation in Scandinavia. Playing guitar and sax on street corners for beer money, he learned something about performing and something more about the universal appeal of rhythm and blues.

Returning to Cheltenham in the first dreary days of 1961, the nineteen-year-old Brian met Pat Andrews in a local coffeehouse and quickly bedded her. Working a factory day shift, his front tooth knocked out in a lorry accident, he was hardly ready for the prospect of fatherhood when Pat told him that she too was expecting. Although he appeared at the hospital with a bouquet of roses for the mother of his child, he was soon off again to London, promising to send for them both when his prospects improved.

Brian's prospects at the time were limited to late nights in London's tiny hive of blues and jazz dives, where he played the occasional set and met some of the scene's earliest and most influential denizens. Included was Alexis Korner, who had graduated from the skiffle days to become the grandfather of British blues. A mix of Greek and Turk with a fierce love for music, Korner had been on hand for Chris Barber's trad jazz breakthrough and had subsequently launched his own group, fronted by a two-hundred-pound auto body worker named Cyril Davies on harmonica and twelve-string guitar.

That band, Blues Incorporated, became the first to play a full blues repertoire in the UK. With a rhythm section that included a thin-lipped drummer named Charlie Watts, the group was, for lack of another, the model for all the aspirants on the edge of the scene.

With the audience for blues growing slowly but steadily, Korner decided to start his own club under a tea shop in the West London suburb of Ealing. The doors opened in March 1962. A month later, Brian was in attendance for a Blues Incorporated gig at what had been dubbed the Ealing Blues Club. Korner called him up on stage and Brian joined the band to deliver a burning slide guitar solo on Elmore James's "Dust My Broom." Brian's supple playing, nuanced and evocative, shredded the smoky air. Watching from the audience were an awestruck Mick and Keith.

F O U R

Strange Bedfellows

The spring of 1962 was unusually wet, with late winter storms blowing off the North Sea, leaving London sodden, fog-draped, and forlorn. The promise of a new year would come late.

In America, a changing of the guard was signaled by the election of John Kennedy, a vigorous young American president, and the death of his secret lover, Marilyn, the icon of an already vanishing era.

Yet the style and sensibility of the fifties was dying hard. The music charts were as soggy as the London streets, with a ragtag collection of novelty items, teenage pillow wetters, and the occasional flash of real rock 'n' roll. Bobby Vinton's maudlin "Roses Are Red (My Love)" vied with Elvis's salacious "Good Luck Charm"; Little Eva's "Loco-Motion" was outpaced by the Tornados' outer space anthem "Telstar"; Acker Bilk's "Stranger on the Shore" was drowned by the soulful strings of Ray Charles's "I Can't Stop Loving You."

For the tiny coterie of musical coconspirators who gathered weekly at the Ealing Blues Club in London, life was hard. Korner's club was nothing more than an insufferably humid basement. "The Ealing club was so wet," Mick recounts, "that Cyril had to put a horrible sheet, revoltingly dirty, over the bandstand, so that the condensation wouldn't drip directly on you. But it just dripped through the sheet. It was very dangerous because of all the electricity and microphones. It was primitive."

Korner, who had heard a rough tape of the Blue Boys doing some off-the-cuff renderings of "La Bamba," "Around and Around," and a few blues standards, offered Mick and Keith the same chance he had given Brian. By April the two were onstage, jamming with Blues Incorporated and making what one innocent bystander referred to as "a diabolical noise."

Mick is first to agree. "I couldn't ever get in key," he recalls. "That was the problem. I was quite often very drunk because . . . I was really nervous."

"Oddly," says another Ealing habitué, "Mick moved very badly in those days. He just had no idea what to do with his legs and arms. The only thing that really worked was the odd rhythmic way he used to shake his head. That was powerful." Korner concurs: "The thing I noticed about him wasn't his singing. It was the way he threw his hair around. He only had a short haircut, like everyone else's. But for a kid in a cardigan, he was moving quite excessively."

Recounts another Ealing regular, "What you noticed about Mick was that he was really into performing. It was touching, the way he so obviously loved being there, holding everyone's attention. And although he was so bad, he had some quality, presence I suppose you'd call it, that stopped you laughing at him."

As awkward and untried as Mick might have been, Korner kept his faith in the young vocalist, and when Blues Incorporated was offered a regular slot at the slightly less seedy Marquee Jazz Club, he invited Mick to join them. The pay: fifteen shillings a night and all the beer he could drink. Keith, considered something less than a total blues purist for his devotion to the revved-up licks of Chuck Berry, was left out.

"I never really had any desire to join the band," Keith would later sniff. "That band drove me crazy, quite honestly. I thought it was just a very, very amateurish attempt by a lot of middle-aged men." Korner and company were, in fact, well into their thirties at the time.

It was as a member of Korner's outfit that Mick received his first press notice on May 19, 1962, in the British music weekly *Disc*: "A nineteen-year-old Dartford rhythm-and-blues singer, Mick Jagger, has joined the Alexis Korner group, Blues Incorporated, and will sing with them regularly on their Saturday dates at Ealing and their Thursday sessions at the Marquee Jazz Club, London."

It was all great fun for Mick, a weekly romp in London's under-belly, late nights spent rocking and wailing, the sound of his own amplified voice bouncing off the damp brick walls. The intense communion that drew together the blues believers made him feel a part of something close to family.

"Mick was very, very involved in what he was doing," Korner recalls. "But he realized that one of the few ways of retaining your sanity . . . is the ability to laugh at yourself. It's an English tradition to be disrespectful. . . . We rather enjoy poking fun at things. And Mick simply took this a bit further . . . finding the absurdity not only in the world but in his own life as well."

It wasn't just cheeky English tradition that kept Mick from enter-taining the diverting dreams of showmanship: his academic career at LSE was proceeding steadily, if not spectacularly, and nothing, it seemed, could deflect the certain course of his future. One day, surely, he would look back on it all from a desk in a brokerage firm or barrister's office, remembering with a smile Ealing and the Marquee and all his spotty mates and the doe-eyed girls that peered up so promisingly from the edge of the bandstand.

And while it lasted, he would excel in the poses and pretenses of student life, including all its callow political posturing. "We were talking about the blues one day," Korner remembers, "and Mick said, 'Why are you playing our working-class music?' I said, 'Mick, you're at LSE! What could be more middle-class than that?' "

But what seemed a frivolous thrill to a middle-class Mick became a serious matter for Brian. The father of two bastard children and all but disowned by his family, he lived in abject squalor in a Powis Square bed-sitter. Music was perhaps the last career option left open to him. Pat Andrews, the distraught mother of his son Julian—named at Brian's insistence after jazzman Julian "Cannonball" Adderly—had arrived unannounced from Cheltenham with two shillings in her purse and a steely determination to make an honest man of Brian. She settled down with him in a simulation of domestic bliss, while he worked in the sporting goods section of Whiteley's department store.

"Brian didn't want to be with Pat," recounts Dick Hattrell, a friend and fellow musician. "He wanted the high life and the beautiful girls who made eyes at him while he was performing. Pat was a very ordinary girl and not at all artistic. She really didn't appreciate music. She was convenient, someone to clean the flat, cook his food, and provide a sexual outlet."

But it was an outlet for his creativity that Brian really craved, and in May of that year, at the same time Mick began his semiregular tenure with Blues Incorporated, a desperate, driven Brian made his move. Determined to form a band around the more provocative strains of Delta and Chicago blues, he placed an ad for interested musicians in *Jazz News*, a London-based trade paper that catered to the traditional jazz crowd. It was the only outlet that might even remotely yield likely candidates.

One of the first to respond was a Scottish-born, Surrey-raised piano player named Ian Stewart. Known to his friends as Stu, he was only vaguely aware of the heroes in Brian's musical pantheon.

"Brian wanted to form a group," recounted the phlegmatic Stu years later. "I went and saw him. He was a strange character but was very knowledgeable. He'd done his homework and . . . was deadly serious about the whole thing. He wanted to play Muddy Waters, Blind Boy Fuller, and stuff by Jimmy Reed—whom I'd never heard of. He couldn't find the people he wanted because not many people had heard that Chess and Vee Jay stuff."

For all his supposed lack of blues aptitude, Stu's arrival augured well for Brian's fledgling band. Something of a character, stoic and unflappable, Stu had arrived at the audition on a racing bicycle in a pair of black leather shorts, toting his lunch, a pork pie. His hard-driving, barrelhouse rendition of "Bye Bye Blackbird" immediately won the chemical company clerk a place in the group. It was a dubious achievement at best. "Brian was living in an unbelievably awful state," Stewart recalls, "drinking spaghetti out of a cup. I thought it was a stunt, but they had no money whatsoever."

Out of the motley cluster of amateurs that answered his ad, Brian quickly assembled the components of a band and began rehearsals three times a week, after hours in a Leicester Square pub. The prospects, from Stu's skeptical perspective, were hardly promising, particularly when they lost their rehearsal space after Brian crept behind the bar to steal cigarettes.

"The one you could never depend on was Brian," Stewart recounts. "He'd suddenly disappear for a few days, then he'd turn up again and want to get another rehearsal going. I never really trusted Brian—mainly because he was always telling you to trust him."

Yet despite the tenuous reality of Brian's grand scheme, word of a newly minted band began to spread. Members came and went, including a skilled guitarist named Geoff Bradford, his harmonica-playing friend Brian Knight, and a singer named Andy Wren. A new rehearsal site was secured, the Bricklayer's Arms on Lisle Street in Soho, where one day, inevitably, Mick and Keith with Dick Taylor in tow turned up to try their luck.

Musical sparks began flying almost immediately. The creative interplay among the trio would in time result in a synthesis of styles that helped define the shape of the British blues boom.

As Keith recalls, "Brian's version of the blues was Muddy Waters, Elmore James, Sonny Boy Williamson, Howlin' Wolf, and John Lee Hooker. Mick and I were much more into Chuck Berry, Jimmy Reed, and Bo Diddley. . . . Brian didn't consider Berry to be in the same class, but when we proved to him that he was, he really started to dig him. He'd work with me on the Berry things. We really got into that. We were working out the guitar parts and the rhythm, which was 4/4 swing, not a rock beat at all. It was a jazz swing beat."

The three-way musical connection was all the more vital for the fledgling friendships that were developing over the summer of 1962. Restive, riven, with an overlay of adolescent envy, the emerging relationships among Mick, Keith, and Brian would eventually shape the music they made, the band they formed, and the lives they led. It was through the constantly shifting, push-me-pull-you alliances that their creative energies and prodigious talents would be channeled.

"We were really a team," Keith explains, "and there were periods of time when we really had a ball together. But there was always this incredible conflict between Mick, Brian, and myself where it was imbalanced in one way or another. There was always something . . . that didn't quite make it somehow. It started out with Brian and I being more friendly because we were completely dedicated to the idea of getting this band together."

In fact, Mick was still hanging back, conspicuous for his lack of commitment to his bandmates' musical ambitions. With his 7-quid-a-week student grant and occasional fifteen-shilling fee for singing with Blues Incorporated, he was, according to Stu, "rather better off.

Every so often, he'd leave Keith and go off to a slightly better caff. Mick was always very fond of his stomach."

Despite the fact that Stu considered Mick and Keith nothing more than a "couple of Piccadilly panhandlers" he continued to play with the nascent group throughout the summer and early fall. It was during this period of thrice-weekly rehearsals and long nights at the Ealing that Mick's friendship with Brian was forged by an unlikely event.

Dropping by the Powis Square flat one afternoon, Mick found Brian gone and Pat alone, tending to Julian. Keith recalls, "He was a bit drunk and screwed Brian's old lady. Pat and the baby split and Brian got thrown out of his flat. Mick found him a place to stay in Beckingham. It was quite groovy until Brian invited a girl down to cook for him one day and they burned half of it down. He continued living there, with a hole in the ceiling with a piece of canvas above it, trying to hide it from the landlord."

Perhaps Brian felt relief at the departure of Pat and the ghastly prospects she embodied. Perhaps both he and Mick were drawn together because they had shared the same woman. In any event, the spontaneous seduction marked the true beginning of Mick and Brian's star-crossed liaison. The next step was natural. In October of 1962, Mick, Keith, and Brian moved into a second-floor flat at 102 Edith Grove, in the West London neighborhood known as World's End. It was here, in the kitchen of the grubby apartment, that the prescient Judy Credland first divined the star of fame on Mick's palm.

To make the rent, the trio had taken two LSE students and a friend, Dick Hattrell, into the two-room flat as boarders. "It was filthy," Keith says. "It was disgusting. Mold growing on the walls."

But however dire the overcrowded conditions, it was, for Mick, a long-overdue break from his Dartford past. "Dartford wasn't a bad place to come from," he would muse many years later, "but it's not a very good place to go back to."

The move to West London would occasion a peculiar sort of release in Mick, one that pointed intriguingly to an emerging persona that would loom large in his life. "Mick went through his first camp period," explains Keith of those early days together, "and started wandering around in a blue linen housecoat, waving his hands everywhere. He was into that kick for about six months." This embryonic indicator of sexual ambivalence was echoed by his stage presence, as insightfully observed by Alexis Korner. "Mick had a very different kind of showmanship, and he was different from the very beginning. . . . I think you can imagine just how shocking Mick was in the early days when you consider that the kind of theatricality which Mick uses is not the kind of mannerism which you can easily identify with the male role in the theater. It's more of a Marilyn Monroe kind of thing. And frankly, it was wildly embarrassing the first time around."

Mick's camping around could well have been the guileless frolic of English music hall tradition. There were, however, other, less innocent overtones to those early romps at Edith Grove. Intimations of homosexuality would, in time, become a part of his teasing mystique, an is-he-or-isn't-he game Jagger delighted in playing with the world. Perhaps more than any other major pop cultural figure, he served to define androgyny's allure as a final flaunting of dull convention. His persona was both a threat and a promise that appropriated all the mincing mannerisms and narcissistic infatuation of the gay lifestyle with none of the ostracizing oppression. He was, indeed, a "different kind of showman."

But even before the limelight lured him over the edge of outrageousness, Mick's sexual identity was a far from settled issue. While he was active, there was simply no way for Mick to keep abreast of Brian's voracious erotic appetite. The extent of the worldly-wise Welshman's experience could well have extended into bisexual realms. Pat had briefly returned, but after a few weeks' stay at the filthy flat had packed up and returned to Cheltenham with Julian. Brian was free to follow his fancy.

The autumn of '62 turned to a bitterly cold winter. "It was a pisser," recounts Dick Hattrell. "Paralyzing amounts of snow, the temperatures constantly below zero that froze all the water pipes in our flat, thereby cutting off the sink and toilet. Keith's responsibility was getting the coins to feed the electric heater. He wasn't very conscientious and we'd usually run out of coins and really freeze. We were like some kind of outlaw band out of Dickens."

The weather was so severe that Brian, Mick, and Keith took to sleeping in the same bed for warmth. "Space was so limited we had to regulate our breathing" was how Brian described it.

It was during the coldest winter in a century that Brian and Keith's musical partnership began taking center stage. With Mick still attending classes and uncertain when and if he would chuck the band for a respectable career, it fell to the two guitarists to carry on. The result was a shifting dance of jealous alliances worthy of a French bedroom farce. Ian Stewart recalls it best: "Keith and Brian developed a relationship as close as their guitar playing, and I sensed that Jagger was beginning to feel left out, jealous, resentful of Brian. . . . I could see him looking at Brian in a way that was a little bit menacing. I could sense back then the beginning of Mick's desire to distance Keith from Brian."

Brian was dedicated to creating a functioning band. "Even though we were all working together, Brian desperately wanted to be the leader," Mick asserts. "He used to get really upset. . . . I didn't give a shit who was the leader of the band. That was the thing that fucked Brian up—because he was desperate for attention. He wanted to be admired and loved and all that . . . which he was by a lot of people, but it wasn't enough for him."

Whether Brian attempted to placate Mick's wounded feelings by giving him "special" attention; whether he used sexual conquest to assert his control and leadership; whether the two ever did more in bed then simply huddle for warmth—all these questions remain among the murkier passages of the Rolling Stones' legend. But at least one quasi-reliable witness claims insider's knowledge.

Anita Pallenberg, the Euro-trash model and groupie who at one time consorted with all three Stones, has insisted that Brian revealed to her the details of a brief homosexual fling with Mick.

"Brian did break up a lot of things by actually going to bed with Mick," she has been quoted as saying. "And I think Mick always resented him for having fallen for it. In later years there have always been rumors about Mick being gay, but then it was as if Brian had violated Mick's privacy by revealing his weak side."

According to Alexis Korner, "Brian was interested in portraying himself as any of the fantasies he had." Whether those fantasies included the gay seducer of a credulous Dartford boy depends on who wants to know. "Mick was very deliberate about the way he presented himself" is Korner's considered judgment, "and over the course of his career, Mick grew ever more adept at becoming all things to all people."

In any case, the melodrama at Edith Grove would shortly take a backseat to sagas played out on grander stages. The band, still a tenuous entity, was dubbed the Rollin' Stones by Brian, after Muddy

Waters's trademark song, which the band had worked into their pure blues repertoire. It was the band's first and only choice, a telling tribute to their musical roots.

They actually performed their first professional engagement that summer as a stand-in for Blues Incorporated. Korner's group had been asked to appear on the BBC radio show *Jazz Club*, but the broadcast was set for a Thursday night and conflicted with the group's regular weekly slot at the Marquee. Mick and company were recruited to fill the slot, and the July 11 edition of *Jazz News* reported the substitution: "Mick Jagger, R & B vocalist, is taking an R & B group into the Marquee tomorrow night while Blues Incorporated do a *Jazz Club* radio broadcast gig."

The item went on to list the lineup, which aside from Mick, Keith, and Brian (under the stage named Elmo Lewis), included Dick Taylor, Ian Stewart, and Mick Avory (later of the Kinks) on drums. The set list, recorded in Stu's diary, included fifteen songs, among them Chuck Berry's "Back in the USA" and renditions of pure blues standards "Dust My Broom," "Bright Lights, Big City," and "Confessin' the Blues." Stu even went on to record the group's attire: Mick in a tatty sweater, Brian in a cord jacket, and Keith in a dark suit two sizes too small.

"I hope they don't think we're rock 'n' roll," Mick was reported to have fretted, worried about offending the purist audience, which promptly took offense. "Before we played a note you could feel the hostility," Dick Taylor recounts.

From that inauspicious beginning came a dead end. The winter slogged into 1963 and the group grew desperate. Bookings for a neophyte blues band on London's clique-ridden music scene were impossible to come by. As Charlie Watts, the Blues Incorporated drummer who would soon join the group, put it, "The Stones were so disliked inside the jazz world. Nobody had a good word for them. They were complete outsiders."

The twenty-year-old Brian worked briefly at a record shop until he was fired for stealing. Nineteen-year-old Keith had finished his final term at Sidcup but ignored the formal exam and any suggestion of gainful employment. Mick, also nineteen, continued to vacillate, hedging his bets while juggling his time. In September of '62 he passed his first-year exams at LSE with respectable marks, his future still very much on track. That same month, the group had played two shows at the Ealing Blues Club to bored patrons, an appearance at a sedate Surrey hotel, the Woodstock, and the occasional Sunday afternoon appearance in Soho jazz clubs.

With some of the meager proceeds from these shows, the group decided to record a three-song demo. "You'll never get anywhere with that singer" was the considered opinion of a record executive on the subject of Mick's vocals. The sentiment was echoed by a producer who attended one of their early appearances: "The singer sounds too colored."

The winter brought with it unremitting poverty. "We had to become petty pilferers," Keith admits. "We'd go into pads where we knew there'd be parties on and await the opportunity to examine the insides of the fridge. . . . If no one was looking we'd try to lift a couple of eggs or something."

In December 1962 Dick Taylor quit to enroll in school, leaving the group without a bass guitarist. He was replaced by Bill Wyman, a friend of the band's atrocious drummer, Tony Chapman. Hired as much for his stock of musical equipment as his compatibility with the group or its music, Wyman was genuinely shocked at their squalid living conditions.

"The place was an absolute pit which I shall never forget," he would write years later. "It looked like it was bomb-damaged. . . . I've never seen a kitchen like it—permanently piled high with dirty dishes and filth everywhere. . . . The temperature in the flat was the same as in the street and we had to keep our coats on."

In January, after repeated entreaties, Brian and others convinced Charlie Watts, whose late nights with Blues Incorporated alternated with long days as a pasteup and layout man at a Regent Street ad agency, to come aboard, replacing Tony Chapman. "I was into modern jazz," recounts the taciturn son of a London Railway delivery man. "But I had this theory that R & B was going to be a big part of the scene and I wanted to be in it."

On January 14, Mick, Keith, Brian, Bill, Charlie, and Stu—the Rolling Stones plus one—played together for the first time at the Flamingo Club in Soho. The personnel was in place. The music was taking shape. It was time for the Stones to wake up the world.

F I V E

England's Newest Hitmakers

Like the Beatles', the Stones' image came in a finely tuned publicity package. While it may be hard to imagine today—at a time when popular music makes a virtue of outrage—the Stones' calculated cultivation of scandal was a stroke of marketing genius. While both the Beatles and the Stones represented a release from the hidebound conventions of the time, the Beatles took care never to step over the line, while the Stones defiantly stood for everything on the other side of the divide.

In 1963 the very existence of such a line was moot. The Beatles had only recently emerged from Merseyside obscurity to begin their march to world domination. While Mick, Keith, and Brian were freezing and starving in Edith Grove, the Beatles were already getting their grip on the national consciousness. In the summer of 1962, right around the time the Stones had played together for the first time at the Marquee, the Liverpudlians had been signed to a record deal with Parlaphone by George Martin. While Mick and his friends put down a futile cleaning deposit for their communal flat,

40

John, Paul, George, and Ringo were watching their first single, "Love Me Do," enter the lower ends of the British charts.

By the early days of 1963 it was clear that the Beatles had ushered in a whole new era of music, style, and sensibility. As much as their lilting sound—the Beatles' second single, "Please Please Me" arrived on the charts in January—the group's mop tops heralded the changing of the guard: clean-cut decorum was not the order of the new age dawning. Long hair was the telling symbol of the budding counterculture; bangs and collar-lapping locks became a key component of a generational covenant.

Significantly, it was Brian who first picked up on the outlaw allure of shaggy hair. Even at their Edith Grove nadir, he had always managed to wash his flowing blond hair on a daily basis, often coming up with a spare shilling to have his locks primped into an elaborate wave. At one of the group's early auditions, for the BBC musical showcase *Saturday Club*, he turned up with a certified Beatle do, with bangs draped well below his line of sight.

"It even shocked us a bit," Keith recounts. "He looked like a Saint Bernard with hair all over his eyes. We told him he'd have to be careful or he'd bump into things." By the time the group played its first gigs of the new year—at dives like the Ricky Tick Club at the Star and Garter Hotel in Windsor—Brian presented himself on stage with, according to Bill Wyman, "shoulder-length hair and an aura of sad vulnerability." The combination was "a magnet for the girls, who started hanging around us after some of the shows." The other Stones let their hair grow too.

On them, the effect was considerably more unsettling than on the determinedly decorous Beatles. Long hair had the effect of accentuating the Stones' distinguishing features: Mick's lips seemed somehow more feminine and lascivious under his tousled auburn mop; Keith's ears protruded even more comically from their sideburn thatches; Bill and Charlie looked even more sinister when they let their manes grow. Brian was served best by the change. His hair formed a flaxen halo around his head, emphasizing his gray-green eyes and delicate features.

Together they began to take on a collective identity. They would become the Beatles' evil alter egos, a brooding rebuff to the Fab Four's insistence that long-haired rock 'n' roll was all in good fun. What long-haired rock 'n' roll was about, the Stones insisted with their music and image, was unkempt anarchy, libidinous abandon, and a bloody-minded disregard for established order. Theirs was a rallying cry that would echo down the corridors of the culture into the sixties.

For the moment the only available champions of good cheer were the four lads from Liverpool. And before that brutal winter grudgingly gave way to spring, the Beatles would help launch the career of the band forever after considered their rivals.

As if a harbinger of the approaching season, the beleaguered Stones' luck took an abrupt turn in the early weeks of 1963. They landed a schedule of gigs including a Monday night spot at the Flamingo Club on Wardour Street, an occasional spot at the Marquee on Thursdays, a Friday night stand at another club—the Red Lion in Surrey—and rounding out the week, a Saturday gig at the Ealing Blues Club. Paying performances, the shows, more importantly, gave them the opportunity to fine-tune their sound. With Wyman and Watts providing a solid rhythm section, the essential components of the group had finally jelled.

"We knew we were good," Mick asserts. "For the time we were very good. When we started, we were just playing blues and rhythm and blues because that's what we liked. We were doing it well and nobody else was doing it. We were doing up to three-hour sets. Now when we went into the ballrooms we used to see other bands and we listened to what they were playing and picked up a lot of new numbers . . . things like 'I Can Tell' and 'Poison Ivy.' When we saw that those things were popular, we said, 'Well, let's do that.' So we did."

What emerged was a repertoire that depended less on the group's pretenses of purity than on the enormous creative energy that was beginning to flow among them. Mick may have been concerned about their being mistaken for a rock-'n'-roll band a few months back, but it had become apparent that that was exactly what they were. A prodigal offspring of the blues, real rock was something the Stones, in essence, *reinvented* by sending the venerable bent notes of the masters screaming through a tunnel of amplified guitars and ecstatic audiences. Their vitality gave birth to a musical eclecticism that would, in time, come to characterize the melting pot permutations of the decade itself.

"The boys seemed in a world of their own," commented Vic Johnson, who later promoted some early Stones appearances. "They pushed out this supercharged music, which electrified the whole place. The kids watching had never sampled this sort of thing and they didn't know what to make of it at first. They knew they'd heard a violent sound that knocked most trad groups right off the scene."

"There was something different about them," remarked another early witness, producer Glyn Johns. "There was the music, of course, but it was also them. They didn't look like the pop stars we had been brought up with." Those same stars, who had established the safe and sanitary confines of pop music for the past decade, would soon find themselves fighting desperately to retain their followings as this new wave of audacious noise began to leak out from the most unlikely places.

The shift in musical fashion—away from slavish imitation of American jazz and the well-worn paths of skiffle and trad—was noticed first by those for whom it mattered most: the promoters and club owners whose livelihood depended on drawing kids to where it was at. And foremost among pop prophets and profiteers was Giorgio Gomelsky, a flamboyant Russian emigré, avant-garde filmmaker, and ardent jazz and blues disciple. The twenty-nine year-old Gomelsky had set down in London after a round-the-world hitchhiking journey which included sojourns in Chicago and Italy, where he promoted the first-ever Italian jazz festival. There he quickly established himself as an enthusiastic, if chronically underfunded, impresario.

After managing a West End jazz club called the Mississippi Room, he opened his own threadbare venue, the Piccadilly, in 1962, where the Stones had played an uneventful gig before a crowd of twenty, including Mick's brother, Chris. A year later the club had reverted back to a cellar and the bustling Gomelsky was in search of a new showcase. The pub at the Station Hotel in Richmond fit the bill perfectly: it was large, it was empty, and most importantly, he could rent it for a five-pound note. He called his new venture the Crawdaddy, after Bo Diddley's "Do the Crawdaddy," and opened for business in early 1963.

It wasn't long before Brian caught wind of a potential new outlet for his group. He had by now fully assumed the managerial mantle, including the obligatory financial sleights of hand. "Brian's accounting," recalls Wyman, "never seemed to make us any money," while Keith recounts more than one occasion when he uncovered a cache of notes hidden away by his bandmate in the filthy flat.

Brian's initial entreaties to Gomelsky were unsuccessful. The avuncular Georgian had already booked the Dave Hunt R-&-B Band, and despite Brian's offer to play for free, Gomelsky turned him down.

Giorgio picks up the story: "I liked what they were doing. I said, 'Listen, I promised this guy I would give him a job but the first time he goofs, you're in. It was the weather, really, that got them their chance. It was snowing and Dave Hunt's band couldn't make it. So Monday I call up Ian Stewart: 'You guys are on next Sunday.' "

The indefatigable promoter had promised the group one pound each and, to protect his investment, spent a day with Mick and Keith pasting up flyers around London. He even went so far as to place an ad in *Melody Maker*, the first of many highlighting his colorful flair for English: "R & B with the inimitable, incomparable, exhilarating Rolling Stones."

Despite his best efforts, the group premiered at the Crawdaddy on February 24, 1963, to a meager audience of thirty people. "I even went through the main pub to try and round some more customers up," recalls Gomelsky. "Anyone who'd buy a ticket was allowed to bring in another person for nothing."

The Stones' Crawdaddy stint that snowy Sunday night would prove to be the beginning of their meteoric ascent. It was a musical groundswell due, at first, to the prodigious efforts of Gomelsky, whose belief in the band was based almost entirely on an altruistic affection for their music. "I didn't know anything about the music business," he said. "I wasn't interested in making money. I couldn't believe making money from something you liked. We shared everything. If there was ten pounds at the door, I kept five, I gave them five."

When subsequently asked if he would manage them, Gomelsky refused. "I kept telling them, 'Wait. Get strong so that you can handle it all yourselves and don't have to ask anyone for anything. Don't run the risk of someone walking in here and taking you over.' "

Within a month of that first show, the hotel pub was filled to overflowing with hard-core music fans, thrill-seeking mods and rockers, and an ever-expanding crowd of the curious.

"It was like really a *scene*," Gomelsky recalls. "What I love about that period more than anything else was that you had the feeling of being in a clan of people who were into the same thing. And that's what made the whole thing gel."

Gomelsky produced a series of ever-more purple promotions. "The unprecedented, incontestable, inexhaustible purveyors of spontaneous combustion," read one *Melody Maker* ad. Another trumpeted the "untamable, wildfire explosion of impetuous R & B with the unsuppressibly storm-raising Rolling Stones."

"We had to teach people how to react to the Stones," Gomelsky explains, "because at first they were all standing there immobile. I encouraged people to dance on the table tops, so they could be seen and to encourage others to join in. The beginning of the whole real Stones thing was audience participation. I can't tell you the excitement in that place in those months. It was like, all of a sudden, you hit civilization on the head. There was something between the band and the audience . . . a ritual, tribal thing."

It was only natural that Mick, as the vocal front man, should be at the center of that ritual. So potent was Brian's star-crossed charisma, however, that the group's shows were initially both a communal affair and a competition for the limelight. According to journalist Peter Jones, an early insider, Brian was "the organizer. It was he who laid down the guiding policies of the band. It was Brian that supervised every single move they made."

As for the music, Mick's gift of mimicry served him well as he wrapped his lips around the salacious blues howlers that were the backbone of their set. Brian's talent, by contrast, was more original, his slide guitar and harp work driving and audacious. But there was one trait they had in common, and recognized in each other—the passion for the limelight.

"The stage was such a tremendous altar of pleasure for Mick that he'd do anything to keep it that way," says Gomelsky bluntly. "He finally had some power and it came to him that he could invent for the world whatever came to his mind. He started conceptualizing himself and the Stones."

"The strength of the spotlight on the singer is so much brighter than on the rest of the musicians," Keith said, explaining the increasing rivalry between his bandmates. "No matter how much you want to upstage the singer, you can't possibly do it. Brian really got off on that trip of being a pop star. . . . He was the only guy in the world who thought he could take on Mick as the head onstage personality."

Gomelsky, agreeing, recalled the moment when he recognized Brian's star-struck ambitions. The two had gone to see the Beatles in their first big London showcase at the Royal Albert Hall. Backstage after the show, Brian, with his flowing blond mane, was mistaken for a Beatle by some indiscriminate fans. After autographs and lingering looks, Giorgio dragged him off down the street. "As we walked away from the Albert Hall," the Russian recalls, "he was almost in a daze. 'That's what I want, Giorgio,' he kept saying. 'That's what I want.' "

With nights full of music and an ever-growing crowd of adoring fans—up to three hundred a performance within months of their Crawdaddy arrival—anything seemed possible.

For Mick, career calculations were suddenly turned on their ear. He was already picking up pointers in stardom from watching the Beatles. Years later, at the induction ceremony for the Beatles at the Rock 'n' Roll Hall of Fame, Mick would wryly recount, "When the Stones were first together we heard there was a group from Liverpool with long hair, scruffy clothes, and a record on the charts with a bluesy harmonica riff. The combination of all this made me sick."

The first encounter between the Beatles and the Stones predated Brian and Giorgio's Albert Hall visit by a week. The meeting had been arranged by the tireless Gomelsky, who had once approached Beatles manager Brian Epstein about a projected film on the group. He subsequently invited the Beatles to the Crawdaddy and in mid-April, after an appearance on the TV show *Thank Your Lucky Stars*, they showed up unannounced at the club, decked out in pricey leather overcoats. "It was a real rave," George Harrison would later recall. "The audience shouted and screamed and danced on the tables."

Following the show, the two bands lingered over pints in the pub and later, back at Edith Grove, Brian played several demos the Stones had recorded in early March, including some rock solid two-track renditions of "Road Runner," "I Want to Be Loved," and "Bright Lights, Big City." The two bands compared musical notes. Mick's interest was piqued when he learned about the publishing company Lennon and McCartney had recently set up. Perhaps there *was* a way to bring his LSE education to bear after all.

Not everyone in the group picked up on the obvious connection between what was happening with the Beatles and what could happen for the Stones. "It was the beginning of Beatlemania," Richards remembers. "The first Beatles records came out. They had harmonica. We'd heard they did Chuck Berry songs, but being a pop star did not even come into the realm of possibilities. We saw no connection between us and the Beatles; we were playing the blues, they were singing pop songs dressed in suits . . . to be pop stars—we were almost a reaction against all that. We were hip not to be pop stars, it was like the only dignity we had left."

As evasive as Keith's account may sound, the Stones were still caught between two worlds. The frenzy that seemed to feed on itself each week at the Crawdaddy sharply contrasted with the hard knocks reality of Edith Grove, where spring was slowly thawing out the garbage-strewn hovel. The band's friendship with the Beatles led John and Paul to drop around one day shortly after seeing the Stones in concert. They arrived to find Mick and Keith in bed together. "I'm not sure about those two," said John, whose own bisexual proclivities were the subject of much speculation.

Yet Edith Grove, with all its indignities, now seemed only a stopover on the way to real stardom's rewards. The prospect of a breakthrough lent a giddy atmosphere to the soggy dive. "Strange things began happening," recalls a downstairs neighbor, Ian Gilchrist. "At two o'clock one morning the lads suddenly hurled all their sheets and blankets out the window and set fire to them." A few nights later, "they came home at three A.M. and played a pop record through one of their stage speakers at tremendous volume. By this time the novelty of living under them was starting to wear thin."

You could feel the excitement in the air and read about it in the papers. "Hyperheterodox R & B voluptuousness for the tempestuously transporting Rolling Stones" read one of Giorgio's advertising blitzes.

"At the Station Hotel, Kew Road, the hip kids throw themselves about to the new 'jungle music,' " ran one of the group's first reviews in the trade paper *Record Mirror*. "The group they writhe and twist to is called the Rolling Stones. Maybe you haven't heard of them—if you live far from London, the odds are you haven't. But by gad you will. The Stones are destined to be the biggest group in the R & B scene."

With that kind of press it wasn't long before well-heeled men with alligator shoes and a glint in their eye began showing up at the Crawdaddy—now relocated to the Richmond Athletic Association after the Station Hotel was demolished. What the Beatles had that the Stones still lacked was someone like Brian Epstein, a manager, rabbi, and father figure adept at turning music into money. But that was about to change.

Enter Andrew Loog Oldham.

The son of a Dutch-American bomber pilot killed in the war, Oldham's personality and portfolio perfectly fit the job at hand. With a nearly albino complexion, gaunt frame, and a nearsighted stare that give him the air of a permanently distracted rabbit, Oldham had become adept at flying in low—under the awareness and expectations of rivals—then leveling them with his cynical wit and air of ennui. Modeling himself on the cool bravura of actor Laurence Harvey, Oldham had taken on several modish stage names—including Chancery Laine and Sandy Beach—during his abortive career as a pop singer. At the same time he had talked his way into an assistant's job with Chelsea fashion maven Mary Quant while managing to moonlight as a waiter in the Flamingo Club. Part-time jobs included doorman at Ronnie Scott's Jazz Club and press agent for crooner Mark Wynter.

The quintessential hustler—a Sammy Glick in Carnaby drag—Oldham was also keenly attuned to the changing of the musical guard happening in clubs from London to Liverpool. Oldham had been in the studio in February when the Beatles performed "Please Please Me" on *Thank Your Lucky Stars* before packing down to the Crawdaddy to see the Stones for the first time. Convinced he had witnessed the future of rock 'n' roll, he cajoled his way into a publicist's post with Brian Epstein, the Beatles manager. Epstein was preparing to launch two more promising Merseyside groups, Gerry and the Pacemakers and Billy J. Kramer and the Dakotas, and appreciated the nineteen-year-old Oldham's audacity and obvious grasp of the new sound. He hired him for twenty-five pounds a week.

Shortly afterward, a chance encounter with Phil Spector, the dark prince of American pop music and architect of the famous wall of sound, gave Oldham's aspirations yet another role model. Eccentric, furtive, and firmly in control of his empire, Spector was the mirror image of Oldham's dreams.

Oldham recalls one April night at the Crawdaddy: "I was drinking with an editor of one of the pop papers and he told me I should go and see this group down in Richmond. It was as simple as that. I was probably forty-eight hours ahead of the business in getting there. But that's the way God planned it."

The next week Oldham went back, this time with a balding, middle-aged theatrical agent named Eric Easton, from whom he was renting office space. Representing such wheezing music hall veterans as Bert Weedon and pianist Mr. Mills, Easton was intrigued by what he saw but hardly convinced. Oldham recalls, "He thought at the time that one of the members we should get rid of was Mick Jagger because technically he couldn't sing."

Oldham saw it differently, although what exactly he was seeing remains a question of much mythmaking. When asked what drew him to the Stones, Oldham's explanation describes either a remarkable feat of entrepreneurial instinct or constitutes some very fast talking by a relentless self-promoter. "I knew that in just months the country would need something different to what the Beatles were doing. It was just an instinctive thing . . . it registered subconsciously that when they made it, another section of the public were going to want the opposite. The Stones were going to be that opposite."

Initially Oldham gained a foothold with the group by merely identifying himself as "one of them." "We just had the same basic desire to do something—a hustling instinct. I wasn't coming on with a cigar and silk suit . . . I was the same age as them. We talked the same language."

It was immediately apparent that Oldham had the Stones' number. "I knew what I was looking for," he insists, adding drolly, "It was sex, the sex most people don't realize is there. Like the Everly Brothers. Two guys with the same kind of face, the same kind of hair. They were meant to be singing together to some girl, but they were really singing to each other."

In early May 1963 Oldham and Easton signed the group to an exclusive management contract, after negotiations with Brian that included Easton's proviso that Mick be dropped. Brian voiced no objection. Stu remembers: "This guy Easton, who didn't know anything about pop music, had seen Mick and said to Brian, 'I don't think Jagger is any good.' And so Brian said, 'Okay, we'll just get rid of him.' I feel sure Brian would have done it. . . . I said, 'Don't be so bloody daft.' "

"Brian wanted to be a star so badly," Gomelsky explains. "He was

in London, totally on his own, with no money because he was in-
capable of working. The others went to school, had parents, jobs. . . .
Brian was very desperate, he really wanted to make it quickly. . . .
He would do anything to make it."

In the end, however, it was Oldham who insisted that Mick should
stay, for reasons that would quickly become evident.

Throughout the summer, the Stones continued to play to packed
houses even as Oldham began tinkering with their image, working
toward casting them in a cleaner-cut, Beatles mode. In the process he
upset the careful balance among the key members. The first order of
business was to dismiss keyboardist Ian Stewart for the sin of "not
looking right for the part." Ever amenable, Stu took up roadie chores
for the band.

The next task required considerably more finesse. "Before this,
everyone knows that Brian considers it his band," Keith explains.
"Now Oldham sees Mick as a big sex symbol." The shift of emphasis,
however obvious a move, would subsequently wreak havoc in the
group as Oldham took his place in what was now a four-way tussle of
shifting allegiances. To secure Brian's compliance, Oldham had arranged a secret deal to pay him an extra five pounds a week over the
others' salary.

Oldham, who had recently celebrated his nineteenth birthday, was
moving fast, utilizing all the shifty skills he had perfected on the
fringes of the British music business. Within a week of firing Stu, he
had arranged for the trimmed-back group's first recording session.
Waiting anxiously to hear the results was Decca Records' A & R head
Dick Rowe, infamous as the Man Who Turned Down the Beatles.

In point of fact, Rowe had already made his decision. After hearing
favorable word of mouth from George Harrison and determined not
to make the same mistake twice, he signed the Stones after seeing
them perform live.

Word of that record deal finally convinced Mick to make his move.
His chronic equivocation had brought matters to a head: there were
rumblings both at home and in the band that if he didn't commit to
either school or show business, the decision would be made for him.
With a recording contract in his back pocket, he announced that he
was leaving LSE.

"I have been offered a really excellent opportunity in the entertainment world," wrote the twenty-year-old Mick in a letter to the

headmaster late that summer, as if he had applied for a position as theater usher. He was nevertheless relieved to find out that the door to higher education was not completely closed. "The registrar said I could come back later if I wanted," he recounts. "It was all surprisingly easy."

A lot of things were coming easy now. It was shortly after he tossed off his long-nurtured ambitions of accountancy that Mick began a tumultuous three-year affair with Chrissie Shrimpton, the perky sister of haute monde fashion model Jean Shrimpton. He had met her five months before when she had been a regular at the Ealing club. With so small an audience, it wasn't long before Mick noticed the pale complexion, silky hair, and huge eyes of the alluring seventeen-year-old.

During one show at Maidenhead, Chrissie boasted to a boyfriend that she knew the singer, and he in turn bet her ten shillings she couldn't prove it with a kiss. After the set Chrissie strolled up to Mick and preemptively planted one on him. A few days later he took her to a movie. What was to be one of the most celebrated rock romances of the era was underway.

They were quickly to become the perfect couple for the fey and dandified crowd beginning to congregate in and around Carnaby Street and Kensington, a new breed of beautiful people celebrated in the photographs of David Bailey. As the scene's court chronicler, Bailey created lushly lit fashion layouts that had already made an international star of Chrissie's sister Jean.

But for the moment, the courtship was a perfectly conventional, if somewhat charged affair, with Chrissie looking for commitment and Mick characteristically leery of making one. They fought, often. Oldham recalls entering through the Crawdaddy stage door the night he first saw the group and passing a couple in the alley having a furious argument. Only later, when seeing Mick on stage, did he realize who it was.

Chrissie was not, however, the first to be lured by Mick's music. The connection between rock and sex had been sparking in more than just the fevered imagination of Oldham. Back in the Ealing and Marquee days, Mick had used a classic come-on to entice an attractive black woman named Cleo Alexander. He asked her to join the band, claiming they had decided to recruit a quartet of American-style backup singers. A hastily arranged rehearsal with the group and a few of Cleo's friends floundered on an off-key rendition of an Ike and Tina Turner standard.

Mick's attempt to woo Cleo continued for months afterward, and included some pining love letters. "Dearest Cleo," read one, "I want somebody to share everything with, someone to respect, not just to sleep with. I feel that in you I've found that something that I've been looking for a long time."

Cleo continued to come around, occasionally cleaning the flat and cooking food. She would eventually become one of Oldham's many clients, recording a version of Spector's "To Know Him Is to Love Him" backed by the band, who were also on hand for the flip side, a ditty titled "There Are But Five Rolling Stones."

Chrissie was, however, an altogether more serious proposition. Attending secretarial college, she would meet Mick in parks and pubs whenever possible. Vowing undying devotion, he was soon suggesting more private rendezvous, refusing, however, to subject her to the chaos of Edith Grove. An opportunity presented itself when Chrissie's parents went away on a weekend to celebrate their twenty-fifth wedding anniversary.

Mick hitchhiked to the Shrimpton estate after a Stones gig, returning to London in time for the evening show. It was only afterward that Chrissie introduced him to her father, Edward Shrimpton, whom he immediately impressed with an informed discussion of economics.

Mick in turn took Chrissie to Dartford for tea with Joe and Eva. Who could blame his parents for hoping for the best? Perhaps, after all, Mick would come to his senses, get a proper job, and settle down.

Yet the Jaggers had no way of knowing that the prospect of fame helped fuel Mick and Chrissie's infatuation. By the closing months of 1963 they were talking about marriage, much to the delight of both sets of parents. The Stones' rapid rise, however, would put the plans on hold and soon in suspension. The compensation for Chrissie was ever-increasing media attention as Mick's main squeeze.

In September Oldham arranged for a move from Edith Grove to a new flat in a slightly better neighborhood, Mapsebury Road in Kilburn. It's significant that the digs were made available to Mick and Keith only. Their new manager's plan to assert his control of the group was proceeding at Brian's expense. Given his increasingly avaricious attitude, Brian's loss of leadership was inevitable. "He didn't have it in him to be a leader," remarks the ever-observant Stu. "As soon as the group became in any way successful, Brian smelled money. He could sniff the fact that he was going to be a star . . ."

Brian had gone off to visit a new girlfriend in Windsor, and in his absence word leaked of his special financial arrangement with Oldham and Easton. "It was such a small thing," remembers Keith. "They made an arrangement that, as leader of the band, he was therefore entitled to five pounds extra a week. Everybody freaked out. And that actually was the beginning of the decline of Brian."

How news of the fatal five pounds got back to the group remains a mystery, but the incident has the unmistakable stamp of Oldham. Within weeks Oldham had moved himself into the two-room apartment with his new clients. The Edith Grove era was over. Something new was about to happen.

Among Oldham's first acts was to book the band into a studio. On May 10, 1963, they recorded their first single, a scrappy, adrenaline-fueled rendition of Chuck Berry's "Come On" backed with a tepid take on the Muddy Waters tune "I Want to Be Loved." Oldham served as the session producer and began the day with the blunt admission that this would be his first stab at record making. "We were a bunch of bloody amateurs," Mick insists, "ignorant as hell, making a hit record."

Released in early June, "Come On" had only a glancing encounter with the Top Thirty. "A bluesy commercial group that should make the charts in a small way" was *Record Mirror*'s prediction. *Melody Maker* was considerably less kind: "Very ordinary," wrote reviewer Craig Douglas. "I can't hear a word they're saying. I don't know what all this is about."

Neither, exactly, did Oldham, as evidenced by his next move, a promotional ploy that throws new light on the claim that he was creating the anti-Beatles. Landing the group a spot on *Thank Your Lucky Stars*, the BBC's premier showcase for new talent, was easy enough. The popular program's smarmy host, Brian Matthews, was one of Easton's clients. How to present the group on their national television debut proved a knottier problem.

The Stones brought up the bottom of the bill that evening with the Viscounts, an ersatz doo-wop group covering the American novelty hit "Who Put the Bomp," and vocalist Helen Shapiro, a little girl with very big hair. When the Stones were introduced, a collective gasp of horror came from the audience. Oldham had decked the band out in absurd houndstooth jackets, uniforms that did the Fab Four one better for cloying cuteness. They looked like nothing so much as a gaggle of East End fox hunters. Years later, Oldham does his best to explain this hilarious gaffe in his master plan.

"There were a couple of compromises we had to make at first," he claims. "We compromised to the extent of wearing some sort of uniform. We knew we had to. The TV people were used to dealing with groups like the Searchers and the Swinging Blue Jeans. If the Stones had dressed the way they wanted, they wouldn't have been allowed inside the building. So they all wore these checked jackets. But we got rid of them as soon as we could."

Not according to Keith: "People think Oldham made the image, but he tried to tidy us up. . . . Those dogtooth-checked suits with the black velvet collars. Everyone's got black pants, a tie, and a shirt. At first we said, 'All right. We'll do it. You know the game.' But then the Stones thing started taking over. . . . I'd pull mine out and there'd be whiskey stains or chocolate pudding all over it."

It was on the evening of their television debut that Oldham made a startling announcement. He had gotten the group their first national tour, sharing the bill with Bo Diddley and the Everly Brothers. It was a collection of exotic American stars whose music had nurtured Mick, Keith, and Brian for years. They had been disembodied voices from a far-off land, plaintive, passionate, possessed, but never, somehow, quite real.

The tour was booked for thirty dates in as many cities. One show a night in towns they had never seen and barely heard of: Cardiff, Doncaster, Nottingham, Bournemouth, Ipswich. The Rolling Stones were about to get used to the idea of things seeming not quite real.

SIX

A Way of Life

Oldham had gotten off to a shaky start with those houndstooth uniforms. But by the time the Stones' first tour got rolling in the fall of 1963, with the group officially together a little less than a year, he had latched on to an essential element of the Stones' appeal and wasn't letting go. It was a campaign of inspired image making that remains one of the most effective marketing ploys in the annals of rock 'n' roll. Oldham, with the canny participation of Mick and Brian, would put together the classic Bad Boys of Rock package, and while it has been the model for countless sneering pretenders since, the original still endures.

While American music stars from Little Richard to early Elvis courted outrage both on and off stage, their antics and indiscretions were carefully constrained. The threat of retaliation from the watchdogs of moral rectitude was always very real. The fate of Jerry Lee Lewis was a sobering case in point. Marrying his underage cousin might not have raised an eyebrow in rural Louisiana, but for the indignant English public on the eve of Lewis's first British tour, the revelation was proof of rock's degenerate effect. The scandal virtually ruined Lewis's career and fueled the fires of repression in the fifties.

But by the waning days of 1963, the moral compass was in flux. The winds of change, only stirring slightly even a year ago, had turned into a generational gale. What had begun as a publicity gimmick would, in time, become a rallying point for rebels, romantics, and reprobates. The Stones' outlaw appeal became a self-fulfilling prophecy. "The Rolling Stones are more than a group," read one of Oldham's early, inspired slogans. "They are a way of life." And it was that way of life that made the Stones quintessential sixties symbols.

That first tour began on a lackluster note with a half-empty house at the New Victoria Cinema in London. The paltry turnout could well have been the result of the erratic talent lineup: the Everlys, fading teen crooners, were paired with Bo Diddley, whose primal syncopation was worlds away from the duo's delicate harmonies. Aside from the Stones, a group of sax honkers called the Flintstones and a bland balladeer named Julie Grant completed the confused bill.

From London the group traveled north. "A few miles out and it was all new to me," recounts Keith. "Up to then, I'd never been further north than North London."

The tour continued to struggle, even after the frantic addition of Little Richard to the lineup. The Stones played two shows a night and quickly learned from their mistakes. "When we went into the ballrooms," Wyman recalls, "we soon found out that you couldn't play those slow Jimmy Reed blues-type numbers. You were expected to play music for them to dance to, but they stood there in front of you and gaped. So at that time we started concentrating on much more up-tempo songs, fast rhythm things, hard rockers that seemed to work out quite well."

The same strategy spilled over into the recording studio. Oldham paid little heed as the tour limped along to ever-dwindling gates. He had turned his attention instead to a follow-up for the group's timid debut, "Come On." Taking time out from the tour, they recorded a dismal version of the Coasters' novelty hit "Poison Ivy," pleasing neither the band nor Decca Records, which refused to release it.

The Beatles stepped in, for reasons not altogether altruistic. "They had this tune and they were real hustlers," explains Mick. "I mean the way they used to hustle tunes was great. So they played it and we thought it sounded pretty commercial, which is what we were looking for."

The tune, "I Wanna Be Your Man," was released that November and immediately climbed into the Top Twenty, peaking at number nine over a thirteen-week run. Fueled by Jagger's unadorned vocals and Brian's slashing slide guitar, the song has an angular menace the subsequent Beatles version conspicuously lacked. The choice was perfect: "I Wanna Be Your Man" was as close to the potent punch of the group's live show as anything they had yet set to record.

But as much as the Lennon/McCartney classic suited the group's sound, it was the power of the publishing deal that really impressed Mick. "The Beatles told me we could write our own songs," he says, "and I said, 'Oh, you're right, that's a good idea.' Everyone just used to redo hits, even hit standards. But then you got the feeling you had to write your own thing because you were running out of them. So we just started writing, but we never really wrote any blues numbers to start off with. . . . The things we wrote were more like ballads or pop songs."

"I Wanna Be Your Man," produced by a nonplussed Easton after Oldham abruptly left for France to recover from a case of food poisoning, had an immediate effect on the band's flagging fortunes. Following its release, the group returned to the road, playing a show at the Odeon in Liverpool, deep in the heart of Beatles country. Under the headline "Stone Us!" writer Derek Johnson's review in the *New Musical Express* helped capture the sense of growing excitement around the band. "The Iron Curtain has been breached, friendly relations have at last been established, and representatives from London have succeeded in creating goodwill in the opposition's capitol. . . . I am talking about the invisible barrier that has for so long divided London and Liverpool," Johnson continued his geo-political metaphor, "and which the Rolling Stones have finally breached."

Hometown rivalry wasn't all that was being breached. On the final date of the tour, November 3 at the Hammersmith Odeon, the MC had to plead with the packed crowd to stop chanting "We want the Rolling Stones" and start up with "We want the Everly Brothers." Richards refers to a "sort of hysterical wail" that rose up to greet the band as they came on stage for the final leg of that first tour. "It was a weird sound that hundreds of chicks make when they're coming. . . . They sounded like hundreds of orgasms at once."

Another concert at the Cavern Club in Liverpool, even then a shrine to the Beatles, produced a line of two thousand fans around the block. Inside twenty-five girls fainted from the heat and excitement.

"It was hot," remembers Mick. "We almost sweated away. They've had so many big groups in the Cavern that you've got to prove yourself."

It was in the midst of this growing frenzy that Oldham's deft promotion blitz began to truly take shape. Like everything else revolving around the Stones, it was happening on the fly, with a seat-of-their-pants spontaneity one step ahead of public opinion.

There's no question that the dismay and sometimes outright revulsion that greeted the group's arrival on the national scene provided the fuel for Oldham's master plan. Early accounts made far more of their alarming appearance than of their orgasm-inducing music.

Much, for example, was made of an early encounter between the group and American lounge sensation Gene Pitney, "When I met them I didn't know whether to shake hands or bark," Pitney is reported to have quipped. It was a line that so perfectly served the group's ends that the suspicion remains that Oldham, who was handling publicity for Pitney at the time, provided it.

There seems little likelihood, however, that the frenetic manager bribed Mr. Wallace Scowcroft, president of the National Federation of Hairdressers, who, with jowls aquiver, delivered this soundbite: "The Rolling Stones are the worst. One of them looks as if he has got a feather duster on his head." Scowcroft then offered a free haircut to any pop star wanting to spiff himself up with a respectable coiffure. Oldham responded by taking out a holiday ad in the *New Record Mirror* picturing the Stones and offering "Best wishes to all the starving hairdressers and their families."

The Daily Express, with a flourish typical of the band's early press notices, described the Stones as "five tough young London-based music makers with doorstep mouths, pallid cheeks, and unkempt hair," adding, "They look like boys whom any self-respecting Mum would lock in the bathroom."

It was all grist for Oldham's publicity mill. He billed the band as "The Ugliest Group in Britian" and followed up with the master stroke, "Would you let your daughter go out with a Rolling Stone?"

The answer, as far as Mr. and Mrs. Shrimpton were concerned, was already out of their hands. After the close of their baptismal tour, the group barely had time to catch its breath before Oldham had them out on the road again, this time as headlines, sharing the bill with yet another catchall talent roster: the Ronettes (the all-girl prodigies of Oldham's idol, Phil Spector), the Swinging Blue Jeans, Marty Wilde and the Wildcats, and others.

In between, Mick and Chrissie found time to move in together, in a basement flat in Bryanston Mews, adjacent to Montague Square. A friend, future fashion designer Thea Porter, helped them decorate it and offers a revealing glimpse of the young couple. "I remember that I found a darling little striped blue dresser. It was very pretty. And they had a huge teddy bear sitting on the bed."

Chrissie was among the first to notice Mick's increasing infatuation with himself and his new persona as Britain's butt-shaking bad boy. Journalist and insider Carey Scofield writes that "Chrissie reported that he would at this time spend ages gazing at himself in the mirror. It was as if he were trying on different variations of the personality that seemed to go down so well in public."

Chrissie, on the other hand, was often obliged to stay well out of the limelight, hidden from fans whose singular fantasy revolved around an available Mick. Most galling of all, when Mick and Chrissie were out on dates together, Mick often pretended not to be with her if approached by his dewy-eyed fans. Chrissie would recall, "If we were holding hands and someone was coming, he'd drop my hand and turn away. Of course I was hurt and humiliated." Only later would Mick lamely excuse his behavior by claiming he acted according to Oldham's publicity demands.

In point of fact, Mick was very much a part of the process of creating the band's image. When drummer Charlie Watts wanted to marry his longtime girlfriend Shirley Shepherd, it was Oldham who forbade it and Mick who backed him up, for the sake of the group's bachelor status.

For Mick's intelligent, strong-willed girlfriend, the demands of their relationship were both humiliating and exhilarating. Graduating from secretarial school, Chrissie was eventually given a job at Decca Records, where, thanks to her proximity to the label's hottest act, she was treated with royal deference, handling only Stones-related business.

But make-work and coattail riding were hardly Chrissie's style. Significantly, she saw as her main competition not Mick's growing female following, but the overweening influence of his manager. She formed an alliance with Charlie Watts's impatient fiancée, Shirley, and would often upbraid Mick on her behalf. At the same time

Chrissie let her feelings be known about Oldham, particularly after one catty friend asked if Mick and Andrew had slept together at the Mapsebury Road flat where Chrissie lived briefly before the move to Bryanston Mews. It was yet another of the shadowy suggestions of homosexuality that would dog Mick throughout his career, suggestions he took no pains to discount. "I did see Mick and Andrew in bed together," Chrissie would later say. "They were undressed, asleep, and I was so naive at the time I thought they looked very innocent and sweet together."

The plain fact was that Oldham's increasingly fey behavior—which included wearing makeup to the office and comparing eye shades with the secretarial pool—was beginning to have an effect on the impressionable Mick.

Chrissie and Mick continued fighting, often escalating to physical violence, with Chrissie slapping and scratching, trying to provoke her increasingly aloof boyfriend into paying attention to their faltering affair.

It was a losing battle. The group's second tour evoked the kind of frenzied response, and abundant female flesh, previously reserved for the Beatles. Bill Wyman's voluminous diaries are full of one-night stands in second-rate hotels. A typical deadpan entry: "Brian and I met two girls, later nicknamed the Pifco twins, and spent the night with them. While I was making love to one, at the last minute she produced an amyl nitrate 'popper' and broke it under my nose."

The pickings were just too easy, both on and off stage. Rumors of a dressing room romance featuring Mick, Keith, and two of the Ronettes was fueled years later by an offhanded remark from Keith. "There was no direct competition in the band for pulling chicks," he remarked, before letting slip, "The only time I remember Mick and me in any slight competition was with the Ronettes. Mick wanted to pull Ronnie and ended up with her sister Estelle." Small wonder Phil Spector, who would subsequently marry Ronnie, sent a telegram on the eve of the tour reading, "Stay away from my girls."

Attracting women provided pleasure, but what really counted was pulling in paying customers. Throughout the early weeks of January 1964, the group generated pandemonium. "The Rolling Stones create a sound so exciting and gripping," wrote one reviewer in *Melody Maker*, "that few other groups can come within shouting distance of it." Their nearly nonstop touring schedule honed their music to whiplash precision, with an attendant flourish of showmanship. Another early witness, Andy Gray of *New Musical Express*, caught a sense of the excitement: "Two packed houses greeted with cheers, screams, and scarf-waving the local lads who have made good—the Rolling Stones. Fever pitch excitement met the announcement of them and they tore into their act with 'Girls,' followed by 'Come On.' . . . Lead singer Mick Jagger whips out a harmonica occasionally and brews up more excitement while three guitars and drums throb away in back."

It was a noise captured with remarkable fidelity on a four-song extended play album the group cut in mid-January. "The idea was to catch in the studio the atmosphere of one of our dates," Wyman explains. "Hence the concentration on strong, beaty numbers." The idea was also to throw something together to satisfy the suddenly spiraling demand for product. The extended play album included the single version of "Poison Ivy" rejected by the record company a few months before.

Oldham's publicity blitz was also in full gear. His love-to-hate-them strategy paid off handsomely and the group was never far from the front page of most British tabloids. Television appearances on *Thank Your Lucky Stars* and another music showcase, *Ready, Steady, Go*, harvested even more outrage: "The whole lot of you should be given a good bath, then all that hair should be cut off" ran one typical protest letter. "I'm not against pop music when it's sung by a nice clean boy like Cliff Richard, but you are a disgrace. Your filthy appearance is likely to corrupt teenagers all over the country."

It was the kind of press you couldn't buy—a made-to-order contrast with the elders' safe and sanitary world. It was also a polarization that demanded a choice—for or against—and Oldham relentlessly pushed the preference as a youth culture mandate. Partisans on both sides of the divide instinctively understood the stakes, as when a Coventry school headmaster expelled eleven students for their Stones-length locks, refusing to reinstate them until they cut their hair back to a "respectable" Beatles trim.

Mused a sage at the *Daily Sketch*, "Who would have thought a few months ago that half Britain's teenagers would end the year with heads like hairy pudding basins? The Stones look straight out of the Stone Age."

Of course, what the men didn't know, the little girls understood.

Stones sightings, both on and off stage, were becoming increasingly frenzied, as nubile teens hurled themselves into the breach. It was a dangerous game, as recalled by Ian Stewart, who was now working full-time as the band's roadie.

On their way into town for a Shrewsbury concert, Stu recounts, "Brian said he wanted to call at a chemist. As soon as he got out of the van, Keith turned to us with a wicked grin and said, 'Come on, let's leave him to it.' We went to the theater and there were only a few fans. . . . By the time Brian arrived, the girls were out in force. They chased him through the streets, tearing the jacket from his back and ripping his shirt. We thought it was hilarious, but Brian didn't see the joke."

When a live Stone was unavailable, a close relative would do. "Many a girl would knock at the door," Eva Jagger recounts. "They would come in all weather and hitch from vast distances. I used to feel responsible, ask them in, and make sure their mothers knew where they were. I still get letters not only from adoring fans but from their mothers too."

A sense of surreal dislocation quickly set in. Edith Grove and the bitter winter of their discontent seemed both a distant memory and the last milestone of normalcy. "It happened so fast that one never really had time to get into that thing," Keith remembers. "We were still sleeping in the back of this truck every night . . . from one end of England to another in Stu's Volkswagen bus."

In addition to the dreamy sensation that it was all happening to someone else, the Stones experienced the low-grade delirium brought on by sleep deprivation. "We only had about four hours' kip each night for most of this week," Mick revealed in the midst of the tour. "When we get back to London, we'd like to do nothing but sleep until it's time to go on the road again. But there's always so much catching up to do on jobs we can't look after on tour."

To dispel the daze, aggravated by a perpetual cold passed from one member to the other, the group eventually stumbled onto that age-old aid for itinerant musicians. "Usually drug taking in music started off on a very, very mundane level," explains Keith, who of all the surviving Stones is best qualified to discuss the subject by virtue of his own prodigious addictions. "Just keep going to make it to the next gig. . . . It's a musician's life. . . . it's an underworld life, anyway. Musicians start to work when everyone else stops working and wants entertainment. If you get enough work, you're working three hundred and fifty days a year, because you want to fill up every gig. And you reach a point very early on when you're sitting around the dressing room with some other acts after the show and you say, 'I've got to drive five hundred miles and do two shows tomorrow and I can't make it.' And so you look around at the other guys and say, 'How the hell have you been making it all these years?' And they say, 'Well, baby, take one of these.' Musicians don't start off thinking, 'We're rich and famous, let's get high.' It's a matter of making the next gig."

Whatever the initial impetus, Benzedrine and various other assorted uppers had become very much a part of the Stones' way of life by early 1964.

It was just one more element that frayed the fragile balance keeping the band afloat. With Mick and Keith beginning to write together, and Oldham's increasing influence on the group's image, Brian's sense of isolation and envy grew. He was caught up in yet another doomed love affair, this time with a fetching model named Linda Lawrence. When she, inevitably, announced herself pregnant, the two had taken up housekeeping following Mick and Keith's move out of Edith Grove.

As with Mick and Chrissie, the two fought, often violently. Moreover, Brian's notoriety and ego destroyed any chance they had of staying together. And, like Chrissie, Linda was privy to Brian's internal struggles.

"Brian and I would talk about his feelings of insecurity," she later recalled. "The boys were one way and he was another. He would question whether the fans came to see the Stones because of Mick, the way he was presenting the show, or did they come because of the actual music, which was what I thought Brian was representing. As long as Brian and I were together, he thought of himself as the leader of the group. . . . He must have foreseen that he would be pushed out because he talked about it. Brian was always looking for ways to stop it or make it right. He always tried to find something to hang on to."

The bandwagon kicked into overdrive with a third British tour in May of 1963, in what was beginning to seem like the never-ending road trip. They shared the bill with an ersatz rocker named John Leyton and the obligatory horde of supporting acts. But the real focus of the group's creative energy was a series of recording sessions beginning late January for their first full-length LP. Legend has it that, to come up with the all-important original material, Oldham had locked Mick and Keith in the kitchen, threatening to keep them there until they put together their own tunes. The duo subsequently emerged with a clutch of droopy ballads, including "It Should Be You" and "That Girl Belongs to Yesterday," subsequently a minor hit for Gene Pitney. Of three Jagger/Richards originals, "Tell Me," a painfully inept, minor chord Beatles imitation, was the only track deemed even marginally worthy of inclusion on the album's projected tune stack.

But it was the rest of the album's cuts, captured at London's decrepit Regent Studios, that remain the best evidence of the group's early, utterly infectious enthusiasm. Numbers such as the hyperkinetic reworking of Buddy Holly's "Not Fade Away," a strutting rendition of Rufus Thomas's "Walking the Dog," and a blatant, sexually seething version of "I'm a King Bee" go a long way toward explaining the band's astonishing appeal. Their instinctive grasp of blues and R & B, and the charged power of their ensemble playing, bristle on virtually every track, making the first Rolling Stones album one of the enduring gems of English rock 'n' roll. The album's twelve tracks ranged from Jimmy Reed's loping "Honest I Do," anchored on Watts's crashing cymbals, to their careening joyride around Willie Dixon's "I Just Wanna Make Love to You"; from "Carol," sporting Keith's faster-than-a-speeding-bullet Chuck Berry riffs, to the sheer, spontaneously combustible joy of "Can I Get a Witness?"

The fans thought so too. The album, featuring a David Bailey deep-shadow portrait of the group with no logo or group name to lessen the impact, logged one hundred thousand copies in advance orders. In an incredible accomplishment for the time, the album reached the top of the charts in a mere eight days, surpassing the Beatles' initial sales performance and securing the Stones' role as pretenders to the Fab Four's throne.

And, like the Beatles before them, the group's next step was across the ocean. "Americans—brace yourselves," read an Associated Press wire story in late May. "In the tracks of the Beatles, a second wave of sheepdog-looking, angry-acting, guitar-playing Britons is on the way." On June 1, 1964, the Stones arrived in New York City to launch their first American tour.

Eric Easton, the group's bean-counting comanager, had worked hard to secure a foothold in the United States. In mid-May an advertisement in *Billboard* set the tone: "Watch Out USA—Here They Are! The Rolling Stones! They're Great! They're Outrageous! They're Rebels! They're England's hottest—but hottest—group!" Once again, the fans seemed to agree. The album debut, released stateside with the subtitle "England's Newest Hitmakers," streaked into the Top Fifteen, remaining in the charts for thirty-five straight weeks. But behind the initial surge of interest was the kind of stubborn resistance America had always reserved for things that are new, novel, and foreign.

The Stones' arrival at Kennedy Airport was a carefully staged photo-op with five-hundred dutifully shrieking fans. The crowd was far short of the thousands who had greeted the Beatles, but Oldham made the best of the occasion, arranging for a symbolic presentation of four English sheepdogs to the bemused and bleary-eyed group.

Canned news items whipped up a contrived tumult. One press release announced: "Teenage fans armed with scissors are keeping the Rolling Stones prisoners in a Broadway hotel, for fans have caught the 'curl for a souvenir' fever." In fact, a subsequent photo shows an anonymous Brian strolling down Broadway unnoticed by anyone.

Back home Oldham publicized remarks such as the one made by a stern MP, warning, "Our relationship with the United States runs the risk of getting considerably worse as soon as the Rolling Stones arrive in America."

He needn't have worried. After the manufactured excitement died down, an uninterested America turned away from the Stones.

SEVEN

Satisfaction

The transformation was nearly complete. Five unlikely louts had joined a line of descent that spanned Sinatra and Presley, Valentino and the Beatles. The adoration, that intense identification exciting so much desire, would soon turn their world into a fish bowl.

And Mick would never look back. Stardom was about to change his life forever, but his essential character, stripped of his charisma, would remain unchanged. As millions of eyes turned to him, he turned inward, crafting an image that concealed as much as it revealed. What was conventional and middle-class continued to exert its pull. In time it would prove the key to his survival.

Mick's pliant vocals and sly, subversive style had become the focal point of the Stones' music. By the summer of 1964 the group had reached their first creative plateau. Revved up and road-tested, their music had a punch that left fans reeling. Their ensemble sound percolated the blues, lacing it with irony and a lot of volume. But it was Mick who was getting the ink, embodying the attitude and capitalizing on the notoriety. The limelight was part of his continuing education, by other means.

The certainty that their lives would never be the same again dawned with prospects of an American tour. "We thought, 'This is the payoff!' " Keith reports. "We got to fly to America, just to get there. . . . Nobody in our lives had a way of getting there, even once, just for a visit."

Brian's approach was cooler, more calculated: "It's people I want to see, not so much the places. I want to meet up with people who have the same ideas on music as we do."

Mick was all business: "I'd like to go to the Deep South and see some of the blues singers there, but we won't be able to on this trip. On a tour like this, you don't get time."

It was the novelty of British bands, an overflow of the Beatles' amazing impact, that accounted for the first surge of excitement that greeted the group in America. "They're so ugly, they're attractive," explained one fan, summing up the uncertainty.

After the manufactured hoopla fizzled, only a few prescient trend-setters picked up on the Stones' significance: "The new spectacular in England is a young man named Mick Jagger," gushed *Vogue*. "The Stones have a perverse, unsettling sex appeal, with Jagger out front of his team mates. To women, he is fascinating, to men, a scare."

The group first appeared with maudlin crooner Bobby Goldsboro before some wildly enthusiastic teenagers in the California farm town of San Bernardino. Shortly thereafter the tour headed for oblivion. "We were very unsuccessful but we still liked it," Mick asserts. "There we were touring all over the place on our own and nobody seemed to know us. . . . There was this total apathy building up from just about everyone."

Sharing bills with trained seals and a rodeo, their music echoed forlornly in one Midwestern livestock hall after another, playing for crowds of a few hundred. Those who bothered to review the pro-ceedings were predictably scandalized by the group's appearance: "Scruffy, undisciplined, ugly, and a menace," chided the *Omaha World Herald*, before pointing out the ultimate affront: "And they're skinny."

"All they've got that our own school groups haven't is hair," quipped one cowgirl at the Texas Teen Fair, where they were billed below a trained monkey.

Their televised appearances proved even more dismal. Oldham's US broadcast coup consisted of an appearance on gadfly Phil Crane's late night talk show on a local New York station late in November. "You guys all dress different," Crane perceptively noted. "How come?"

The nadir of a trip that had begun with such high hopes was an appearance on the L.A.-based TV variety show *Hollywood Palace*. Guest host Dean Martin's aura of inebriation gave license to a series of nasty jokes at the band's expense. Breaking for a commercial, he begged the viewing audience to stay tuned. "You wouldn't want to leave me with these Rolling Stones, would you?" he smirked. Returning to introduce a trampoline artist, Martin just couldn't help himself. "This is the father of the Rolling Stones," he said. "He's been trying to kill himself ever since."

"It was really like being a new group, trying to break through," Mick would later recount. "Hair questions drove me potty in America. I suppose we've got to start from scratch in a new country where they don't know us, but I got cheesed off with the whole thing."

The *Omaha World Herald* review continued, "The first Rolling Stone who poked his shaggy head through the curtain was a sight that belonged to a science fiction movie." It was typical of the stateside response engendered by the Stones: a mix of exaggerated horror and curiosity. "The guitar player came out in a kind of crouch. . . . He stared at the crowd with furtive, almost hostile eyes. Was this the creature from the black lagoon?"

Keith's stare could well have been attributable to something other than hostility or exhaustion. The drug underground proved a natural constituency for the group, their music, and their insurgent image. As the tour wound through hot spots in the emerging counterculture, New York and Los Angeles primarily, the group was introduced to a wide variety of mood-, mind-, and music-altering substances— uppers, downers, mind expanders, and all manner of feel-good concoctions.

But Mick's experiments extended only as far as the possibility of losing control. A casual dabbler, Mick had innate habits of caution that would serve him well over the course of the group's most harrowing drug adventures. And small wonder. Brian and Keith would go on to set examples for excess that would embody all the fears Oldham was working so hard to stir up.

While it's impossible to pinpoint the band's first forays into the cabinet of sixties pharmacopoeia, early evidence of abuse can be seen in Brian's increasing absences from the stage during concerts. Both Keith and Oldham were likewise entranced with the possibilities of drugs.

At the same time Oldham had taken to ever-more-flamboyant expressions of his gender-bending personality, flashy silk shirts with flowery prints and billowy sleeves accentuated his flair for makeup as he flitted around the country, hyping himself as much as his clients.

Like drugs, sex too was a plentiful commodity. "Bill Wyman was the one who lined up the ladies," Oldham insists, "the one who gave out his room number from the bandstand. There were always several girls waiting at Bill's door and he'd parcel them out. There was one, I recall, whose mother was patiently waiting downstairs in the lobby." The result, according to Oldham: "The band got a lot of clap, the price they paid for indiscriminate fucking."

In the end, it was Brian's fond hope—to meet the people who made the music—that would be best rewarded by America. On the lookout again for a new single, Oldham had uncovered a rock-ribbed R-&-B shouter, "It's All Over Now," and booked time for the band to cut it and a few other tracks at the mythic Chess Studios in Chicago, where so many classic blues and R-&-B hits had been recorded.

The trip to Chess, for years a shrine of all that Mick, Keith, and Brian held sacred, was like a visit to holy ground. While band members were helping Stu unload equipment from the van, Muddy Waters—a small, round black man with a pencil mustache—arrived. "He helped us carry out equipment," marvels Wyman, years later. While they were recording Chuck Berry's "Confessin' the Blues" and "Around and Around," the duck-walking guitarist himself stopped by the studios. "You got a real great sound," Berry told his awestruck devotees. "Swing on, gentlemen."

And swing they did. The evidence from those Chess sessions was undeniable: despite the travails of the tour, the group's music continued to take shape. Under the deft hand of engineer Ron Malo, behind the boards for many of the blues sides the band had cut its teeth on, "It's All Over Now," "Down the Road Apiece," and a handful of other tracks took on a round, deep, and fully packed dynamic. The musical momentum carried them back to New York for what would prove to be the best concerts of the tour: a pair of sold-out dates at Carnegie Hall, hosted by manic DJ Murray the K.

But for Mick the lessons of those half-empty halls in the sun-baked heartland lingered. "I give the Rolling Stones about another two years," he told Murray in an on-the-air interview. "I'm saving for my future. I bank all my song royalties for a start."

Chrissie was waiting at the airport for Mick's return to London in late June 1964. She had been enduring Mick's off-again, on-again attention for over a year. She basked in her boyfriend's reflected glory and was in no position to object when Oldham announced a new British tour to wipe the bad taste of America's from their mouths.

Her only recourse was to give Mick a taste of his own medicine. Discovering that Mick had found an American girlfriend and that she had followed him back home, Chrissie promptly got herself involved with singer P. J. Proby. "Whenever he'd stray," Chrissie would later brag, "I'd just go out with someone else and Mick would be back like a shot. He would never let the woman be the one to call things off. Mick *has* to be the one in control—giving the orders, calling the shots."

Another factor in Mick's thirst for control was his passion for upper-class respectability. He cultivated his friendships with anyone of title, including Princess Margaret, whom the British press often reported in Mick's company. "They spoke on the phone constantly and Margaret invited him to social events," one insider recalled. "Like many other women she found him sexy and exciting. If you saw them laughing together, dancing, the way she'd put her hand on his knee and giggle at his stories like a schoolgirl, you'd have thought there was something going on."

The Stones' return home to Heathrow Airport, in contrast to their Kennedy appearance, turned into a spontaneous mob scene of riotous fans being chased through boarding lounges by panting bobbies. The Stones had recently walked away with the Best Group competition in the British music trade paper *Record Mirror*, handily beating out the Beatles. At the same time, Mick was voted Favorite Group Member by readers and, most surprising of all, Sixth Best Dressed Man in the country, an honor that was particularly galling to Brian's vanity. "No comment," he growled to reporters who dared bring it up.

The struggle for control of the group was, in fact, virtually settled. Oldham's maneuver to put Mick and Keith together as songwriters effectively shut Brian out of the most creative, and potentially most profitable, aspect of their burgeoning career.

"Things got more complicated when Andrew got Mick and me together to write songs," Keith reflects. "It was the final full circle back to Mick and I being more together and Brian feeling the tension. Eventually it was standard procedure that Mick and I wrote the songs for the Stones. After that Brian felt completely disillusioned. . . . He felt this was a scene between Andrew, Mick, and me, and he was being left out."

Brian's deep distrust of Oldham exacerbated the rift. Music writer Peter Jones had an inside track on the unfolding feud: "There were a lot of things Andrew regarded as triumphs of promotion, in terms of getting space for the Stones, that did upset Brian. . . . The sensitive side of Brian made him think that the Rolling Stones were in danger of being classified as morons."

Peter Jones, a chief writer for the group's fan magazine, *Rolling Stone Monthly*, recalls numerous editorial meetings between the group, their manager, and the magazine staff. "Brian was terrified of being dated. After the image was done, the music would be done and people wouldn't take the Stones seriously. Brian especially felt this way after Andrew made one of his famous speeches that the 'Rolling Stones are not just a band but a way of life.' Brian questioned this all the way. I think it must have taken a fair amount of nerve as the months went by to speak out against Andrew, because Andrew wasn't listening to anybody."

Brian was, of course, free to take his talents elsewhere, but, from the heights the group had so quickly attained, there was no place left to go but down. "The hostility he felt from the other group members was very strong," recounts one close associate at the time, TV journalist Ellen Grehan. "He felt they were presenting a united front. But the saddest part was that he felt he was no longer a Rolling Stone."

"Although Brian mentioned to me a couple of times that he was going to leave the group, he never actually did it," recounts girlfriend Linda Lawrence. "Something held Brian to the Stones. I guess it was the beginning . . . the first thing he created. And it's scary to go out on your own after having all that success."

Despite the fact that Mick and Keith had been singled out by Oldham as the group's resident songwriting team, it was still Brian who put the top spin in the sound. "He was really incredible," recounts engineer Glyn Johns. "A lot of Rolling Stone records were built on riffs and Brian invariably played those riffs."

His harmonica work, his slide guitar, his wide-ranging and restless musical appetites—together they elevated the band from slavish blues purity to something utterly unique and audacious. "Some groups give performances," Brian himself would boast. "We have a rave, a mad, swaying, deafening, sweating half hour of tension and excitement that gives us just as big a kick as the kids."

In late July the Chess-recorded "It's All Over Now" was released and immediately shot to the top of the charts, giving the band their first number-one single. By then Mick had his Oldham-crafted attitude down pat: "I don't care a damn if our new record has reached number one. . . . What's it matter, anyway? . . . None of us have been worrying about it." He couldn't, however, help but engage in sales speculation: "I reckon it will do a half million in this country and others."

The arrogance was justified. Since their return home, and throughout their second UK tour, the band had inspired a frenzy. The barnstorming itinerary kicked off in late July of '65 before a packed house of seven thousand at the Empress Ballroom in Blackpool. Before it was over, two policemen and thirty fans were injured in a melee sparked by a gang of drunken Scots, in town commemorating the Battle of Culloden.

The band presented an irresistible excuse for hell-raising wherever they appeared throughout that balmy summer. And Oldham's publicity machine could do no wrong. "Rude," "boorish," the tabloid banners read, while one publication dismissed them as "anthropoid." Accounts of concert mayhem became more and more outlandish: a gig at the Boom Boom Room in Belfast, where screaming girls were carried out in straitjackets, seems an event sprung directly from Oldham's fevered imagination.

But this time there was a genuine hysteria to fuel. Crushed fans, rushed gates, battered bouncers, and regularly recurring episodes of nubile fans getting their clothes torn off were glorious grist for Oldham's publicity mill. In August a leap across the Channel for a first-ever European performance proved that continental fans had picked up the slack for the Americans. A crowd outside the Hague concert hall, unable to get into the show, inflicted major damage on the building and each other. Later that same year the group was besieged in the Brussels airport by 5,000 screaming faithful. For their Paris debut, at the Olympia, they were treated to a full-scale riot that spilled into the streets and resulted in 150 rock-crazed Parisians being tossed into jail.

Before it was all over, the Stones played fifty-four delirium-inducing shows between early July and October 1964. It was a punishing pace, but the music again proved that the group's sap was running high. Gathering the remainder of the Chess tracks, Decca released a second extended-play album, *Five by Five*, to advance orders of 200,000. The magic of those Chicago sessions was potent, and Mick's performances on cuts like "If You Need Me," "Confessin' the Blues," and "Empty Heart" were the musical equivalent of spontaneous combustion, his voice kindled by the excitement of the sounds it was capable of making.

The collection also featured a sterling token of Brian's continued creative influence: "2120 South Michigan Avenue," named for the studio address, was a loping, laid-back instrumental that ignites with Brian's soaring harp solo, one of the most exhilarating and unfettered of his recording career. *Five by Five* proved that the Stones were more than the sum of their hype. They could sustain.

In late October, on the heels of their British tour, they returned to the US after only a four-month absence, this time bolstered by the chart success of "Not Fade Away" and the growing American awareness that the Rolling Stones were, after all, the Next Big Thing.

The tour, launched with another pair of sold-out shows, this time at the New York Academy of Music, was hampered by Brian's increasingly erratic behavior. His drug use, nurtured on their first American swing, had sprung into full bloom, and there were dark rumors of a sleeping pill overdose on the eve of their departure. His absence from the stage prompted a statement that denied a little more than was absolutely necessary.

"I'm not on my last legs and I'm not leaving the Stones," Brian was quoted as saying. "I felt ill during our first American tour and I wasn't enjoying good health when we arrived back in Britain. That's why I have to take things easy for a while. The thought of leaving the Stones has never entered my head."

Leaving Linda Lawrence, Brian took up with a petite Scottish girl named Ronny Money. "He left Linda because he thought he was hurting her with the drug and star pressures," Ronny would later write, trying to justify Brian's erratic and often cruel behavior. "Brian was taking all sorts if amphetamines, which made him really paranoid."

Another friend, Dave Thomson, concurs: "Brian was paranoid because he had every reason to be: it was a paranoia based on reality. In a hotel I saw Brian standing outside a room with his ear to the door. When he saw me, he said, 'They're talking about me. Go in and find out what they're saying.' When I went in, I found out he was right. Brian was definitely being excluded. He thought Mick was at the root of it."

Peter Jones saw another side of Brian's increasing substance abuse. "Brian got very heavily into drinking," he reports. "The point is that if somebody starts behaving strangely you can never really put your finger on what it is that's causing it. You don't see them doing anything but drinking, so you obviously tend to blame the drinking."

Brian in turn blamed his increasing estrangement from the band on the machinations of Mick and Oldham. The manager's campaign to tie himself to the singer's increasingly high profile generated a lot of ego-stroking coverage that angered Mick's bandmates and enraged Brian.

"The most important thing about Mick is that he is such a distinct personality," Oldham asserted in an interview. "A very intelligent and creative one. . . . To get the best from him and the other Stones at a recording session, I aim at the right atmosphere, a relaxed and informal one . . . plenty of tea, Cokes, and gags. I also hold the session in the evening if I can. That's the time when Mick is in the right mood."

Mick's former Edith Grove roommates could see right through Oldham's panderings. For Mick it was another voice proclaiming him the prince of pop culture.

Chrissie did not join in that chorus of praise. Her identity now entirely submerged by her association with Mick and the Stones, Chrissie had left her job at Decca to work directly for Oldham. It was, perhaps, a ploy to get nearer to her wavering suitor, but the move didn't help her self-esteem. Nor did the move to a larger flat in a prestigious neighborhood, Harley House in London's Marleybone Road. While the pair took high-profile forays to the antique stalls of Portobello Road and Kings Road's fashionable boutiques, the house remained stubbornly half-furnished, a testament to their half-finished affair. A friend, Maldwin Thomas, reports "famous, plate-throwing, Hollywood-style rows" emanating from the apartment. Another aquaintance confirms that "they were always, always arguing."

And when they weren't fighting, Chrissie capitalized on her famous boyfriend, writing charming fabrications about domestic life with Mick in "From London with Luv," her monthly column for *Mod* magazine. "Recently had my 21st birthday," ran one cloying snippet. "Mick gave me a huge rocking horse which I named Petunia."

The fact that Mick stayed with Chrissie as long as he did, well over two years, is yet another clue to the conventional aspirations that formed his persona. He was not willing to forgo marriage and a family, despite the endless opportunities for debauchery offered on the road and his own carefully calibrated reputation for hedonism and heroic nonconformity.

Even as the Stones' trajectory flew toward the pinnacle of fame, there was something that held him back, something between a lingering sense of unreality and the stubborn virtues of his upbringing that held him. Chrissie, every inch a prize for an ambitious bourgeois boy, became the last vestige of all those simple aspirations. As such, he was as loath to let her go as he was to make the plunge into marriage.

"Actually, if you're a musician I think it's very good not to be with anybody and just live on your own," he would muse years later, long after the options had been all but foreclosed. "Domesticity is death. You see, the trouble with most musicians is that they're too domesticated. A musician doesn't spend too much time at home; he's on the road, living out of a suitcase. Then, when he gets home, he tends to become very domesticated. In fact, you enjoy the best of both worlds."

Without, it might be added, the real rewards or responsibilities of either.

The second American tour was attended by all the requisite folderal, assiduously milked by Oldham. An October 25, 1964, appearance on *The Ed Sullivan Show* prompted another, by now routine burst of righteous indignation, this time from the lantern-jawed host himself, responding to a switchboard jammed by irate viewers.

"I had not met the Stones until the day before they were due to appear," ran Sullivan's disavowal. "They were recommended to me by my agents in England. I was shocked when I saw them. I promise you they'll never be back on the show."

The impresario went on with a revealing observation that illustrates just how far removed the Stones were from both the musical mainstream and their rock 'n' roll competition. "Now the Dave Clark Five are nice fellows," he allowed. "They are gentlemen and they perform well. It took me seventeen years to build up this show, and I'm not going to have it destroyed in a matter of weeks."

The notion that the Stones could singlehandedly scuttle such an American institution only added to an allure that would guarantee them a return spot on *Ed Sullivan*, more than once as their career mushroomed.

The conspicuous success of their return American swing set the tone for what was, indeed, to become the Stones' way of life for the foreseeable future: a chaotic blur of dim-lit hotel lobbies, frantic concerts pitched against the roar of their fans, and recording studios where the band struggled to chronicle changes in their music as urgent and unmanageable as the shifting aspects of their lives.

By the end of 1964 they had released another album, *12 × 5*, recorded in London and Los Angeles. The album highlighted an ethereal version of Willie Dixon's barnyard lament, "Little Red Rooster." Despite the qualms of Decca Records at releasing pure blues, the cut climbed to number one in the space of a fortnight. A second single, a cover of Irma Thomas's "Time Is on My Side," took the group into the US Top Ten for the first time.

On hand for the L.A. sessions at RCA's Hollywood studios, producer and engineer Jack Nitzsche offers compelling proof of what made the Stones, and their records, so different. "There was no guidance at all on those records," he explains, "and very little need for it. . . . This was the first time a band got together and just played. They changed my whole idea of recording. Before I'd just been doing sessions, three hours to get the tunes down. Working with the Stones made sense right away: book studio time for twenty-four hours a day for two weeks and if you didn't get it, fuck it."

Brian's ongoing physical deterioration landed him in a Chicago hospital in mid-tour. Though he was ostensibly admitted for pneumonia, the rumors of yet another drug overdose grew more persistent. But nothing could slow the careening course of the band, least of all the intractable soap opera that Brian's life was becoming.

The group roared into 1965 with the announcement of another tour, this time to Australia and New Zealand, back to Eva Jagger's dimly remembered homeland. The Stones had now been on the road continuously for over a year. And things were beginning to fray a little.

"Nineteen sixty-five was the year it all came together for the

Stones," recounts Oldham, "but for me personally it started to come apart. . . . I got heavily into drugs and I was in no shape to contribute much to the Stones."

If the band was too busy to enjoy their success, their manager certainly found time. "My memory of their US tour is fuzzy and full of gaps. I vaguely recall lying on the beach in Miami or somewhere warm while they were slogging around the States performing."

By Oldham's estimation, "By July of 1965 the Stones had sold ten million singles, five million albums, and had earned five million in personal appearances."

They were breaking records certainly, but it wasn't until Mick and Keith discovered the true strength of their songwriting partnership that they began making history. There was a comradeship, a creative connection stretching back to Dartford, that would have brought the two together even without Oldham. In combination, the pair would take the group, and the state of the rock 'n' roll art, to a whole new stage. There was a potent blend of the blues and the British in both of them, a distillation of irony, braced by demanding passions. And it all came together in a cut called "Satisfaction."

The first hint of things to come could be heard in "The Last Time," released in February of 1965 on the heels of a new American album, *The Rolling Stones Now.* "The Last Time," with its low, hovering guitar hook and lyric ambivalence, was the first true rock song written by the team of Jagger/Richards.

" 'The Last Time' was the first of our own songs that we really liked," admits Mick. "I suppose we'd been writing for almost nine months to a year by then, just learning how to put songs together. And with 'The Last Time' it became fun. After that we were confident that we were on our way, that we'd just got started."

Fans agreed. "The Last Time" went Top Ten in the States, setting expectations high for the group's follow-up. Returning to Chess Studios in early May, the band recorded a handful of new songs, including "The Under Assistant West Coast Promotion Man"—an ode to London Records' obsequious George Sherlock—along with a tenuous new number built around a lick Keith had thought up while driving through Clearwater, Florida.

"If I'd had my way, 'Satisfaction' would have never been released," he insists. "The song was basic as the hills and I thought the fuzz guitar thing was a bit of a gimmick." According to legend, the decision to release "Satisfaction" was put to a vote. It was Mick and Keith against the rest, with Stu and Oldham weighing in for good measure. "Satisfaction" it was.

And "Satisfaction" it would be, a song full of sexual urgency and contempt for convention. It was a call to arms for a generation too impatient to wait for the privileges of adulthood, too angry to endure the indignities of youth. The song wasted no time getting straight to the point, that gimmicky fuzz guitar lick becoming one of the most universally recognized refrains in modern music. But it was the lyrics, the deadly accurate evocation of tongue-tied frustration, that would forever express the surging discontent of the time. More than simply the song that brought international renown to the Stones, "Satisfaction" was the key to understanding the emotional investment in change being made by millions of the disenchanted, disenfranchised, and disillusioned. Mick was the voice, but they were all doing the singing.

EIGHT

Convent Girl

It was Andrew Loog Oldham—with his flair for the dramatic, his gift of provocation, his instinct for outrage—who discovered her. He was the first one to see her delicious antithesis, the whole Madonna/ whore paradox that gave her innocence its edge, her sensuality its ethereal aura. It was Oldham who pegged her for stardom, as a pale-eyed sixties remake of a de Sade heroine—all breathless passion and defiled virtue. But he could never have come up with so perfect a name for the creature, Marianne Faithfull.

As Mick Jagger's consort through the prismatic shadow play of Swinging London, Marianne Faithfull embodied a paradigm of beauty, an ideal of pallid glamour perfectly in keeping with the enraptured vanities of the time. She was a lacy English wraith, her gaze so wan it seemed all but transparent, her lips as bruised and tremulous as her lover's, her vulnerability suggesting a kinky new variation on Ophelia. Like Twiggy and like Jean Shrimpton, and like the thousand other "birds" that flitted through the London underground, Marianne was a walking invitation to violation, an ideal of womanhood so frail and exposed, it could excite the most unseemly passions.

And that was the whole idea. If Marianne hadn't existed to present herself a living sacrifice on the altar of Mick's flamboyant narcissism, someone would have had to invent her. As they strolled together through Hyde Park in boas and bangles, she both enforced Mick's masculinity and enhanced his androgyny. They were less like lovers than like brother and sister, tied by some incestuous fate, in an affair that blurred the boundaries of identity. It was not the first time Mick would look into a woman's face as if looking into a mirror. But for Marianne the gaze became unendurable, the reflection cracked, and the reverie rudely laid to rest.

If Chrissie represented the sort of lass an LSE graduate with good prospects might one day hope to marry, Marianne carried with her the rich scent of the monied class and all the dreams of social ascent that came with it. She was the daughter of a heroic British intelligence officer and a genuine Austrian baroness, Eva Sacher-Masoch, the Baroness Erisso. Scion of an illustrious Middle European dynasty stretching back to Charlemagne, Eva's most famous ancestor was the nineteenth-century novelist Leopold von Sacher-Masoch, who first posited the notion of pain producing sexual ecstasy. It's a condition that still bears his name: masochism.

A beautiful woman and a talented dancer, Eva, Marianne's mother, lived in Vienna throughout the war and was active in the effort to rescue Austrian Jews from the Nazis. Glyn Faithfull, a liaison officer with Tito's partisans in Yugoslavia, rescued her brother from the Germans and, so the family legend has it, was repaid with an introduction to the radiant Eva. The two were married after the war and their first child, Marianne, was born in 1947.

When her parents separated six years later, Marianne moved with her mother to the bucolic confines of Reading, where she lived in genteel poverty among the musty reminders of Eva's regal past. Stricken twice with tuberculosis, Marianne survived, retaining that fashionable Dresden pallor left by the illness.

By all accounts Marianne was a remarkable child, encouraged by Eva to develop her gifts of intellect and art. "My mother taught me that to be beautiful—as I knew I was—shouldn't be a passive thing," Marianne recalls. "It was something to be put to use, the way that, in the past, she had put her own beauty to use. I was trained by a highly trained professional. There was no doubt, in my mind or my mother's, that I'd go on the stage."

Before the limelight, however, it was the cloistered glow of a convent that lit her days. Marianne was taken in to St. Joseph's, a local Catholic convent, as a charity case boarder, and it was that lingering image—the virginal convent girl—as much as any education in sin, guilt, or redemption that would shape her career and her life.

She began to sing, folk tunes in a lilting mezzo-soprano, in the local coffeehouses, passing her teenage years, as she puts it with a fitting poetic flair, "living in a Renoir: long blond hair, sunny days, straw hats with ribbons." Eventually she fell into the orbit of a Cambridge fine arts scholar, John Dunbar, with connections to the London music scene. It was in the summer of 1964, on Good Friday to be exact, that Dunbar escorted his lissome find to a promotional party in London to launch a singer named Adrienne Posta. In attendance, Andrew and Mick.

"The minute I saw her, I knew she was something special," Oldham recounts. "She had this fantastic virginal look. I mean, at a time when most chicks were shaking ass and coming on strong, here was this pale, blond, retiring, chaste teenager looking like a Mona Lisa, except with a great body. And what a name—Marianne Faithfull." It was, in fact, his opening gambit to her: "With a name like that you ought to be making records."

"Looking at Mick and Keith and the rest of them, I thought, 'My God, what truly awful people,' " Marianne recalls of that fateful evening. "Awful, mind you, but a bit fascinating, especially Andrew Oldham, who was wearing feminine silks and had on makeup. They took notice of me . . . even though I was only a shy girl of seventeen from a convent in a little town. And I looked very different from everyone else, I think, because I wasn't dressed up and I wasn't made up either. And also I was very, very still. I picked that up from the nuns . . . that business of not really showing your hands, keeping very still, and moving sort of all in one piece."

Oldham's offer was in earnest. "He showed up with a personal management contract and a recording session at Decca," Marianne remembers. Still a minor, Marianne required the consent of her mother. Eva readily gave it, no doubt convinced that the curtain was rising on her daughter's career. "Her one stipulation was that when I went out on tour, I must always have a chaperone," Marianne recalls.

Oldham picks up the story: "So now I've got this convent girl with the sexy body and the virginal smile, daughter of a countess, name of Marianne Faithfull, a potential hot property, but I haven't got a thing for her to sing. So I go to my resident songwriters, Mr. Jagger and Mr. Richards, and I ask them to write a nice ballad for a convent girl to sing, a song with brick walls around it and positively no sex. . . . Well, what do the two fuckers come up with? An absolute knockout, 'As Tears Go By,' sentimental, lyrical, melodic—for the first time they had composed something original out of themselves and not tried to echo stuff they had heard."

Oldham's relentless revisionism notwithstanding, "As Tears Go By" *was* an inspired match of music and maiden. "Greensleeves goes pop" was how the *Daily Mirror* put it as the tune slowly climbed into the Top Ten on British charts throughout that summer and early fall.

With such a promising response, Oldham wasted no time in putting his new client out on the road, with scant regard for the jarring dislocations that might ensue. In point of fact, Marianne adapted quite well. There was a streak of steely ambition in the gamine, no doubt an offshoot of Eva's genes. "I had gone from the obscurity of a convent right smack into the limelight," she explains. "It was fabulous when I first started singing in front of an audience. I loved it."

Considerably less appealing to her were Oldham's star clients. "They looked very common to me," she says. "I liked John, doing his fine arts at Cambridge and all that. The Stones didn't have that superficial undergraduate education that I liked, to be able to talk about paintings, reading Camus, and going to see foreign movies. They weren't into that."

Eventually, after the first flush of excitement sparked by "Tears" evaporated, Marianne married the solid, dependable Dunbar. It was not a match made for love. With characteristic candor, she recounts: "I wouldn't have married John Dunbar if I hadn't been pregnant. He didn't mind marrying me, and in a way I think he thought it was the only way to pin me down. Because I was very much on the verge of realizing my power, and I think I was frightened of it too. I thought that getting married would tie me to the ground a bit. I needed to touch the hand of reality, I really did."

It wouldn't exactly be reality's hand that she would hold for the next six years. Marianne became a star in London's swinging orbit, wowing Gene Pitney and stealing the heart of an adenoidal Minnesota poet named Bob Dylan who had just burst onto the scene. Dunbar had set himself up on the cutting edge of the scene by opening an underground art outlet, Indica Gallery, but it was quickly apparent that he was being badly outclassed by his wife's rich new friends. The couple gamely struggled to raise their new son, Nicholas.

"I did want that baby," Marianne recalls. "I was trying to become respectable, I think. I was looking for myself, who I really was." She would find some semblance of that identity among the whimsical menagerie inhabiting the paisley corridors of sixties London. By 1966 her marriage was over and Marianne was free to follow her elegant fancy through a world awash with drugs, money, and damp secrets.

That world was increasingly populated with big-league players, both in the bedroom and in business. The Stones had begun to attract a whole new class of hustlers and hangers-on, people who knew just where to sink the hooks and just how deep. People like Allen Klein and Anita Pallenberg.

The success of "Satisfaction," number one in America for a solid month in the summer of '65, and the brilliant licks they were laying down on their new album, *Out of Our Heads*, signaled the band's continued creative vitality along with their earning power. Oldham had read and rejected a number of film projects for the band in his quest to take them to the inevitable next step. With *Out of Our Heads* topping album sales charts for three weeks in that long, hot, and riot-torn summer, Oldham leaked reports that the group was on the verge of signing a ten-million-dollar multi-movie deal.

In truth, the drug-addled dandy was losing his grip on the group. At the end of the day Oldham was simply too light in the loafers to take hold of the exponentially expanding enterprise that was the Rolling Stones. He much preferred to pass himself off as the man behind the curtain, controlling the events that had already begun to control him. "Andrew wanted to be the star of the Stones and that's what got him in trouble," asserts Stones confidant Cynthia Stewart.

That trouble started in the summer of '65 when Oldham first met New York music accountant and attorney Allen Klein. The two had done business before, negotiating a rate for "It's All Over Now," administered by Klein's publishing company. The squat, scheming son of a Newark butcher, Klein quickly presumed on his passing aquaintance with the famous group's famous manager.

"How would you like to be a millionaire?" he asked Oldham, then promptly promised to make him one. "What do you want for now?" Klein then asked, offering a good faith token.

"A Rolls-Royce," replied Oldham off the top of his head. A day later Klein arrived at the hotel door behind the wheel of a Silver Shadow.

Subtlety was not the strong suit of a man whose holiday cards read,

"Though I walk through the valley of the shadow of death, I will fear no evil, for I am the biggest bastard in the valley."

A legendary music business operator whose client roster included Sam Cooke, Scottish Dylan manqué Donovan, and a clutch of Merseybeat acts, Klein was also up-front with the Stones. He shrewdly played on the vague fears of all stars that someone is stealing their money. Scoffing at the lucrative deal with Decca that Oldham and Easton were completing, Klein offered to do better. He did, landing the group a 1.25-million-dollar advance against royalties.

Klein's arrival naturally necessitated the departure of the long-suffering Eric Easton. Easton blustered and filed suit, but it was no use. Klein, with a feral prescience, had taken on the role of avuncular sugar daddy to Mick, Keith, and Oldham, playing them like proverbial fiddles.

Keith was especially taken with this pugnacious thirty-four-year-old CPA. "Klein was young and he knew what was happening," Keith explains. "He made us laugh. We liked him. We decided on an American for our business manager because we did so much business there it was very useful to have a man on the spot. We kept in touch by phone."

Klein was hardly the sort to be left to his own devices. By late August of 1965 the money, and the possibility for more money, seemed staggering. Klein's new deal with Decca and, in the States, London Records, called for over three million dollars in American rights alone. The group's 1965 tour of America was fueled by "Get Off My Cloud," a jokey variation on the "Satisfaction" theme that nevertheless went to number three. With Klein putting together the concert itinerary and handling the gate, the group, over the course of a grueling thirty-two dates in the dead of winter, would gross an unprecedented two million dollars.

The gates earned in night after sold-out night, along with much of the funds to come, would subsequently be sucked into a shell company Klein ostensibly erected to run the group's American interests, a company controlled outright by the real man behind the curtain, Klein himself.

With oily aplomb Klein became the group's comanager. Oldham was given charge of vaguely defined conceptual conceits, a calling accepted with embarrassing relish. "The sound, face, and mind of today is more relative to the hope of tomorrow and the reality of destruction than the blind who cannot see their children for fear and division." So ran Oldham's oblique copy on a sixty-foot Times Square billboard announcing the group's new album, *December's Children (and Everybody's)*. "Something that grew and related. Five reflections of today's children. The Rolling Stones."

December's Children was the group's first serious mistake on record. A muddy hodgepodge of outtakes and dusted-off tracks, the album sounded exactly like what it was: fodder for the fans that snapped up everything the Stones created, good, bad, or indifferent. "It's difficult to realize the pressure we were under to keep on turning out hits," Keith remembers. "After 'Satisfaction' we all thought, 'Wow, lucky us. Now for a good rest.' And then in comes Andrew, saying, 'Right, where's the next one?' "

Aftermath was the next one, recorded in Los Angeles in December of that bustling year. The record offered the strongest evidence yet that Brian, whatever his political standing in the band, continued to exert a powerful creative pull. The songs were all Mick and Keith's and the lyrics were pure Jagger, spraying the petulant venom that was becoming the substance of his trademark anti–love song, cynical, cutting, and cruel.

But it was Brian's deft touches that gave the album its ghostly aura and gossamer textures. From the rounded marimba notes that introduced the scabrous "Under My Thumb" to the winsome dulcimer tones of "Lady Jane" and the languorous "Waiting," from the sitar runs of "Mother's Little Helper" to the mellifluous melancholy of his "Out of Time" arrangement, *Aftermath* was an album that fashioned subtle nuances and fleeting beauty from the base metal of rock 'n' roll.

It was all the more impressive considering Brian's fleeting sanity and weak grasp on reality. Working twenty-hour shifts in their downtime from the last numbing days of the tour, Brian and the group managed to turn their exhaustion into a musical statement. Here was lassitude you could dance to.

"Brian would be down on his back, laying around the studio with his guitar strapped around him," Keith recalls. "Then he would contribute amazing things. Suddenly, from nine hours of lying there, he'd just walk in and lay some beautiful things down on a track— piano, harpsichord—something that nobody'd even thought of."

It was an alchemy most evident on the album's centerpiece and the band's new single, "Paint It Black," which would reach number one in the US by the spring of '66. With its galloping Gypsy cadence and modal chanting, "Paint It Black" was an electrifying example of Brian's increasingly esoteric approach to the backbeat. His growing infatuation with North African culture—now the decor *du jour* in London's psychedelic dens—fed his musical imagination, as did the raga rhythms brought into the mix by the Beatles' George Harrison. More than a novelty hit, "Paint It Black," with its Middle Eastern echoes, pointed the way toward the coming Rococo Age of rock 'n' roll, with its drug-drenched experimentations.

A fellow traveler on Brian's agonized journey had made her dramatic entrance earlier that year. When, following the *Aftermath* sessions, the group returned to London, it was to Anita Pallenberg that Brian turned for solace and succor.

It was not an especially perceptive choice. With her lanky blond hair, lean curves, and Swedish pedigree, Anita Pallenberg was to love what Allen Klein was to business, an inside operator. Descended from the medieval painting clan of Holbein and Böcklin, Anita had hung on the fringes of the international art scene in New York, London, and Rome as a teenager. By 1965, at age twenty-three, she was a well-established model and aspiring film actress.

"Anita in those days was absolutely electrifying," recalls a friend, antique dealer Christopher Gibbs. "There was a sense of mischief about her . . . of naughtiness. Something kittenish."

A beautiful woman of voracious appetites, she would become a sort of depraved den mother for the band, seeking advantage with her body and her wicked imagination. "There was nothing genteel about Anita," explains another friend, Jane Ormsby-Gore. "She had an almost masculine sense of humor, which could be very savage, and had a completely unrestrained laugh. She was very wicked, very intelligent."

To hear her tell it, Anita arrived in Brian's life not a moment too soon. "The first night that Brian and I spent together," she recounts, "he cried the entire night." It was September 1965, and Anita had talked her way backstage after a Munich concert. She was thin and blond with hooded eyes, it was not the first time that a Rolling Stones was drawn to his own image in the face of a woman. "We were in bed and I held him in my arms and he couldn't stop crying, like he'd been holding back all this pain and now he was able to let it go. It was all about Mick and Keith and the others."

For Anita it would always be about combinations—in partners, drugs, and allegiances. "We got along very well, right from the beginning," she recounts, "liking to investigate, experiment, get into mischief. Brian looked kind of like a girl. . . . Sexually I like girls as well as men and Brian seemed to combine both sexes for me."

There were, in fact, few things that Anita did *not* like. She had a Pandora's box of kinky secrets and control trips waiting for Brian and his bandmates. Mick, as usual, was wary of the new power equation brought on by Anita. She was a stunning prize for the discredited Brian to suddenly have on his arm. "I was aware that these other Stones didn't approve of me," Anita continues. "Especially Mick. Mick really tried to put me down, thereby putting Brian down in the process."

Anita Pallenberg did not suffer fools, even a famous one, gladly. Hardly a simpering groupie, Anita ran with a very fast, very savvy crowd, the vanguard of Europe and England's psychedelic art dandies, "a fascinating group of people who were on the cutting edge of what was happening in high society," Anita attests without apparent irony. "Great cultural evenings, wonderful intellectual talk, plenty of hash and marijuana and speed and LSD. Brian and I were having a ball."

Mick of all people was powerless to stop the ball from spinning. "There was no way this sort of crude, lippy guy was going to do a number on me," Anita insists. "I was always able to squelch him. I found out, you stand up to Mick, he crumbles. He tried to order Brian to stop seeing me, called me poison. He ordered his girlfriend Chrissie not to go near me."

Mixed with Mick's suspicion of Anita and his anxiety of a new power balance in the band, there was certainly a tinge of envy over the exotic, risky new woman in Brian's life. Whether it was Anita's arrival which would finally prompt him to find his own fitting femme fatale is a matter of opinion.

His decision to finally cut loose the increasingly despondent Chrissie seems more likely the result of an indiscretion named Marianne Faithfull. With her marriage over, she turned in late 1966 to an unlikely source of comfort. "I went to Mick because I needed a friend," she says, before adding, with compulsive honesty, "Mick was a friend who also happened to be a millionaire."

Honesty and an innate intelligence were to help Marianne cope with life among the Stones. It was more than her serene good looks that set her apart from the perky Chrissie. Her trembling innocence was a simple trick of nature, a disguise to hide the complex, questing woman within.

From late summer of that year onward Mick and Marianne did little to hide their liaison. That winter he took her for a leisurely cruise along the French Riviera to proclaim his love, leaving Chrissie behind.

Chrissie and Mick had a harrowing argument in early December of 1966. "We had loads of rows," Mick had declared, "and it reached a point where a split was the only wise thing left."

For Chrissie it wasn't so simple. Three years of indecision, suspicion, and benign neglect had culminated in a kiss-off. A subsequent suicide attempt landed her in a Hampstead hospital. At a bedside visitation Mick revealed his ill-concealed affair with Marianne and, on his way out, told the front desk he wouldn't be footing the bill. "On Christmas Eve," writes Wyman, "Mick hired a van to collect all of Chrissie's personal belongings from the Harley House flat and return them to her." It was over.

NINE

Traps for Troubadours

When the pressures of stardom began to take on a routine of their own; when excess yields only crushing ennui; when you're not quite sure in what country you are for another one night stand, it's time for a break.

But for the Stones, pacing had always been a problem. It wasn't exactly impossible to stop, it's just that no one knew where the brake was or even wanted to admit they were looking for it. Oldham's palaver about a "way of life" was coming back to haunt them. The Rolling Stones *were* a way of life that consisted of one cavernous stadium after another, all filled with undulating screams from a faceless crowd. It was a world of maddeningly sanitized hotel rooms and room service carts overflowing with stale breakfast, bottles, and butts, of women without names wrapped in every imaginable package.

Each Klein-catered tour ratcheted up the group's bone weariness. The release of *Aftermath* in July of 1966 mandated a fifth American swing, with Klein pulling all the strings from an office on a yacht anchored in New York Harbor.

Like the ones that preceded it, the Stones' new itinerary was an exhausting string of twenty-eight dates in twenty-seven days, playing regularly to crowds of ten thousand. The summer was a numbing blur of packed houses and music cranked to the threshold of pain. It was the only way the band, who had once reveled in their ensemble playing, could even hear themselves. The orchestrated outrage continued, a testament to Oldham, who had by now nearly faded. But it was all just another too-familiar routine. The group's goading of the gray flannel types had become uncomfortably like a Punch and Judy publicity show, each side using the other to score points.

Still the band played on. "They didn't have the confidence to deal with success," Mick's brother Chris was to observe years later. "Not the sudden success of the rock world with all that adulation and enormous money. They were poor boys, from provincial places. . . . Success overwhelmed them. It's much harder to deal with success than to deal with failure, because with failure, you keep trying."

The pressures—private and public—that were warping the Stones' lives also had an effect on their music. Despite its title *Aftermath* was more a harbinger of things to come, as the group began to deconstruct its own sound, pulling it apart and fitting it back into the oddest, most appalling and intriguing combinations.

The first alarming indication of the Stones' strange new sound was the September 1966 release of the single "Have You Seen Your Mother, Baby, Standing in the Shadows?" Recorded on a cheap tape deck for maximum distortion, the song opens full bore on guitars droning like a hive of angry bees, then rapidly plummets into a bewildering cacophony of strife and incoherent violence. Tin trumpets blare, pianos are pounded to splinters, the air is full of snarls and wheezes and demented caterwauling.

Mick's lyrics, previously poised in their mincing misogyny, erupted into curdling contempt, fueled by sputtering rage. It was a terrifying tour de force and a hair-raising representation of the angst that swirled around the band. The sleeve for the single raised the ante with a perverse joke on the group's drag queen subtext. The band was pictured decked out like nightmarish maiden aunts, Wyman in a wheelchair and Mick in a tacky flowered hat. It was a twisted take on Mick's tradition of cross-dressing. The Stones were pushing the envelope—and their luck.

An in-concert recording, *Got Live If You Want It*, continued the descent into disintegration. With a title that could be construed as either an invitation or a warning, the album, released in November 1966, was a raucous recording of the group's frenzied stage show, in which music was decidedly beside the point. According to Marianne, the raw passions of thousands of unhinged fans had a sometimes horrific effect on the objects of their adoration.

"I went once to meet Mick on a European tour," she remembers. "He came straight off the stage to the hotel where I was waiting, and he was absolutely terrifying. I was really, really scared. . . . He was like someone possessed. . . . He still had his makeup on and there was a froth of spittle around his lips. His eyes were violent. He was making sounds, guttural sounds. . . . After that I never went to any of his performances if I could help it."

"I get this strange feeling on stage," Mick himself would admit. "I feel all this energy coming from the audience. They need something from life and are trying to get it from us. I often want to smash the microphone up because I don't feel the same person on stage as I am normally."

Normalcy was a word best used advisedly in the supercharged circuses that the Stones' shows had become. "What really upsets people," Mick would say, "is that I'm a man and not a woman. . . . What I do is very much the same as a girl's striptease dance. Those screaming girls at our shows: their emotions are affection with violence and sex on top. They're all charged up. It's a dialogue of energy. They give you a lot of energy and they take a lot away."

What time and energy he had left he lavished on Marianne and their enchanted love affair. The two were the toast of London's haute monde, regal as they strolled down King's Road or breakfasted at the Chelsea Antique Mart. Evenings were spent at the Chelsea Potter, the Pheasantry and Kenco Coffee Bar, or over the sumptuous spread at the Baghdad House on Fulham Road. They attracted to their inner circle such charmed confidants as photographer David Bailey, now one of Mick's closest friends, painter David Cammell, American alternative filmmaker Kenneth Anger, and in Mick's first brush with European royalty, the Swiss playboy Prince Stanislaus Klossowski de Rola. Their standing as London's premier rock aristocrats eventually led them into the upper reaches of the social register. Papparazzi regularly caught them ducking in or out of the latest nightclub with the likes of Cecil Beaton, Princess Margaret, and others in the junior division of the royal set.

The aura of the era was epitomized by the ongoing Moroccan craze, essentially started by antique dealer Christopher Gibbs— billowy drapes, satiny pillows, Persian rugs and strings of Goulimane beads hung about high-ceilinged Kensington flats with calculated abandon. The fashion was sheer, loose-fitting, and languid, a mix of Gypsy panache and Berber chic. It was as if clammy old London had suddenly become sweltering downtown Marrakesh. Clothes, furniture, the hazy glow of scarf-covered bulbs through thick incense smoke—it was the expression purely and simply of a culture drenched in drugs. Miles distant from the colorful, confrontational extremes of the Mods—the last great moment of British fashion—the new style was closer to the muted lights and silky textures of a richly appointed opium den.

The nineteen-year-old Marianne took to the metaphor rather more avidly than Mick. The couple went to the French Riviera in early '67 for a holiday. Marianne had become an accomplished devotee of herbs and chemicals. She had been introduced to psychedelics by John Dunbar, who had a habit of mixing LSD and methedrine in his coffee for a morning cocktail, and who cultivated a discriminating taste for cannabis. She took pains to catalog the combinations of effects. "The thing about drugs," Marianne would later explain in her remarkable interviews with A. E. Hotchner, "is that when you are taking drugs, you simply don't speak. You are. You don't talk about anything. You just are." For the convent girl, drugs were more than a pastime. They were the keys to a world where all things were held in an exquisite balance between ecstasy and oblivion.

Mick was another matter entirely. "They laughed at him," she says, recalling Keith and Brian's disdain for Mick's cautious habits, "because he was so straight and so conventional and terrified of hash or acid or whatever. He was really out of step, not part of the scene. Mick is very frightened of drugs—always was."

" 'This is all getting out of hand,' " Donald Cammell, a friend of the couple's, remembers Mick warning. " 'I don't know where it's all going to end.' "

The beginning of the end—as far as the group's dangerous disdain of authority went—began with what seems a blatant setup by the tabloid *News of the World*. Under the banner headline "The Secrets of the Pop Stars' Hideaway," the writer purported to have spotted Mick at LSD parties with the Moody Blues, later trailing him to an

Oxford Street club where he "took about six Benzedrine tablets . . . and showed a companion and two girls a piece of hashish and asked them to his flat for a smoke."

The colorful invention of a copywriter who himself may have popped one too many bennies, the story nevertheless provoked a panic in Mick. Alone among the group's inner circle, he seemed to sense the impending crackdown. On a talk show that same Sunday, he announced that he would be suing the *News of the World* for libel.

At this point Mick's unerring sense of self-preservation deserted him, with disastrous results. Perhaps he simply bridled at being bluffed by the newspaper; maybe he was beginning to believe the talk about a psychedelic revolution sweeping the streets; or possibly he simply gave in to the blandishments of Marianne and the ridicule of his friends. Whatever the case, on February 12, at age twenty-two, he motored to Keith's new Redlands estate, where he had agreed to swallow his first dose of LSD. It was going to be a bad trip.

T E N

Breaking the
Butterfly

If a bomb had gone off that day at Keith's country hideaway, Swinging London would have lost its A-list. The party of eleven included, aside from Mick, Marianne, and Keith, friends and hangers-on Christopher Gibbs, Robert Fraser, and Michael Cooper—all part of Mick's inner orbit. The guests of honor were George and Patty Harrison, and the day's entertainment would be provided by a California drug dealer nicknamed the Acid King. Remembers one initiate, "He had this enormous chic briefcase, absolutely brimful of every possible kind of narcotic, mostly with initials that no one had ever heard of." It was the Acid King who woke everyone that morning with a stiff hit of Sunshine-brand LSD.

After a bedazzled afternoon drive in the country, the revelers returned to Keith's high, half-timbered walls, where they were served a Moroccan feast by Fraser's African servant, Ali. The Beatle and his wife had since left and the starry-eyed fellow trippers settled down to watch a Jack Webb movie on the telly while listening to Dylan on the stereo. Marianne, whose single change of clothes were muddy from the day's romp, joined them after her shower, wrapped only in a fur rug.

It was at this point that Chief Inspector Gordon Dineley and a force of eighteen West Sussex policemen arrived with a search warrant. "Through my acid haze I remember being amazed at the number of policemen who were crowding into the room," Marianne recalls. "Eighteen or nineteen of them. The whole raid, we believed, was a setup triggered by the *News of the World*. . . . We suspected that they had picked up the information on a phone bug and surveillance." Whatever the case, a subsequent search turned up enough traces and residues to result in Mick and Keith's being charged with violating the Dangerous Drugs Act of 1964.

At least that's what Inspector Dineley told them. But Mick could hardly be blamed for not paying attention. "Poor Mick," says Marianne, "he could hardly believe his bad luck. The first day he ever dares take an LSD trip, and eighteen policemen come pouring in through the window."

"Drug Squad Raids Pop Star's Party," crowed the *News of the World*, while another paper quoted the prosecutor describing "a strong, sweet smell of incense" wafting from the premises. More intriguing still was the story of "Girl in a Fur-Skin Rug." Detective Sergeant Stanley Cudmore would testify that Marianne made deliberate attempts to distract him from his sworn duty by letting the rug slip "and disclosing parts of her nude body."

The multicolored acid haze would part quickly enough. Mick had been caught in the middle of a scene he had feared and from which he had tried to distance himself. "We are not old men," Keith would later say at his trial. "We are not worried about petty morals."

The incident dominated newspaper headlines for weeks afterward. Even Brian, for whom drugs had long ago become a daily requirement, sensed a subtle shifting of the Stones' sense of themselves. The group had laid claim to the mantle of rock's unrepentant troublemakers with all the cynical élan Oldham could muster. But heresy—deliberate, premeditated—carried a price, one that they now began to tally. The Stones, a role model for millions, were about to be made into another kind of example. Faced with the consequences, exposed and vulnerable, the group did what they knew best: they hit the road.

In late February 1967, with the band now together five years, they and their girlfriends submerged from public view, lying low until their scheduled European tour in March. They left behind yet another album recording the effect of drugs and the centrifugal force of fame. Alternately limp-wristed and rabid, droll and contemptuous, *Between the Buttons* became a harrowing but now forgotten masterpiece of the era. With songs alternately cynical, petulant, and sinister, the album's twelve tracks were stories of betrayal and thwarted love.

The attitude is summed up on the LP's best-known hits, "Let's Spend the Night Together" and "Ruby Tuesday," the closest the Stones could come to love songs at that point. On "Miss Amanda Jones" (a thinly disguised diatribe against Brian) and songs like "All Sold Out" the group let it all hang out—Keith's guitar making vile noises, while Mick rants against the treachery of woman.

The album's cover also reveals the band at their rawest edge. Huddled in overcoats in a bleak winter park, the band stared defiantly into the camera of photographer Gered Mankowitz. It was the apex of antiglamour, a postlogical extension of the image that had made them famous four long years ago. Mick's famous lips are cracked and parched, while Brian stares from slitted eyes, his face broken by a leering smile.

The boys needed a change of scenery, and for reasons that had as much to do with habitual scene making as any notions of privacy, they chose Morocco. Mick and Marianne would fly first to Paris, then join the others—Keith, Brian, and Anita—in Marrakesh.

The two-thousand-mile trip through France and Spain in Keith's Bentley reinforced the notion of a desperate flight from reality. Anita, watching firsthand Brian's descent into drug delirium, had turned her considerable charms on Keith. Stricken by a bout of asthma in Toulon, Brian was left behind while Keith and Anita continued south.

By the time they arrived in Tangiers, where Mick and Marianne were already waiting at the Hotel Minzah, the deal was sealed. A haggard, still-hacking Brian arrived to discover Anita's betrayal and began to beat her up. Brian also became enraged when Anita would not participate in an orgy he had arranged with two Berber whores.

"I was in fear of my life," Anita remembers. "I was hysterical. Keith saved me."

What Keith did was spirit Brian's Nordic doppelganger into the night without a word to the cuckolded star. "I was just so disgusted with the way Brian treated Anita," he recounts, "I just threw her in the back of the car and split."

Brian turned up a few days later at the Paris apartment of Donald

Cammell, who recalls: "Brian was always so fastidious about his clothes, but when he came up to my place he was filthy. He hadn't changed his shirt and was wearing bedraggled lace and tattered velvet. He was alone, a figure of great pathos."

Losing Anita proved the final indignity to Brian's battered pride. He began to drown himself in abject self-pity. "They took my music," he told a friend, "they took my band, and now they've taken my love."

"Just because a chick leaves somebody to go with somebody else is no reason to feel guilty," Keith insisted. "It could have been someone twelve thousand miles away, but it happened to be the guy who stood on the other side of Mick on stage." Anita, having deftly switched Stones, set about to consolidate her new position. It was a very thorough job. Her relationship with Keith would last thirteen years and produce two children.

For Mick the Moroccan sojourn did nothing to dispel the pall cast by the Redlands bust. The always-delicate power balance inside the Stones had been completely upended by Anita's defection to Keith, and Mick had neither the time nor energy to sort it out. Events were beginning to overtake him and it was pointless to remain in exile, pretending it might all dissolve like that sugar cube on his tongue. He returned to London to face the dissonant and demanding music.

His arrival was greeted by an indictment for possession of four amphetamine tablets, while Keith was brought up on the charge of allowing his premise to be used for pot smoking. "I don't think it occurred to Mick that he would ever get into real trouble," confides a friend. "He worried about what the folks back home would think."

There wasn't much time for worry, however. A week after the charges were announced, the group roared off on a three-week European tour. Yet even the frenzied concert itinerary couldn't distract them from their looming legal difficulties. Of no help in the matter were squads of zealous customs police who tore apart the baggage and conducted cavity searches at nearly every airport on the route. Mick, his short fuse already frayed, punched out a French official at Le Bourget Airport over one such delay.

The tour plowed on through the Iron Curtain for the group's first swing through the Eastern Bloc. An appearance in Warsaw proved that even the grip of communism could not quell the excitement for the Stones and their decadent Western music. A crowd of two thousand Polish fans unable to gain entrance to the concert engaged the police in a running street battle, replete with water cannons, that resulted in thirty arrests.

In April the band was off the road and scattered again: Brian in Cannes, Keith and Anita on another cross-continental motor jaunt, and Mick back in London, holding forth on his upcoming trial. He told the *Daily Mirror*, "I see a great deal of danger in the air . . . Teenagers are not screaming over pop music any more, they're screaming for much deeper reasons. We are only serving as a means of giving them an outlet. Teenagers the world over are weary of being pushed around by half-witted politicians who attempt to dominate their way of thinking and set a code for their living. They want to be free and have the right of expression, of thinking and living without any petty restrictions."

It was hardly the contrite note Mick's barrister, Lord Michael Havers, would have preferred, but even as he assumed the mantle of revolutionary firebrand, Mick hedged his bets. "This doesn't mean they want to become alcoholics or drug addicts or tread down on their parents. This is a protest against the system. I see a lot of trouble coming in the dawn."

Lord Havers was busy denying the rumors that swirled around the impending trial. He recounts, "One of the peculiar aspects of the case, widely reported in the press, was the infamous Mars Bar rumor. When the police entered the living room, so the rumor went, they found that the woman on the couch had a Mars Bar protruding from an intimate place in her anatomy. . . . The tabloids continued to refer to the proceedings as the Mars Bar Trial, replete with rather graphic references to what occurred."

The hearings, which began May 10 in a Chichester police court, started to go badly for Mick, Keith, and Robert Fraser almost immediately after their not-guilty plea. The more sensational facts of the case were spelled out in testimony by the stolid Inspector Dineley.

The speed pills Mick was being accused of possessing actually belonged to Marianne, who had begged him to let her reveal the truth. "Mick kept saying that his career could stand a drug bust and mine couldn't," she recalls. "I could tell it pleased him to think he was playing the English gentleman, that he wouldn't let me be thrown to the wolves."

But while the Fleet Street reporters waited for the eventual announcement that a trial date had been set for late June, they were missing the day's big story, taking place that afternoon at Brian's Courtfield Road flat in Chelsea. At about four P.M., dressed in a Japanese kimono and coming off an all-night drug binge with a few close friends, Brian answered a knock on the door to find the Scotland Yard Drug Squad ready for business. Moving into the house, they deferentially informed Prince Klossowski, the last of Brian's party guests, "I'm afraid we have a warrant to search these premises for drugs."

This time is wasn't stash box scrapings and the odd prescription pill that were carted away for analysis. After fifteen minutes' work, the search team had discovered eleven different suspicious substances, later to be identified as hashish, Methedrine, and a small amount of cocaine. "No man, not cocaine," Brian told the arresting officer. "That's not my scene. I smoke hash, but I'm no junkie."

Brian's arrest, dramatically timed to coincide with the beginning of Mick and Keith's trial, convinced many that the Stones were serving as convenient scapegoats in the authority's losing battle with the chemical crimes of the counterculture. With a knack for publicity that was by now routine, the group played off the spreading generational warfare by rushing to the studio to record a furious response to the oppressive hand of the Man.

"We Love You" featured guest vocals from Lennon and McCartney. Despite its title, the song was a rant against the other side of the us-or-them equation. The fashionable conceit of loving your enemy was a thin veil draped over the Stones' outrage: the song began and ended with a slamming prison door.

Brian, meanwhile, was constitutionally incapable of cleaning up his act, despite his fear of going to prison. Continuing to inhale and swallow every available substance, including increasing amounts of brandy and scotch, he fought to hold off approaching disaster. While awaiting a court date, he flew to the Monterey Pop festival to watch new friend and fellow acid adventurer, Jimi Hendrix, perform. Together they dropped the latest in psychedelic elixirs, an exotic combination of Methedrine and LSD known as STP. It was a trip that kept their fried synapses sputtering for seventy-two hours.

Returning home at the start of Mick and Keith's trial, Brian began seeing a psychiatrist in a desperate attempt to find his footing. "Anxious, considerably depressed, perhaps even suicidal," ran the diagnosis of Dr. Henry Flood, "he is easily thwarted. He cannot sort out his problems satisfactorily and has not a great deal of confidence in himself. He is still trying to grow up in many ways."

Sensing the impending implosion of the group, Mick steeled himself to carry on, arranging for recording sessions to follow up *Between the Buttons*, which had performed poorly. Aside from everything else besetting the beleaguered group, the Beatles had reestablished their progressive rock hegemony with the June release of *Sgt. Pepper's Lonely Hearts Club Band*, hailed as an instant masterpiece and immediately held up as a standard for modern songwriting, studio sophistication, and psychedelic pioneering. The Stones had been neatly trumped by their longtime rivals.

Mick had prevailed on the band's rhythm section, Bill and Charlie, to get to work on new material while he oversaw the legal maneuvering of his case. Through sheer force of will, Mick tried to keep all the scattered elements of his life under control. Keith, caught up in his affair with Anita, and Brian, in the grip of his own deadly preoccupations, were of little help. Photographer Gered Mankowitz was present at some of the initial sessions for the new album: "Brian was a very screwed up boy with a major personality problem," Mankowitz said. "Once he was in such an awful state in the studio. . . . He had to play a little recorder part. In a side booth where they did the vocals, he was propped up with chairs so that he wouldn't fall over. But he played and did so very well. He was a natural musician who could play almost anything."

On June 27, nearly five months after the Redlands raid, Mick and Keith's trial began in the court of Judge Leslie Block, a former Royal Navy commander. The defense strategy for Mick, who was tried immediately after Fraser, was revealed by the one defense witness called, Dr. Raymond Firth, who had been the singer's physician for nearly three years. Under oath Dr. Firth testified that he had given Mick "permission" to use amphetamines for relief of stress. The contention was that such advice constituted a legal prescription and that, therefore, Mick was breaking no law by possessing the four pills.

Judge Block could hardly have disagreed more. "These remarks cannot be regarded as a prescription," he instructed the jury. "I therefore direct you that there is no defense to this charge." The jury took six minutes to convict.

Mick was to be remanded in custody awaiting the outcome of Keith's and Fraser's trials. Handcuffed to the stunned and silent Fraser and running a gauntlet of reporters and distraught fans, he was driven to Lewes, a dank Victorian prison, where he passed the night in the infirmary.

"I was deathly scared and in tears," he would later admit. Marianne paid him a visit, bringing with her a touching collection of small comforts: cigarettes, a checkerboard, newspapers, and fresh fruit. He would lodge at Lewes for another night as well, awaiting the outcome of Keith's trial.

When it occurred, detailed testimony replayed the entire episode for a voracious press. It was prosecutor Malcolm Morris's relentless probing of the fur rug affair that finally set off the guitarist. "There was, as we know," Morris droned, "a young woman sitting on a settee, wearing only a fur rug. Would you agree, in the ordinary course of events, you would expect a young woman to be embarrassed if she had on nothing but a fur rug in the presence of eight men, two of whom were hangers-on and another a Moroccan servant?"

The exact point of the attorney's grilling remains somewhat unclear, but Keith understood the implications. It was then that he declared the Stones and their charmed circle above the "petty morals" of "old men." In so doing, he all but sealed their collective fate.

Judge Block sternly admonished the jury to "put out of your minds any prejudice you may feel about the way Richard dresses, or his observations about petty morals" and to disregard "the evidence as to the young lady who was alleged by the police to have been in some condition of undress." The jury then retired, returning after an hour with a unanimous guilty verdict for all defendants on all counts.

The news was met by horrified gasps from the packed courtroom, but the real shock was yet to come. Addressing the convicted Stones one at a time, Block sentenced Keith to one year in prison and Fraser to six months. Last up was Mick, pale, trembling, and all too aware that the magical ride that had taken him so far from Dartford might be about to come to a screeching halt.

"Michael Philip Jagger," Block intoned, "you have been found guilty of possessing a potentially dangerous and harmful drug. You will go to prison for three months. You will pay two hundred pounds towards the cost of the prosecution."

Jagger, already bloodless, began to tremble, head in hands. "I was stunned," recounts Marianne. "In fact, I didn't quite grasp the impact of the judge's penalties. Mick and I looked at each other as the bailiff handcuffed him and led him away. There were tears down his face, as there were down mine."

Pushing her way through an unruly crowd, she hurried to Mick's holding cell to spend a few minutes before he was driven off to Brixton, handcuffed to a policeman. He spent another sleepless night in jail, while three hundred fans protested under the statue of Eros at Piccadilly Circus.

"I visited Mick in Brixton Prison the morning after his imprisonment," Marianne recalls. "He was terribly frightened and very, very upset, in fact, freaked out. . . . I also felt a terrible guilt because he was really sacrificing himself for me since those were my amphetamine tablets. I don't think he had any inkling when he took the blame that it would turn out as bad as it did. . . . He sat with me and I held him and he wept in his frustration. But I think that was a great thing for him, to be able to let go like that, to rebut his whole attitude of staying cool no matter what. This was a real feeling, and he was showing it, crying, and why the hell shouldn't he?"

It was more than simply a case of being in the wrong place at the wrong time. Mick was spooked by the whole notion of drugs, of the threat and promise of losing control, which is exactly what had happened. "That was a brick wall for Mick," Keith asserts. "Mick came up against the brick wall of reality."

The group's attorneys, meanwhile, worked feverishly through the night to have a bail granted while the appeal got underway. Their task was aided not only by Lord Havers's reputation in legal circles as a respected, aristocratic barrister, but by the general perception among cooler heads that Judge Block had overreacted.

It was not a response universally shared by the man on the street. "Good stiff sentences will deter others and we know that youngsters copy the Rolling Stones," ran one sample of public opinion, echoing another's conviction that enough was enough: "The sentences were too lenient. It is time drug taking was stamped out." A poll conducted by the *Daily Mail* found that 56 percent of the twenty-one- to thirty-four-year-old population thought the sentence was not hard enough while a mere 12 percent thought the judge was too severe.

But it was in the power centers far removed from London street corners that the fate of the band was ultimately decided. The Rolling Stones had become a highly visible British export. Whatever the personal distaste of the establishment for the band and its lifestyle, photos of young men being hauled off in handcuffs tarnished the Empire's image of tolerant magnanimity.

The *London Times* led the defense in William Rees-Mogg's enlightened editorial, entitled "Who Breaks the Butterfly on a Wheel?" in reference to the persecution of Oscar Wilde. "We have, therefore, a conviction against Mr. Jagger purely on the ground that he possessed four Italian pep pills," the editorial stated. "Four is not a large number. This is not the quantity a pusher of drugs would have on him, nor even the quantity one would expect from an addict."

Rees-Mogg saved his most eloquent appeal, however, not for legal niceties but for a rather bemused sympathy for the rock star's trying lifestyle: "In any case Mr. Jagger's career is obviously one that does involve great personal strain and exhaustion; his doctor says that he approved the occasional use of these drugs, and it seems likely that similar drugs would have been prescribed if there was a need for them.

"It should be the particular quality of British justice," he concluded, "to ensure that Mr. Jagger is treated exactly the same as anyone else, no better and no worse. There must remain a suspicion in this case that Mr. Jagger received a more severe sentence than would have been thought proper for any purely anonymous young man."

"There are many people who take a primitive view of the matter" was the *Times*'s lofty contention. "They consider that Mr. Jagger has 'got what was coming to him.' They resent the anarchic quality of the Rolling Stones' performances, dislike their songs, dislike their influence on teenagers, and broadly suspect them of decadence."

However well founded those suspicions might prove, public opinion was hardly the point. The Stones, after all, had gotten this far by goading the very primitives who now saw justice long delayed but finally served. Oldham himself could not have come up with a more fitting picture than the broken butterfly. But what really did the trick was not a fanciful appeal to tolerance; it was the prospect of what the *Daily Mail* called "a one-million-pound-a-year empire of pop," grinding to a halt.

A battery of high-priced barristers pulled the requisite strings. Mick's bail was set and, pale and rumpled, he was freed. Asked what he did in jail, he replied that he had been writing poetry, underlining again the *Times's* fanciful notion of a man too sensitive for hard facts and harsh treatment.

"The appeals took two weeks or so," recounts Lord Havers, "and Mick's anxiety during this period was intense." And for good reason. "It was imperative that I get those convictions overturned," he continues, "or Mick and Keith, with drug convictions on their records, would not be able to enter the United States to perform their concerts." An appeals hearing was set for July 31, on the grounds that Judge Block's summing up was prejudicial; he had referred to Keith as "scum" and "filth." Mick's sentence was upheld but commuted to a conditional discharge.

"If you keep out of trouble for the next twelve months," the judge admonished him, "what has happened will not go on your record as a conviction. . . . You are a model to a large number of the young in this country, you have grave responsibilities."

No one needed to tell Mick twice, although he was certainly not above taking advantage of his new status as persecuted symbol of youthful extravagance. He was taken from the courtroom directly to a press conference, where he insisted, "My responsibility is only to myself. I've been pushed into the limelight. I don't try to impose my views on people. I don't propagate drug views, such as some pop stars do."

"He'd been given a lot of Valium beforehand," Marianne recounts, "and he still seemed very scared. You got the feeling he only had to say one word out of place and he'd have been taken straight back to Brixton."

Instead he was taken by helicopter to the Georgian country estate of the Lord Lieutenant of Essex, Sir John Ruggles-Brise, for a taping of the television program *World in Action*. Conceived as a sort of generational summit, the program featured Mick, engaged in a cozy garden chat with a variety of distinguished venerables, including the

Bishop of Woolich, all earnestly seeking to bridge the dreadful gap between young and old. "You are often taken as a symbol of rebellion," intoned Rees-Mogg, an obvious, and highly partisan, program participant. "Do you feel that society has a great deal in it today that ought to be rebelled against?"

It was all very polite, even if the assembled graybeards could not quite hide their fascination with the exotic creature before them. Commented Stephen Jessel, who interviewed Mick for the *Times* the day after the appeal, "He is so unlike the cartoon stereotype as to be almost unrecognizable in reality. He is a slighter figure than you expect. . . . He is quieter and has more grace of manner. . . . He is articulate, and the philosophy he outlines is obviously the product of sustained consideration."

Even the most objective observer, it seemed, could be starstruck, and Mick played his role to the hilt. He had, with the arrest and his subsequent vindication, elevated the Stones' image to something altogether more purposeful and serious. More than simply a pop star, he had become, in a single stroke, a spokesman. It's hardly surprising, however, given his natural caution and his recent unpleasantness, that he chose his words carefully. "I am a rebel against society, but not an obvious one," he said with an intriguing ambiguity refracted through his Valium haze. "People should be punished for crimes, not the fears of society."

It was a telling phrase. For if society feared Mick Jagger and his band, it was also true that the Stones' boundless contempt had backfired on them at last, teaching them the limits of their rebellion, no matter how lofty its banner. Mick still had places to go, things to do, and the notion of being martyred for making a stand on drugs or anything else was not only foolish, it was stupid.

"I hated the bust," he confided years later, "because I felt it stopped the band and slowed it down. I think being busted still does slow the band down. And I'm trying to kick the habit. That's why I turned bourgeois."

He's only half kidding. "It wore me out," he says. "It wore my bank balance out. Cost a fortune. And those horrible gray people that get you off. . . . The whole thing is a sort of a game between lawyers."

The game was over, at least for now. Wherever the excesses of his bandmates might lead them, Mick's experience had steeled him to the purpose at hand: stardom and the perquisites of stardom.

Later that year in a speech before the Horsham Plowing and Agricultural Society Judge Block summed up the affair: "We did our best to cut those Stones down to size. But alas, it was not to be, because the Court of Criminal Appeal let them roll free."

If only being free was that easy.

Satanic Majesties

The Stones' brush with British justice affected them each in his own way. Mick became more wary, having grasped the essential difference between show and business. Oldham's bad boy creation might have served them well, but the trick was not to believe one's own press.

Along with whatever predispositions to addiction he had going in, Keith brought along all the cherished musician's traditions of the high life. He would do his best, in years to come, to live up to the image that Oldham and Mick and all the flack troops had fashioned, a brave stand that all but doomed him. His spirited testimony at the Redlands trials stood in marked contrast to Mick's muted performance, just as his prodigious excesses so sharply contrasted with his old friend's careful calculations. For Keith, there was no turning back.

For Brian, there was no place left to turn. "Please don't worry," he had telegrammed his parents after his May 10 arrest. "Don't jump to nasty conclusions and don't judge me too harshly."

But harsh and nasty things were already closing in on the hapless musician. His drug use had reached that point where pain and pleasure merge; death hung like a shadow over his face. "He was just so messed up in his mind," recounts Suki Potier, the blonde who had replaced Anita. "He used to have terrifying dreams and wake up screaming. His big thing was that he was afraid he wouldn't be liked by anyone. He was so paranoid."

He had good reason to be. Mick and Keith's ordeal, short-lived as it was, preyed on Brian during the five months between his arrest and trial. In combination with a drug habit that had extended deeply into LSD and other psychoactives, the anxiety produced a nervous break-down. He was admitted to the Priory Nursing Home in July, where he rambled on to staff doctors about Mick's plot to steal the Stones from under him.

The group had begun work in earnest on a new album, their ostensible answer to the Beatles' *Sgt. Pepper*. Decca Records, des-perate for new product, had in the meantime released *Flowers*, a collection of singles and outtakes, in August of 1967. But the group's latest project would be an important response to the profusion of drug-influenced music that had sprung up everywhere in rock 'n' roll.

The result, *Their Satanic Majesties Request*, fell far short of the goal, although it still clung to the premise that the band could make intriguing music, almost by reflex. Amidst noodling, extended jams and special effect segments, the album boasted a few good tunes and evocative performances: "2,000 Man," with its plaintive future-shock sentiment; "She's a Rainbow," as prettified a Flower Power bauble as anything the Beatles concocted; and Bill Wyman's droll "In Another Land," the album's only quasi hit. While the blurry 3-D cover photo—an overdone attempt to outdo *Sgt. Pepper*—could not dis-guise the album's patched-together quality, *Their Satanic Majesties Request* still pushed the Stones' music in interesting new directions.

"The only time Brian looked like he was coming into his own was when they did that awful *Satanic Majesties*," Ian Stewart remembers. "He got a chance to dabble with the Mellotron. . . . He would turn up at the studio with saxophones and he even played a harp on one number. . . . He had the ability to actually sit down and fiddle with it, and got something out of it fairly easily. The talent and ability were there, but he had just screwed himself up."

It was in the midst of recording the album that Oldham, sensing his rapid approach to the abyss of his own uncontrolled drug use, simply walked away from his association with the band and, with it, a defining chapter of his career, if not his life.

"They realized that Andrew's ideas were only ideas he'd got from them in the first place," asserts Stu, describing the group's final split from the man who shared their fame but stopped short of sharing their fate. "Everything the Stones have done has been natural," Oldham would later graciously insist. "They were not puppets. They were people. . . . As people we went in different directions. There was no definite decision. It was just over. We split because we all got to a stage of mutual boredom."

Photographer Gered Mankowitz remembers it differently. During the photo session for *Satanic Majesties*, Mick told Oldham in no uncertain terms what the album's cover should look like. Mankowitz recalled to author Christopher Anderson, "When it came to the look, the image of the Stones, they had always deferred to Andrew's genius. But not this time. By not consulting Andrew on this, Mick was basically telling him he was finished. I remember the look on Andrew's face so clearly. He knew what was going on and that he was powerless to do anything about it."

With Oldham out of the picture, the Stones' financial empire was left largely to the tender mercies of Allen Klein. Mick was sobered by his recent brush with justice and determined to keep a firmer grasp on the group's fortunes. He had grown increasingly suspicious of the pudgy wheeler-dealer. He would eventually act on his doubts by hiring a personal financial advisor, Prince Rupert Ludwig Ferdinand zu Lowenstein-Wertheim-Freudenberg, a jet-setter of dubious lineage into whose sphere Mick was increasingly drawn.

Explains another member of the circle, Sir Mark Palmer, "There was this whole group of us from 'better homes,' and title and all that, who had told our families to fuck off. Terrible rows with them. Disinherited and all that. Mick and Marianne fitted in with us rather nicely."

Lowenstein was described by a wag in the *Tatler* as "a princely German dumpling." His mother was rumored to have worked in a button factory in Bavaria, but his reputation for scrupulous honesty and high-level banking connections clinched the job. "I had met Mick Jagger at some function or another," Lowenstein recounts, "and we got to talking about finances, and he told me the Stones had been in the grip of a character named Allen Klein who had done them in financially."

It was all part of Mick's new down-to-business approach. He rented a new office for the group, on Maddox Street in the building where stage star Lily Langtry had once lived.

"Mick loves the idea of having an office to go to like a business-man," says the Stones' longtime fan club president, Shirley Arnold. "We had four rooms with sloping walls and original fireplaces. The lift had been especially installed by King Edward VII so he didn't have to walk up all those stairs. We had someone whose job it was to go around the country buying antique furniture. . . . There was a lovely atmosphere around that time. People were always coming in for a drink, it was very friendly. . . . It was all because of Mick. He loved it all."

But Lowenstein and a lovely office were only a part of the funda-mental changes Mick, at age twenty-four, had set about to make in his life and career. The spring and summer of 1967, the period imme-diately following the Redlands bust, was filled with moves and ma-neuvers aimed at stability and a long overdue sense of decorum. Marianne was very supportive, won over by her lover's show of chivalry and anxious in her own way to find the center of their life together.

In the manner of Chrissie Shrimpton, Marianne was a prize to be displayed, a beguiling accoutrement to Mick's rock star wardrobe. "You could see it on Mick's face every time they were at a party together," recalls mutual friend Donald Cammell. "It was pure pos-session."

Yet behind the often insufferable swagger, Mick was making a sincere stab at domesticity. Shortly after the trial, he bought a lavish apartment in one of Chelsea's most prestigious addresses, Cheyne Walk, near the Albert Bridge overlooking the Thames. He arranged for Nicholas, Marianne's three year-old-son by John Dunbar, to move in with them, creating a family with a single stroke.

"He insisted that we have a nanny," Marianne recounts. "He interviewed all the applicants himself. You'd have thought he'd been dealing with servants all his life."

Christopher Gibbs was hired to decorate Mick's new home. Ex-pense was no object, starting with a chandelier costing six thousand pounds. Mick, with mock horror, pointed out the fixture to visitors, never failing to remark on its extravagant price tag.

A place in the country was the next order of business. "We looked at a lot of very nice houses," Gibbs recalls, "including a wonderful William and Mary house in Shropshire with Chinese wallpaper." The estate Mick and Marianne settled on, however, was a ramshackle

Victorian affair on the edge of the Berkshire downs called Stargroves. Visions of grand restorations danced in the couple's heads, but, according to Palmer, "It was a grim place. . . . Mick and Marianne stayed for a bit but before long they took off."

The pair could be excused their flightiness. Despite their resolve to make a home for themselves, the undertow of fame drew them away. According to one visiting reporter, "They have the air of children left in charge while grown-ups are away."

Marianne explained, "Mick prided himself on being so cool, but he realized he'd got nothing on the real upper class for coolness. The cool they had was centuries old. They were the most restful people to be around because nothing we did ever seemed to shock them."

Mick's middle-class upbringing and education left him woefully unprepared for life in such aristocratic precincts. Marianne took it upon herself to educate him, arranging for enchanted evenings at the theater, opera, and ballet. Together they delved into the prismatic wonderland of hippie mysticism, exploring a variety of esoteric disciplines with their charge account at the Indica Bookstore, a well-known London haunt for affluent seekers. *Secret Tibet, Fairy-Faith in Celtic Countries, The Masks of God, The Golden Bough, Book of the Damned*, and *Manuscripts of Witchcraft* were a few of the works that opened Mick's world to the spiritual, the sacred, and the just plain spooky.

In the latter category must be included the couple's friendship with Kenneth Anger, the American avant-garde director whose avid interest in the occult had led him to become the foremost disciple of Britain's infamous black magician, Aleister Crowley. Anger saw in Mick's charisma all the manifestations of a latter-day Lucifer, and it was a role that appealed to the rock idol, not the least for its intriguing sense of purpose. If Mick's spectacular career really *was* the incarnation of some eternal battle between dull rectitude and liberating abandon, it would certainly explain a lot, including all those "horrible gray people" who had lately invaded his life.

Yet satanism, like drug use, was hardly the sort of excess his practical nature could fully embrace. After going as far as composing the synthesized score to Anger's short film *Invocation of My Demon Brother*, Mick precipitously backed off from the black arts, declining to star in Anger's proposed film version of the satanic textbook *Lucifer Rising*. In fact, he subsequently took to wearing a crucifix around his neck to proclaim, quite clearly, his allegiance to forces of light. "Mick will never play with anything really dangerous," asserted one friend from the period. "He's not going to mess with the devil. It's just one of his games to pretend he is."

Keith and Anita were another matter. "Anita was certainly into black magic," Marianne later said. "And although I can't really say whether she was a witch or not, there's no denying the fact that Anita was sort of a black queen, a dark person." Rumor had it that Keith and Anita were contemplating a pagan marriage with Anger officiating.

Mick and Marianne's dabbling with invisible realms reached an apex of sorts when they accompanied the Beatles on a trip to Bangor, Wales, to sit at the feet of the wizened salesman of transcendental meditation, Maharishi Mahesh Yogi. The pilgrimage trailed a cloud of incense smoke and flower petals, but was cut short by the news of Beatles' manager Brian Epstein's death.

The two supergroups, while ostensibly at opposite ends of the rock spectrum, had maintained close ties since their initial encounter back at the Ealing Blues Club. After Epstein's death by drug overdose, there was even some active discussion of a joint venture between the Beatles and Stones, a studio and management concern. It came to nothing when Allen Klein discovered that a Beatles functionary, Peter Brown, had been tapped to run the proposed complex, to be housed in a refurbished brewery in Camden Town. Klein, determined to keep his grip on the Stones' affairs, quashed the project.

For Mick such schemes were part of a continuing campaign to pull together his prospects and take charge of his future. Yet beneath the bustling exterior, pitfalls, personal and professional, continued to loom.

Among the most troubling aspects of Mick's burgeoning new world was his relationship with Marianne. The inbred caution and the habits of distance and disdain he had nurtured along the road to stardom were difficult to keep out of his love life. It was simply too trying to make the transition from the public persona to the private lover.

Marianne would tell A. E. Hotchner, "For a while I had a great time with Mick and everything was all right. When we were together, we had a lot of power. And that's where it all started to go wrong. . . . We were the beautiful couple of the sixties and for me it was very, very exciting. To be very young, very free, very rich, and very careless. But then it went too far. . . . That's when it really became a nightmare."

The nightmare for Marianne (now dubbed Marijuana Faithfull by the magazine *Private Eye*) was happening through a heroin haze. Her voracious consumption of drugs had led to its inevitable terminus and by late 1967, at age twenty, she was well over the line of helpless addiction. She said there was a part of her "I disliked terribly, something I wanted to crush."

It is clear that Mick, wrestling with his own demons, wasn't much help. Their sex life, never overheated, was sputtering out entirely. "Whatever sexual drive Mick had," she says, "he used it up on stage and there was very little left over for his personal life."

"There I was," she laments, "trapped in an image I couldn't stand." According to confidant Mark Palmer, her solution was oblivion. One of the reasons Mick and Marianne's stays at Stargroves were infrequent was its distance from Marianne's London drug connections. She was enmeshed in a world where image was everything, peering in a mirror whose reflection was distorted by chemical ecstasies. "Drugs as an escape were a fallacy," she allows, but the truth goes deeper: "To be honest, there is something—how shall I say— romantic about it."

There was nothing romantic about what was happening to Brian. Following the release, and critical drubbing, of *Satanic Majesties*, he faced the immediate prospect of a kangaroo court, with the grim, gray people determined to inflict on him what they couldn't on Mick and Keith. It was too much, and like Marianne, he sought to change reality from inside.

The signs of his decline were abundant. Brian's doctor at Priory, where he convalesced during the first of his nervous collapses, recalls a revealing episode: "Brian came back at seven in the morning, after having taken something—so much that he couldn't stand straight." It turned out to be a megadose of Mandrax, a powerful downer. "One of the reasons he had done this," the psychiatrist continues, "was that . . . he had a heard a rumor that while he was at the nursing home, the police planned to plant more stuff in his flat. This threw him completely. . . . There was an incredible degree of paranoia about him. . . . I don't think Brian was living in a real world."

A friend recalls another frightening evening in the grip of Brian's madness: "We were going to stay at the Hilton Hotel in London for a night. . . . There were shoes to be cleaned and people had put them out in front of their doors. Brian ran down the hall, swapping shoes and throwing them down the chute. Then he ordered five portions of chips from room service. . . . He tried to stuff some in the mouth of the waiter and threw the rest out the window. We weren't in there two hours before they kicked us out."

The court date for his South Kensington bust arrived October 30, a day on which all of the twenty-four-year-old Brian's worst fears were realized. After plea bargaining away the Methedrine and cocaine charges, he then pled guilty to smoking pot and letting drug use happen in his flat. The sentence: eight months in Wormwood Scrubbs. Like his bandmates before him, Brian was subject to the terrifying humiliation of being handcuffed and taken to jail to begin immediately repaying his debut to society.

Wormwood was the prison where another famous rocker had recently bunked. "Wormwood is a hundred and fifty years old, man," recalls Keith with a shudder. "They don't give you a knife and fork, they give you a spoon with very blunt edges so you can't do yourself in. They don't give you a belt, in case you hang yourself. It's that bad in there."

In Brian's case, such precautions were probably a good idea. "We finally got one of those bloody longhairs," prison guards were reported to have snarled.

A rowdy demonstration the next day—resulting in a few arrests of incensed friends and fans, including Mick's brother, Chris—had less to do with Brian's quick release than did the Stones' by now well oiled legal corps. In preparation for the appeal, Brian was interviewed by a battery of doctors, who together concocted a convincing case for innocence by reason of impending insanity.

According to the report of Dr. Walter Neustater, "Mr. Jones's thought processes do reveal some weakening of his reality ties as a result of intense free-floating anxiety. . . . He thus urgently needs psychotherapy to assist in mustering his considerable personality resources and capacity for insight to contain his anxiety. . . . It is likely that his imprisonment could precipitate a complete break with reality, a psychotic breakdown, and significantly increase the suicidal risk for this man."

A sorrowful sight with his pin-striped suit and hollow eyes, Brian was given three years' probation and a one-thousand-pound fine.

Brian celebrated his release, according to scene maker Al Aronowitz, "by pouring bottles full of pills into his mouth. He didn't care what the hell they were: acid, coke, speed—anything that would make the world go away. Then after a day and a night of being totally strung out, he went to a club in Covent Garden with one of his many women. . . . The resident band invited him to play with them and he did. He picked up a big double bass and started to play it fluidly, though as he played, he kicked it with his Cuban-heeled boots until it was smashed to matchwood. Brian was so far gone he carried on playing an invisible instrument, pumping out invisible music only he could hear. The crowd cheered, believing . . . that the whole thing was intentional, but by then he started to weep uncontrollably."

"He could be what he wanted to be," his Priory doctor would later maintain, "so long as he didn't step outside of what is a sort of funny corridor, a Milky Way upon which Brian Jones is walking."

T W E L V E

Requiem

Brian's tortured journey had blazed a trail of chaos across too
many other lives, and Mick, typically, was among the first to consider
cutting his losses. "Mick was very forceful about Brian," Ian Stewart
recalls. "He said that it was imperative that we get rid of Brian and
replace him with someone who could perform."

It turned out Brian still had one incredible musical performance
left in him. The Stones' flourishing legal hassles would have sunk
another band without their rugged endurance. But their next album,
which got underway with producer Jimmy Miller in the early spring
of 1968, was more than a testament to their survival instincts. It was a
feat of sustained brilliance that marked the group's triumphant resurgence.

An early indication of this burst of sheer bravura was the single
"Jumpin' Jack Flash," whose title character summed up the Stones'
stance. It exploded in charts on both sides of the Atlantic. With
Miller's concise, uncluttered mix replacing Oldham's total lack of
production chops, the song crackled like ominous heat lightning, the
guitars glancing off each other, the rhythm section pumping like an
infernal machine. The song's title character was another stroke of
genius, the distillation of the band's bad boy persona, writ large.

Mick was doing his part to lay the groundwork for a new, focused,

116

and forceful group, a band with its shit together. His trademark disdain was undercut by a canny political agenda. He could hardly miss the rumbling of social upheaval quaking the status quo. And he could not resist positioning himself on the cutting edge.

He asserted in a May 1968 *International Times* interview, "I'm interested in the idea of an alternative society growing out of what's been happening the last few years. Not a specific drug or hippie thing, but a general reevaluation of things that a lot of people are getting into, which is beginning to threaten a lot of the barriers which old-style society has put up. I think it will mean the ending of one society and the starting of another rather than a natural flow of change."

The only obstacle in Mick's natural flow continued to be Brian. While the group continued work on their new album through the spring and summer, Brian was arrested again for cannabis consumption and released at Marlborough Street Magistrate's Court on two-thousand-pounds' bail to await the distinct possibility of serving real time. There was little doubt now that the police and the powers behind them had found their weakest link in the enemy camp. Mick would later reflect, "Now, if you do that to some people it makes them strong, and if you do it to others it can quickly destroy them. . . . Brian came really close to doing six months. . . . He was followed all the time, but we all were. It was a systematic campaign of harassment which brought Brian down and destroyed the musical side of him as well."

Not quite. The music emanating from London's Olympic Studios by mid-summer was the best the group had made for a long time, perhaps ever. And it's in the touches, shadings, and sorrowing moments of *Beggar's Banquet* that Brian's haunting musical legacy endures.

Despite his legal travails, despite the doom that hung over him and the demons that tormented him, Brian lost and found himself again in the power of the band. It was a rare alignment that made them, together, great. "We've been in the studio all morning and we're going back to rock 'n' roll," Brian enthused to a friend. In point of fact, Brian's final album with his Ealing Grove flatmates would go back considerably further, to that place where music had touched a troubled soul.

It was the same for them all, a return to basics, a stripping away of the artifice that was choking off the wellspring. Mick and Keith's writing reached back to the blues, pulling them up through the ragged rock 'n' roll years to a moment fraught with personal meaning.

Beggar's Banquet would be a work full of moments, a big, stunning delivery of maximum impact tracks like "Sympathy for the Devil," "Salt of the Earth," and "Street Fighting Man," released as a single in late 1968 while the album was delayed in a cover art dispute with the label. But it was in the ephemeral passages of such blues-drenched cuts as "No Expectations" and "Prodigal Son" that Mick and Keith revealed their true brilliance.

Brian journeyed with them, enhancing the essentials of their remarkable compositions through performances that carry the heartbreaking certainty of death. His slide guitar work on "No Expectations" is the most enduring example, but his poignant presence echoes through a hundred moments in the multilayered masterpiece.

The evolution of an album one critic would call "as near-perfect as any rock record should ever possibly be" was captured in an extraordinary document. French director Jean-Luc Godard, a cinematic anarchist with a penchant for polemics, approached the group to participate in his new movie, *One Plus One*, another of his films reflecting all the rigorous obscurity of the New Left.

Remarked Mick, "We're very excited about this. We have been great admirers of Godard's work for a long time and have great respect for him."

Few but the most rarified Marxist cinesthetes could actually decipher the intention behind Godard's endless slow pans and convoluted dialectic. What the Stones were meant exactly to symbolize in *One Plus One* is unclear, but the footage itself—shot in a beautiful, muzzy black and white—is as accurate a portrait of the original Stones at work as exists.

In long, in-studio set pieces, Godard chronicles the evolution of *Beggar's Banquet*'s centerpiece, "Sympathy for the Devil." The track evolves from a shuffling mambo, on through a half-dozen permutations, each moving closer to the center of the song. When the breakthrough comes, the group's detached cool hardly cracks. Godard's static shots reveal the Stones working together but distanced by their own auras of fame and hubris and doom. It is the music that binds them together, uniting them again for the length of a song.

In its final incarnation "Sympathy for the Devil" reached the wailing pitch of creative interplay among Mick, Brian, and Keith. Like a field recording from the Congo, "Sympathy for the Devil," an ode to Lucifer, opens with smoke-smudged drum beats, gourd rattles, evil anticipatory yelps and moans. The song lurches into its pounding groove, a furiously fretted samba, as the band fights to keep it all under control. Session pianist Nicky Hopkins is the unsung hero of these six incendiary minutes, his spot chording cohering into a great rolling progression, hurling the song headlong into Keith's solo, a rending, clawing attack.

The lyrics of the song had come to Mick after he'd read Mikhail Bulgakov's *The Master and Margarita*, a surrealist Russian novel in which Satan visits Russia after the revolution. It was given to him by Marianne as part of her continuing tutorial in art and literature. But what struck Mick about the book was the devil's urbane, ironic manner. It was a voice that became his own on "Sympathy for the Devil."

Finally released in December of '68—after a nearly four-month delay while the record company fought the band's cover art depiction of a graffiti-festooned loo—*Beggar's Banquet* marked the resurgence of the Stones as a commercial and creative entity.

Mick had meanwhile been working assiduously throughout the year to enhance his personal stature. In May he announced that he had signed to star in *The Performers*, a surreal sex and drug saga, opposite British film star James Fox. The Stones, of course, had been named to appear in innumerable film projects since as early as 1963, all with a conspicuous lack of success, especially considering the Beatles' money-making movie output.

It's not hard to understand why. For all their internal dissensions, the Beatles existed in the public mind as a single entity of four complementary parts: cute, acerbic, shy, and cheeky. The Stones had become a battle of personalities, and it was Mick who defined the style and substance of the group for mass consumption. Mick, in short, had marquee value. *Performance*, as it was quickly renamed, would be his breakthrough.

It was painter Donald Cammell who pulled the project together. Cammell had worked with early Stones promoter Giorgio Gomelsky on a film about the early British blues scene. Cammell then turned to screenwriting and concocted an intriguing plot that paired a retired rock star and a vicious gangster. When Mick agreed to appear, the movie was approved by Warner Brothers, although what, precisely, they thought they were getting remains unclear. Certainly not *A Hard Day's Night*, *Performance* had the queasy, vertiginous feel of a bad peyote trip. But it was a trip of chilling brilliance, a potent evocation of a time when drugs and music were signposts to a new reality.

Cammell had wanted to direct his script, but without the slightest experience, he brought in cameraman Nicolas Roeg and also recruited his girlfriend Deborah Dixon and Christopher Gibbs as set designers. Three London locations were scouted and filming began in mid-September of 1968.

James Fox was cast in the role of Chas, a thug on the lam, after Cammell's first choice, Marlon Brando, couldn't decide whether to take the role. To prep for the part, Fox moved into a flat above an East End pub to soak up the seedy atmosphere. "He turned into this young hoodlum, East End character in front of your eyes," Cammell recalls. "His best friends became two or three wide boys . . . really frightening people."

Playing opposite an intense and absorbing Fox, Mick portrayed the retired rock star Turner, living in opulent decadence with his harem. The concubines were portrayed by Michèle Breton, a rail-thin waif Cammell had discovered in France, and the sultry, sinewy Anita Pallenberg.

The film's druggy internal logic and kinky complications soon spilled out onto the set. Cammell recalls Keith sitting in his car outside the Lowndes Square location, while Mick and Anita made love for the camera in one of the film's many erotic couplings.

"Although what ended up in the picture was a lot of vague, tumbling bodies in the sheets," Stu recounts, ". . . there was a lot of explicit footage of Mick and Anita really screwing, steamy, lusty stuff that was edited into a separate X-rated short feature and shown all around."

"There was the unbelievable soap opera that had been scripted by Mick and Keith," Cammell continues. "Anita was just having the time of her life with everybody. And my romance with Anita was on during all this time too."

Pallenberg, as usual, was playing the angles, looking to hook Mick into her orbit. "She seemed to be teasing Keith about wanting Mick,"

The original Rolling Stones, circa 1962: from left to right, Ian Stewart, Keith Richards, Brian Jones, Charlie Watts, Mick Jagger and Bill Wyman.

Mick and his trademark maracas.

England's Newest Hitmakers: The Rolling Stones in 1963: from left to right, Mick Jagger, Charlie Watts, Brian Jones, Keith Richards, Bill Wyman.

Mick makes a friend, circa 1964.

Portrait of a rock star as a young man.

The Rolling Stones, sitting on top of the world in early 1965: from left to right, Mick Jagger, Keith Richards, Charlie Watts, Bill Wyman and Brian Jones.

You're so vain: Mick reveals his beauty secrets.

Marianne Faithfull, circa 1965.
(Michael Ochs Archives)

Pandemonium: The Rolling Stones in concert.

Mick in the studio, circa 1966.

Mick and Bianca, 1971. (Michael Ochs Archives)

Mick performing at the Hyde Park memorial service for Brian Jones, July 5, 1969.

The Jagger Family: Mick, his brother
Chris and Eva and Joe Jagger.

Disaster at St. Tropez. The Jaggers at Mick and
Bianca's wedding. From left to right: Chris Jagger
and friend, Eva and Joe Jagger.

Mick, at his most precious, singing "Angie."

The mercurial Mick Jagger in concert.

Glam Rock summit. Lou Reed, Mick and David Bowie, 1973.

The Glimmer Twins:
Keith and Mick make nice.

The Rocker and the Cowgirl:
Mick with Jerry Hall.

Jade Jagger and her father.

The Stone keeps rolling: Mick at forty-six, with children James and Elizabeth Scarlett.

The Rolling Stones at the Rock & Roll Hall of Fame Awards, 1988.

"Wandering Spirit: Mick at fifty." (Paul Cox)

Cammell continues, "the way she'd teased Brian about wanting Keith."

Cammell goes on to claim that before it was all over, even Mick and James Fox had a brief fling. "They disappeared into the woodwork and there was a sort of romance. . . . It was a joy to watch."

It was just another of the gay innuendos being bandied about at the time. The beat godfather Allen Ginsberg regaled friends with his account of spending the night at the Cheyne Walk house in a ménage à trois consisting of Mick and inner circle intimate, Socialist MP Tom Driberg, who had once suggested that Mick stand for Parliament. Driberg was later revealed to be a spy, working closely as a double agent for the KGB and Britain's MI5. According to a report by the British secret service, Driberg "reported on the personal and political activities of friends and colleagues in Parliament."

The goings-on before and after hours on the *Performance* set, along with Mick's bizarre yet surprisingly nuanced screen presence, further fueled rumors. According to Cammell, "The role brought out the most contemptuous side of Mick, an almost arrogant side, prancing around, preening himself." Whatever the sordid details behind the scenes, the experience left Fox, a classically trained actor, deeply shaken. Years would pass before he returned to the screen.

In the end *Performance*, for all its jumbled subtexts and mystical posturing, does have a dangerous, disturbed edge. An exotic relic of psychedelic London, the film comes on like an acid rush of surreal scenes such as the one in which a malevolent Anita, naked beneath a floor-length fur, perches in a steaming kitchen, chopping the heads off live eels.

It was, finally, all too much. An early Warner Brothers screening actually induced vomiting in one executive's wife and the studio demanded extensive edits. Finally released in 1969, it was a commercial failure and garnered only sporadic critical approval. Mick's first movie outing had misfired badly.

In early October of 1968, the twenty-one-year-old Marianne announced to the world that she was pregnant. Mick pronounced impending fatherhood as "groovy. We'll probably have another three," he said, adding the by now obligatory, "but marriage? Can't see that happening. We just don't believe in it."

Behind the studied pose Mick was genuinely excited. It was a natural response for a man who still harbored the deep-seated need for security and stability. He wanted a girl and had already picked the name, Carena.

For Marianne, motherhood necessitated an immediate change in her reckless habits. What doctors referred to euphemistically as "complications" led to orders for strict rest away from the pressures of London. What her extended hiatus in a seaside house in Ireland's County Galway really constituted was an attempt to wean her from the drugs that threatened the health of mother and baby. She remained in her Irish cloister during the filming of *Performance*, although friends kept her informed of Mick's more blatant indiscretions, including a gift of exotic orchids he sent to Anita the same day he wired roses to her bedside.

It is unfair to speculate what either Marianne's drug-weakened condition or the stress of Mick's casual adultery contributed to the ultimate tragedy. In November, fully seven months pregnant, Marianne returned to London and was admitted to a nursing home in St. John's Wood, where she miscarried. It was a girl.

The news shook Mick deeply. More poignantly, his grief at the loss seemed to seal the estrangement between himself and Marianne. "I think Mick and I could have overcome all our problems if I hadn't had a miscarriage in my seventh month," she insisted. "If we'd had that baby, I think we would have stayed together, and I believe I might have pulled myself together. When I became pregnant, I began to have feelings that I think would have liberated and removed all those negative elements. But what happened with that baby was a tragedy. Mick commiserated with me very little, but I don't think he realized how bad I felt. Once it was over, he hardened toward me. He really wanted that baby. And so that miscarriage did us both in."

Mick responded by throwing himself into work. In mid-December, following the release of *Beggar's Banquet*, he and the Stones hosted an ill-fated variety show called *The Rolling Stones' Rock 'n' Roll Circus*. Conceived by Mick as a three-ring attraction spotlighting the heftiest names in British rock 'n' roll—including the Who, Eric Clapton, Jethro Tull, and John Lennon and Yoko Ono—the extravaganza's Big Top motif included trapeze acts, wild animals, clowns, strong men, fire-eaters, and other circus accoutrements, with Mick as the master of ceremonies.

The result was a chaotic, underproduced debacle that petered out way before its forty hours of continuous shooting. Mick would not allow the special to be aired in its scheduled Christmas slot. He was unhappy with his performance and was convinced that the Who had upstaged the Stones.

With the almost instant success of *Beggar's Banquet*, it was obvious that the group needed to go back on the road. But Brian Jones presented a very real problem. In September Brian's second trial for drug possession ended with more dire doctors' reports, a fine of two hundred pounds, and another conviction. His voracious drug use continued unabated, as did his obsession with Anita and all the paranoiac delusions of his bandmates' treachery.

His fears, once again, were well founded. After one of many return trips to Morocco, this time to indulge his wide-ranging musical eclecticism by recording the legendary dervish pipers of Jojouka, he bought his own country estate, Cotchford Farm. The bucolic spread had previously been owned by *Winnie the Pooh* author A. A. Milne. Brian alternated his time between the estate—uneasily playing the role of country squire—and London, where his behavior was becoming increasingly erratic.

"He looked like Louis XIV mummified," recalls Alexis Korner, who was working for the BBC at the time and spotted his one-time disciple at a fashionable watering hole. "Brian wore even more foppish clothes than usual, and he put on some very unhealthy fat, like the cats who drink too much and their faces go white and puffy and pockmarked. He had gotten a bit of a gut as well."

It was clear that Brian, with two drug convictions, mushrooming health problems, and a shattered psyche, no longer fit into Mick's plans for the Stones. "We wanted to play on stage and Brian was in no condition," Mick said. "He was far too messed up in his mind. I don't think he wanted to and it was this that pissed me off. He didn't have the desire to go on stage."

It was a protest more than a little self-serving. In point of fact, Mick had been scheming for some time to ease Brian out of the band. He had secretly auditioned replacements and had been introduced through Stu to a cherubic twenty-one-year-old guitarist named Mick Taylor. A gifted player, Taylor had served a stint with John Mayall's purist band, the Bluesbreakers, and in May he was invited to Olympic Studios for an audition to become the next Rolling Stone.

It was an event that coincided with Brian's own suggestions that it was finally time to leave; he cited his ill-defined desire to, variously, return to the group's blues roots, form a traditional jazz combo, or further explore Moroccan music. He would spend long hours at the Haywagon, the Sussex pub near Cotchford Farm, where, after one evening of drunken revelry with the locals, he drove his Triumph motorcycle through the window of the village grocery store.

In June of 1969 Mick, Keith, and Charlie drove to Brian's house to confront him with the reality of an upcoming tour.

" 'I can't do it again,' " Keith recalls Brian pleading. " 'I don't think I can go to America and do those one-nighters anymore.' " It was an intensely painful moment for old friends who had been together seven long years, a parting of the ways not made easier by Mick's offering Brian a hundred thousand pounds a year for life.

"Firing him was hard for Mick and me," Keith continues, "but he could hardly play, hardly stand up, hardly breathe. We'd come to a point where we could not bring the guy around."

A sense of relief can be read between the lines of Brian's official statement: "I have a desire to play my own brand of music rather than that of others, no matter how much I appreciate their music concepts," it read in part. "The only solution was to go our separate ways, but we shall still remain friends."

"It was almost like someone had taken a big weight off his shoulders," asserts Ian Stewart, who goes on to describe Brian's attempts to make good on his promise of a new band, bringing in blues musicians to jam at Cotchford. "He had Alexis down there, John Mayall. . . . In fact, he was on to me to go down there and play, but I said, 'I've started one group with you and that's enough.' "

Brian, now twenty-six, made the first tentative steps toward salvaging his ruined life, swimming regularly for exercise and trying to regain his fragile health. "He knew he'd done something disastrous, careerwise," comments old friend Peter Jones. "But even though he was not too sure of the outcome, he was glad he did it."

But the slide had simply been too precipitous. On the humid evening of July 2, he and his new live-in girlfriend—another Swedish blonde, Ann Wohlin—spent the evening at Cotchford, drinking and watching television. The summer air was thick with pollen and Brian's chronic asthma had worsened over the course of the day. An inhaler was never far from his side. Around 8:30 P.M. he went to the apartment above the garage to invite two other guests, contractor Frank Thoroughgood and Janet Lawson, to dinner. The meal was marked by what Lawson later described as Brian's "garbled conversation" and the consumption of an entire bottle of brandy and nearly a full bottle of vodka, as well as whiskey and wine.

At around 10:30 P.M., with the farm still under a blanket of summer heat, Brian invited the others for a moonlight swim. "They were in no condition to swim," Lawson recalls. "I felt strongly about this and mentioned it to both of the men. They disregarded my warning."

After about twenty minutes Lawson and Wohlin left to return to the house. Thoroughgood followed shortly afterward, in search of a cigarette. Lawson, with a sharp foreboding, returned quickly to the pool. She saw Brian lying on the bottom, "quite motionless," his blond hair floating around him like a halo. Brian Jones had succumbed.

Mick got the news at the studio, where the band, their new guitarist in tow, was mixing new tracks. He was stunned to silence. "They were all in a terrible state," Shirley Arnold, the band's longtime fan club president, recounts. "Charlie was crying. Mick was wandering to and fro and tripping over the dog's bowl that was on the floor."

"An advanced state of fatty degeneration" was the coroner's description of Brian's liver. The cause of death was listed as drowning associated with ingestion of alcohol and drugs. The verdict, death by misadventure, was rarely more apt.

The Stones, and by extension a whole wing of modern music, would be altered forever by Brian's death. His individual contribution to the vitality of sixties rock 'n' roll is echoed in a dozen variations today—his World Beat eclecticism, his interpretative instincts, his infinitely supple playing. Brian Jones moved the rock enterprise into whole new fields of expression. He was a pioneer, his music laying claim to all the right and true and real things that had been gone so long from his life.

The Stones would roll on, but an essential ingredient in their appeal, that sense of spontaneity and surprise, would be muted after Brian's departure. The group would continue making great music between ever-longer stretches of indifferent music. Brian had kept them honest in ways they would only occasionally recall without him, as they relied increasingly on the sheer stature of their legend.

Brian, too, was a legend—a legendary loser, whose pathetic end never quite overshadowed that lingering image of one too beautiful for this world. Like most legends, Brian's was full of half-truths and outright lies. The music was real. It just wasn't enough.

Street Fighting Man

The demise and death of Brian Jones neatly broke the history of the Rolling Stones in half. Whatever the band had been—that magical confluence of talents and temperaments—was forever altered with his passing. Whatever they were yet to become—junkies, jet-setters, jaded survivors—would begin in earnest with the severing of this last link to the past.

Brian's contribution to the group and its music was, at best, an ephemeral, on-again, off-again proposition. But it was in his absence that the ballast of the band begin to shift, listing as the always volatile balance of power began to realign itself. It was truer for the Stones than perhaps any other major rock 'n' roll enterprise that their creativity depended, in large part, on conflict and competition. With Brian a fading memory, their dynamic would have to find new expressions if the group were to maintain its vitality.

As much a fait accompli as Mick's assumption of creative and commercial leadership may have been, it was far less certain that he could sustain the requisite conditions for the band's continued growth. The juggernaut would doubtless continue to roll; the Stones had become a fact of life for a whole generation, with the gate receipts and chart numbers to prove it. But what had died with Brian was a special gift of spontaneity that could not easily be coaxed back to life. The original Rolling Stones were gone forever. What replaced them would be, in essence, a new band, with new approaches.

"I wasn't surprised about Brian," Keith said. "And it was hard to shed a tear about his demise, quite honestly. Cold blooded as it sounds, he was a passenger for us. We had to cover his ass. But you don't leave the Stones singing, you just get carried out. Brian was already effectively dead when he died."

Mick was more circumspect. "I'm wordless and sad and shocked," he said in an interview shortly after Brian's dismal passage. "We were like a pack, we Stones. Like a family. I just say my prayers for him. I hope he is, at last, finding a peace."

As with Keith, Mick too felt relieved once the real shock wore off. "It's more of a band now," he would say. "It's definitely a different band. It's fucking incredibly hard now. I mean, we haven't got a lot of the things Brian could do. Like none of us play dulcimer and those things. Those were things Brian did that we don't have now. But we're so hard now as a band. There's more time to think. It's something we've never gotten into just that way before."

What Mick couldn't get into—what he tried his best to stay away from—was any sentimental summing up. "It just seemed like he decided that he had done what he set out to do," he insisted. "I was sad when he left the band, but I had to carry on. I had to keep going. I was trying desperately to put the band back together and Brian just went and died."

Like most statements he made on subjects close to him, Mick's pronouncements were disinguous, dissembling, and evasive, disguising emotions difficult to express. He came closest to articulating the truth of the frustrating relationship when, in an unguarded moment, he stated simply, "I wasn't ever really close to him."

Under the circumstances of their tumultuous seven-year relationship it was a sad commentary, especially considering the depth of feeling generated in the rock community at the news of Brian's death. "I got to know him very well, I think," said Beatle George Harrison, "and I felt very close to him. I don't think he had enough love or understanding. He was very nice and sincere and sensitive, and we must remember that's what he was." Jim Morrison, heading toward his own addled apocalypse, even wrote an ode celebrating Brian's song "Porky Satyr's Leer."

But it was the Who's Pete Townshend, never at a loss for words, who devised the most fitting tribute among Brian's peers. On hearing the news, Townshend recorded a song titled "Brian Jones, the Man Who Died Every Day."

If Mick had been less than generous in his praise of his former bandmate and more than a little guarded in his grief at Brian's death, he was hardly at a loss for a grand gesture at the birth of the new Stones.

Following the decision to recruit Mick Taylor, the group had announced they would perform a free concert in Hyde Park on July 5, 1969. Brian's death two days before had momentarily put the event on hold, but Mick, who had masterminded the show, made a virtue of necessity by announcing that it would now go on as a memorial. "Brian would have wanted it," he avowed. "We will now do the concert for him. I hope people will understand that it's because of our love for him that we are still doing it."

Whether the 300,000 who jammed the park on that stifling summer day understood the band's motives didn't seem to make much difference. The sunny Aquarian aura clung to the event like a pungent whiff of patchouli oil. Death was far away that day. It was rock 'n' roll that ruled. The concert, thanks to Mick's consuming attention to detail, was the seminal event of the season for Swinging London.

A genteel lovefest captured on film by six Granada TV film crews, the day began with Mick emerging from his Cheyne Walk home, dressed in a billowy apricot blouse and accompanied by Marianne and his surrogate son, Nicholas. He and the rest of the band arrived at the park later that afternoon in armored personnel carriers, climbing onto a stage festooned with a looming photograph of the freshly departed Brian. The moment for Mick's arch eulogy had arrived. He hushed the crowd and began reading passages from Shelley's *Adonais*, evoking a far different Brian than the one who had stymied him for so long. "Peace, peace!" he read as a crowd listened in eerie silence.

> He is not dead, he doth not sleep—
> He hath awakened from the dream of life—
> 'Tis we, who lost in stormy visions, keep
> With phantoms an unprofitable strife . . .

As the last words faded, roadies opened cardboard boxes to release a swarm of white butterflies, designated to fly among the crowd like the shattered remnants of Brian's soul. What hadn't been accounted for, however, was the sweltering heat, which killed most of the insects and left the survivors feebly fluttering about the stage. The band launched into their new single, "Honky Tonk Woman."

"That performance in Hyde Park was one of the worst, if not *the* worst concert we ever gave," remembers Stu. "Now I admire Mick for a lot of things, but one thing he ain't is a reader of epic poems. Keith showed up in terrible condition, off some kind of dope binge."

It hardly mattered. The crowd sensed the significance of the event and erupted into a frenzied celebration of the sixties spirit, which was fading, even then.

All that talk of being "lost in stormy visions" and "unprofitable strife" could well have sprung from something closer to home than Shelley's dark musings. Brian's death was, in fact, only one in a escalating number of ill omens plaguing the Stones in general and Mick in particular.

Keith and Anita had moved into a posh Cheyne Walk address nearby, which they promptly turned into a funhouse for their increasingly drug use. The relationship between the couple was still marred by Anita's on- and off-screen escapades with Mick during *Performance*, and the bed she shared with Keith in their new home was the same one on which she had done the deed with his partner.

The arrival of a son, Marlon, born August 10, 1969, did little to anchor the pair, for whom hashish and LSD had long since yielded to the somnambulance of heroin.

Rumors of late-night rituals, witchcraft, and hauntings were given credence by their mere persistence. "Kenneth Anger told me I was his right-hand man," Keith recounts. "Left-hand path. Right-hand path. How far do you want to go down? I mean, what is evil? There are black magicians who think we are acting as unknown agents of Lucifer, and others who think we *are* Lucifer. Everybody's Lucifer."

The Stones' reputation for nasty habits remained untarnished, a perception that proved as important in their worldwide prestige as the caliber of the music itself. Quite a feat, considering the quality of sound the band was producing despite Brian's absence.

"Honky Tonk Woman" was first played during that indifferent performance at Hyde Park. The song, an ode to easy women the world round, represented an impressive leap forward in the group's technical prowess as well as a stunning distillation of the Jagger/Richards school of rock writing. Under the expert production prowess of Jimmy Miller, the number crackled with an intensity and precision that placed the band's music in a whole new context. It was a textbook exercise in rock dynamics, centered on Keith's riveting guitar line, which seemed at times to swallow itself whole before emerging, ever more rapacious, on the other side of the refrain. "Honky Tonk Woman" was the first fruits of Mick's reformulation of the group, focusing on the quality of the music and putting their personal problems behind them. The rewards were an indisputable justification of his strategy and leadership: the song shot to number one throughout the United States, Europe, and Asia, reaching into such unlikely outposts as Turkey, the Philippines, Bermuda, and the Soviet Union.

The flip of the double A-sided hit, "You Can't Always Get What You Want," revealed yet another facet of Mick's and Keith's sure-footed songwriting. The track was a testament to the simple fact of their endurance, a worldly wise lament backed by a fifty-voice chorus. "Mick and Keith . . . were a party the moment they arrived," recalls Al Kooper, a session musician who played keyboards on the cut. "Everyone sat around on the floor with either an acoustic guitar or a percussion instrument. There was a conga player who could play congas and roll huge hash joints without missing a lick."

The Rolling Stones' new sound, leaner, mean, and produced with polished professionalism, added a luster missing from their earlier work. Mick was running the band now like a business and, like a business, they were geared to produce.

The focus and attention he brought to the music was in sharp contrast to the crumbling center of his personal life, where external pressure met internal crisis, with the hapless Mick and Marianne trapped and torn between. In May, shortly before Brian's death, the couple experienced another bust. They were having tea in the sunny Cheyne Walk kitchen when a half-dozen police arrived. After a search Mick and Marianne were formally charged with cannabis possession. The amount was a quarter ounce in a small wooden box. "I didn't get a chance to say anything," Mick remembers. "One of them stuck his foot in the door and the rest came barging in."

The timing could hardly have been worse, with the publicity

machine immediately cranking up for yet another round of us-against-them. It was getting tiresome and the wear was showing, most of all on Marianne. The distance Mick kept between them, his reserve and inability to express what was genuine about himself, drove her deeper into heroin, often in the company of Keith and Anita.

"The worst thing of all about being with Mick was the rule he laid down that you must never show emotion, in case people realized you weren't cool. Over the months everything got bottled up inside me."

A casualty waiting to happen, she had reached that place of exhausted desolation where disaster lurks. Her sense of self-preservation demolished, it was only a matter of when and how her sadness would overtake her.

The moment was reached in Australia. A few days before the May 28 bust, it was announced that Mick and Marianne had signed to star in a biopic of the legendary Australian outlaw, Ned Kelly. Shooting was to start in July, with Tony Richardson, best known for his rousing *Tom Jones*, as director. The news was hardly met with pleasure by the Aussies, who accused the production of portraying their ruddy hero as a "limey pantywaist." A petition was even circulated to that effect.

The arrest, and its resulting immigration questions, briefly threatened the shooting date of *Ned Kelly*, but by early July the Stones' lawyers had cleared the way. Mick and Marianne arrived in Melbourne on July 7.

For Mick the endless demands of a starring role in a major motion picture was the last thing he needed. The arrest, Marianne's deteriorating condition, and a looming financial disaster brought on by Klein's large-scale pilfering were turning his life into one long, convoluted emergency. There was, however, a small consolation to the trip: he would be out of town for Brian's funeral. "He did feel awful about Brian's death," one friend reports, "but it's the kind of thing he can't cope with. He wouldn't be able to see Brian's parents and say how sad he was and all that."

Their presence was missed. "We've had no cards at Christmas," Lewis Jones told reporter Stanley Booth as the funeral party disbanded across the verdant lawns of Cheltenham Cemetery. "Nothing from the boys. If you see them, remember me to them. Tell them that if they want to write or call, I'd be happy to hear from them."

Ten thousand miles away, Mick would have other things on his mind. In a room at Melbourne's Chevron Hotel, with Mick lost in a jet-lagged slumber, Marianne methodically swallowed 150 Tuinal capsules, washing them down with a cup of hot chocolate she had ordered from room service. Mick awoke and found her on the floor, a deathly shade of pale. He immediately summoned help. He had found her, and saved her, with literally seconds to spare. The massive overdose was enough to kill three men.

It is impossible to fix precisely what finally pushed Marianne over the edge. "When I started to take them," she told A. E. Hotchner, "I only intended to take a few, enough to get me to sleep, but watching myself in the mirror of the vanity table, sipping hot chocolate and carefully placing each pill on my tongue, I somehow couldn't restrain myself."

In a coma for the next six days, she recounts in vivid detail a hallucinatory dream she had, providing another glimpse into her shattered psyche: "I remember finding myself in a big, gray, still place where there was no climate at all—no wind or cold or sun, no weather of any kind. And Brian Jones was there. Brian was talking in just the way Brian would, hopeless, but funny as well: 'Man, what a jolt I had waking up here, no pills, no smokes, no Valium, a real drag, but then it came to me that I was dead and that was another jolt. But man, I can adjust. You tell Mick, I can adjust.'"

Adding to the aura of doom and disease was Marianne's identification with Ophelia, a role she had recently been playing in a London production of *Hamlet*. "I'd will myself into a suicidal state of mind," she says, "quite apart from what was going on around me. . . . All the business of Brian and Ophelia seemed to get mixed up in my mind."

There is no doubt Mick played a significant role in Marianne's desire to commit suicide, including his habitual womanizing, which had led him to a number of casual indulgences, most notably with a statuesque black American actress named Marsha Hunt.

One of the stars of the halcyon hippie musical *Hair*, Marsha had been on conspicuous display at Hyde Park, decked out in a stunning white buckskin ensemble. Her flat in St. John's Wood, a quick stroll down from Cheyne Walk, was the sight of an increasing number of assignations. Marsha had even given Mick a token of her regard: a basset hound puppy named Grits. Mick in time would reciprocate with a love child.

But adultery and benign neglect aside, it was Marianne herself who had failed a fundamental life lesson. She simply didn't know how to look out for herself. "Mick's other affairs did bother me," she revealed years later. "But that wasn't as bad as being pinned against the wall by the whole superstar thing."

In Australia Marianne had finally come apart. Perhaps it was the prospect of eternity in that gray, cold place with Brian Jones. Perhaps it was the prayers of Canon Hugh Hopkins, rector of the church where Brian had sung as a boy. After preaching Brian's eulogy from the parable of the prodigal son, Hopkins had petitioned the Lord to preserve Marianne. Or perhaps it was simply the knowledge that she had finally gotten Mick's attention. Whatever the reason, Marianne at length willed herself back from the edge. She would spend the next two months convalescing at Mount St. Michael's Hospital outside Sydney.

Meanwhile Mick, faced with breach of contract, had no choice but to continue with the grind of shooting *Ned Kelly*, a film version of the life of the legendary Australian outlaw. It was obvious almost from the start that the production had more troubles than just miscasting. With Marianne incapacitated, her understudy, Diane Craig, stepped into the supporting role of Ned's outback lover without having learned the lines. It didn't matter. The abysmal script and endless days on location completely exhausted everyone. Symbolic of the disaster, a prop gun exploded in Mick's hand, leaving a gash that took sixteen stitches to close.

The film opened to a chorus of critical hoots in the summer of 1970. The movie finds Mick floundering in an ill-conceived role, sporting an Irish brogue. Its most memorable image showed Mick as a chin-bearded outlaw, miked for heavy breathing, inside a suit of home-made armor made to repel the bad guy's bullets. "*Ned Kelly*—that load of shit!" he would later say in an effort to distance himself from the fiasco. "I only made it because I had nothing else to do."

"Mick thinks he needs to do those things," Keith would later assert. "We've often talked about it, and I've asked him why the hell does he want to be a film star. But he says, 'Well, you're a musician and that's a complete thing in itself, but I don't play anything.' "

The truth went much deeper. For Mick film was the arena for establishing the sort of stature that music could never provide. The music still mattered, of course; it was the commodity that secured the band's market share, but the trick was to make *oneself* the commodity—to sell the masses on nothing more than personality and perceived charisma. To become an actor, to fill a screen with the minute details of face and form, was to transcend the notion of entertainment and reach the next plateau of adoration.

It's a measure of Mick's power as a rock 'n' roll deity, however, that he could never really lose himself in a character. *Ned Kelly* was ludicrous precisely because the rough-hewn outlaw was so far from the public notion of who Mick Jagger was supposed to be. *Performance* had come closer, if only because he had essentially played himself, a rock-'n'-roll idol sunk into a world of his own creation. Mick would never fully emerge from that world and, as a result, it was impossible to see him on screen and forget who he really was.

Filming finally concluded in September of 1969 and Mick, the frail Marianne in tow, returned home. He was immediately immersed in another mammoth undertaking, the band's first US tour since 1966, three years before. Plans for the tour had been delayed following Brian's death. Now with the enormous success of "Honky Tonk Woman," and on the strength of tracks the group had been recording off and on through the year, the time was finally ripe.

The band's financial circumstances, however, were decidedly rotten. Stones bassist Bill Wyman recounts a time in spring of 1968 when he had less than fifty pounds in his bank account, thanks to Klein's varied schemes to separate the group from their enormous profits. In 1968 the attorney had landed three of the four Beatles as clients, realizing a long-sought ambition to have the group, or at least the majority of it, under his control. For their part Mick and the rest of the band could not decide which was worse: having Klein ignore them in favor of his latest coup or having him give them, and their money, his full attention.

In any event, it was decided that he would have to be eased out, if for no other reason than to keep him away from the projected record-breaking proceeds from the upcoming American extravaganza. Because shooting *Ned Kelly* kept Mick in Australia that summer, he had to handle the disentanglement from a distance. "The trouble is that it disorganized our plans," recalls Keith. "It happened just as we got Mick Taylor into the band and just as we were finishing the album."

The lack of a firm hand resulted in all sorts of mistakes. "We had one track to do and we accidentally wiped Mick's voice off when we were messing around with the tape," Keith continues. "Then there was Mick, stuck down in Australia, three thousand miles from the nearest studio."

Erased vocals could be fixed. An irate Klein was an entirely different matter. Mick, ever more adept at navigating the band's murky financial waters, deftly recruited Klein's nephew, Ronnie Schneider, to their camp. Schneider had made it his business to ingratiate himself with Mick and Keith, even to the point of sharing their disgust with Klein. By bringing him on board, Mick had engineered a change in management, getting Klein's agreement to let Schneider handle the band's affairs from his uncle's New York offices. The arrangement, as it was meant to, proved unwieldy and Schneider relocated to London, smoothly stepping into the role of full-time manager.

Also waiting in the wings was Prince Rupert Lowenstein, who hoped to prove himself by landing the band a new record deal after their contract with Decca expired in a flurry of acrimony and accusations.

It is a measure of Allen Klein's obsession with the Beatles that he hardly noticed all the maneuvering just beyond his sight line. As news of a new Rolling Stones tour spread through the music business grapevine, Schneider was deluged with offers from American promoters willing to guarantee virtually any price he named, up to and including four million dollars for broadcast rights to a single concert. On November 1, 1969, a week before the tour's scheduled appearance at the Los Angeles Forum, a fourth date was added to three already sold-out appearances at Madison Square Garden. In like fashion, all tickets for the show were bought within two hours of the time they had gone on sale.

The Stones, freed from Brian and his entangling problems, continued to have mixed feelings about performing. Mick, particularly, worried about developing a stage persona to do justice to the myth that now defined him.

Increasingly, that myth centered on the group's evocation of dark forces, an identification that seemed to suit Mick's notion of the larger-than-life role he wanted to fulfill. Ossie Clark, a fashion designer who was hired to put together the group's onstage attire, recalls one harrowing encounter with Mick's alter ego.

"One night I was in Mick's house in London. He'd put on a tape of the music that would be played on tour and he'd dance around . . .

with great intensity, and he was telling me in a stream of what seemed subconscious feelings, somewhat incoherent, what he wanted to convey. It was more than just describing costumes or anything like that, it was as if he had become Satan and was announcing his evil intentions. He was reveling in this role. Frightening, truly frightening. He was rejoicing at being Lucifer."

The effect the new Stones would have on eager American fans became evident from the start of the tour. As the first notes of "Jumpin' Jack Flash" careened though the cavernous stadiums and Mick leapt to the stage in a half-black, half-red jumpsuit topped by an Uncle Sam top hat, the answering roar quickly subsided as audiences strained to catch every gesture and nuance. Mick remarked, "On the Coast and a lot of other places, there was a very large cross-section of people, all kinds of people, and they listened. A lot of them did. That was new in some ways."

For the Los Angeles opening a $230,000 box office broke the Beatles' previous record and kicked the tour off to an eventual $2 million gross. As the dates continued, the band's confidence grew. "Compared to the way we sounded later along, we were terrible in San Francisco," Mick recalls. "By the time we got to Detroit, I'd say it was like a one hundred percent improvement."

One factor of the barnstorming itinerary that did not improve, however, was the pervasive aura of bad vibes that clung to the group and its entourage. Ossie Clark recalls, "I flew with the Stones to their first date. I remember vividly that from the moment I set foot on that plane, before it took off from London, I felt a kind of oppressive fear. There was a negative electric charge in the atmosphere. The flight over was a nightmare, truly scary. The way the Stones were toward each other, toward me—an insistent, brooding, uncontrolled intimidation. In Los Angeles we were put up in a big house and the evil vibes intensified. The Stones were taking all kinds of evil drugs, particularly a new kind of potent acid that they had gotten hold of. But it was more than that. They were getting deeper and deeper into black magic. Led by Anita Pallenberg, Keith and Mick had developed a kind of Satanic indentification, as if they were openly dealing with the devil."

The ominous atmosphere increased with each stop on the tour: San Diego, Phoenix, Dallas, Chicago. The show stormed across the States, leaving in its wake the supercharged hysteria that always precedes flashpoint violence. "The Rolling Stones are violence," asserted *Rolling Stone* magazine critic Jon Landau. "Their music penetrates the raw nerve endings of their listeners and finds its way into the groove marked 'release of frustration.' Their violence has always been a surrogate for the large violence the audience is so obviously capable of."

Mick denied the obvious. "I don't understand the connection between music and violence. People are always trying to explain it to me and I just blindly carry on. I just know I get very aroused by the music, but it doesn't arouse me violently. I never went to a rock 'n' roll show and wanted to smash a window or beat somebody up."

He was about to become the star attraction in just such a convocation.

Danse Macabre

Coinciding with the Stones' triumphant return to the road, America was convulsing from internal contradictions that threatened to tear it apart at the seams. In Vietnam, 567 people had been slaughtered in a town called My Lai. Half a world away, a quarter of a million Americans marched on Washington to protest the war, while headlines were filled with the news of the murders carried out by Charlie Manson and his bizarre clan.

With the hippie utopia going up in flames, the time seemed right for the street fighting man the Stones had so gleefully evoked. With that song's surge of revolutionary rhetoric, the group naturally gained stature as antiheroic icons. The tune declared that "the time is right for violent revolution," but Mick was careful to cast himself as only a "poor boy in sleepy London Town." But no one paid much attention to his disavowals. Small wonder "Street Fighting Man" had been banned in certain law and order outposts across the country. America was under siege and the Stones were leading the charge.

A broadside distributed on the streets of San Francisco gave shape to the fears of the old order. The band was greeted as "our comrades in the desperate battle against the lunatics who hold power. The revolutionary youth of the world hear your music and is inspired to even more deadly acts. We will play your music as we tattoo 'burn, baby, burn' on the bellies of the wardens and the generals and create a new society from the ashes of our fires."

After his narrow escape as an unwilling symbol of the drug culture, Mick should have known better than to allow too close an identification with the radical revolutionary politics of the moment. But once again he couldn't resist the temptation to make the most of his radical chic status. In a 1968 interview for London's underground paper, *International Times*, he was asked how he felt when students rioted while the band was on stage: "Do you pick up on that energy?"

"Yes! Wow! Tingle with it!" was Mick's reply. "The energy's great. . . . I never went on stage with the idea of keeping everything cool. I never wanted it to be peaceful. . . . I mean, they were totally in control as much as I was. I mean, I was in control but they were also."

Control, finally, was the issue, and as the Stones flaunted their power, it focused the pent-up rage of a purposely alienated generation. "We're so violent," Mick would proclaim in the same interview. "We're violently frustrated. And it's our excuse, see? We can't be guerrillas."

What they could be, however, were highly charged symbols of the new political order, anxious to kick out the jams regardless of the consequences. "I'd just call it us versus them," Mick would avow. "It's all political, whatever you want to call it. I'll take my chances on the outside. We'll just keep on doing it our way." The group's leftist posturing was all the more potent for its lack of definition: this was a fill-in-the-blanks uprising against anything, everything, or nothing in particular.

It was an attitude that, fused with the group's equally broad attachment to Satanism, became the clenched fist at the heart of *Let It Bleed*.

Their follow-up to *Beggar's Banquet*, the album was released at the height of the US tour frenzy. Cut in the spring, *Let It Bleed* contained the last faint echoes of Brian's input. It was the album the band had been working on that night at Olympic Studios when they got news of his death.

More to the point, *Let It Bleed* raised the stakes on the band's incendiary potential. The album core consisted of a pair of songs that touched on the Stones' twin conceits: "Gimme Shelter," a roiling, gospel-rooted anthem, bristled with warnings of impending apocalypse, a cleansing rain of "rape and murder" that sounded like divine retribution. It was as fitting a soundtrack for the end of the sixties as any band would offer, even as it prodded the faithful to new heights of paranoia.

"Midnight Rambler," a loping paean to Boston Strangler Albert DeSalvo, was a blatant escalation of all the demonic innuendo of *Beggar's Banquet*, a crude, cruel, and pernicious tone poem for homicidal maniacs, replete with images of breaking and entering and gruesome execution.

Once again the group's image had run away with them. If the urbane sophisticate of "Sympathy for the Devil" sent shivers down the spine, why not an explicit account of a knife murder? If "Street Fighting Man" got people's blood boiling, what would "Gimme Shelter," the group's anthem of anarchy, incite in them? *Let It Bleed*, an out-of-the-box smash, had the answers, layered between the standard-issue rockers and one-off blues and country ditties that comprised the remainder of the album.

It wasn't that the Stones had exceeded the bounds of good taste or social responsibility: that, after all, was what was expected of them. *Let It Bleed* was something else, proof that Mick and Keith could no longer control, much less direct, the course of the band and its music. The forces that defined the Stones, set them apart as exemplars of contempt, anarchy, and outlaw excesses, were now dictating the terms of their success. It was too late to turn back, to suggest that it was all just a shadow play, a publicity ploy, a way to fleece the faithful. What they had set in motion would now be played out to its dreadful conclusion.

Musically, *Let It Bleed* continued the trend begun with "Honky Tonk Woman." The addition of Mick Taylor and his seamless guitar technique had snapped the band to attention, reenergizing the interplay, at least initially. "He's really good," Mick would say of Taylor. "And it means that Keith can sort of lay out. . . . There's more time to think. And sometimes they'll get to tossing solos back and forth between guitars . . . and it's just great. It's beautiful to hear."

If beautiful meant every musical shading and texture carefully crafted and consummately performed, then *Let It Bleed* was a beautiful album. What it conspicuously lacked was a soul. For the first time in their recording career, the Stones had gotten all the parts right and missed the point. Jimmy Miller's production once again was an awesome balancing act, with the band's aural dynamics caught in perfect suspension. But the cost of all the technical sizzle was music that strived shamelessly for effect. Mick and Keith's songwriting was concerned more with getting the attitude right than with expressing something original or instinctive, living up to the legend instead of living it out.

Not that it much mattered. The legend had taken on a life of its own. The four Madison Square Garden shows had grossed $100,000 each and had been taped for a projected live album. At a November 28 press conference, the group announced that as a thank-you to American fans, they would perform a free concert in the counterculture's capital, San Francisco.

The group had broken every available box office record. But there was more to the event than mere gratitude. "It was when we first fucking got to Los Angeles," Mick recounts. "We decided right then that we wanted to do it when the tour was over. We wanted to do Los Angeles, because the weather's better. But there was no place to do it there, and we were assured we could do it much more easily in San Francisco."

Mick proposed to stage his own Woodstock, the rock 'n' roll bacchanalia held the previous August and instantly proclaimed one of Flower Power's defining moments. Although the Stones still stood outside the pale of the Aquarian Age, the notion of so grand a gesture as a massive free concert in the hippie heartland appealed to Mick.

It was also a neat bit of one-upsmanship. The group's Hyde Park appearance, after all, had drawn a bigger crowd than Woodstock, held that same summer in upstate New York. Yet it had hardly drawn the kind of cultural milestone comparisons heaped upon the muddy three-day festival. This time around, the Stones would trump all comers with the mother of all rock spectacles.

The bandwagon proved big enough to accommodate a full complement of artists and hangers-on. San Francisco's premier psychedelic conglomerate, the Grateful Dead, volunteered to coordinate the event as well as play an opening set. Other support acts quickly queued, and while announcement of the concert was delayed to maximize the box office of the remaining dates, an all-star lineup began taking shape. Aside from the Dead, Santana, the Jefferson Airplane, Crosby, Stills, Nash and Young, and the Flying Burrito Brothers were slated to appear.

The site Mick had in mind was sun-dappled Golden Gate Park, but negotiations proved fruitless. The City of San Francisco rightly sensed a lack of direction and control at Stones Central. "Meetings of two or three or ten people in every side office broke up in confusion after a few minutes," wrote one reporter, describing the scene at the event's Marin County headquarters. "There was an air of frantic activity about the place. But in fact, nothing was happening."

And a great deal needed to happen to ensure the kind of epoch-making moment Mick had in mind. The four-million-dollar insurance bond demanded by San Francisco made Golden Gate a definite nonstarter, even as the announced date for the free concert, December 6, drew near. A second site, Sears Point Raceway, was secured and a stage hurriedly constructed before the offer was withdrawn at the last moment. No less a legal wizard than Melvin Belli, then at work on the Charlie Manson murder trial, was retained by Mick to smooth out the difficulties and secure a last-minute venue.

On the day before the date, Belli delivered, striking up a bargain with Dick Carter, owner of a barren stretch of parched hills forty miles east of San Francisco called Altamont Raceway. Charmed by the silver-tongued Belli, Carter agreed to lend out his property for the event, asking only a million-dollar insurance bond and a five-thousand-dollar cleanup fund. With less than twenty hours until showtime, the stage was dismantled at the old site and reassembled by crews working through the night in a surreal setting lit by diesel-driven klieg lights.

By dawn the first of the fans appeared, shouldering backpacks and making the long trek from the roadway across a desolate landscape littered with the carcasses of gutted hot rods. The Stones had already arrived by limousine at 3 A.M., wandered among their dazzled disciples, sharing joints and a growing sense of anticipation.

As a feeble winter sun crested the horizon, the arid expanse was crawling with rock 'n' roll pilgrims who had abandoned their cars in a solid ten-mile traffic jam to make their way on foot to the concert site. Many, lost and drug-dazed, paid the five dollar fee charged by locals to guide them across the trackless expanse. Some who lacked the money were found the next day, still wandering lost among the dry brown hills.

By ten o'clock the security forces had arrived, straddling the backs of Harleys and decked out in their finest fascist regalia. They were the San Francisco, San Bernardino, Oakland, and San Jose chapters of the Hell's Angels, hired by the Grateful Dead to maintain order. The bikers were escorting a school bus brimming with cold beer, red wine, and a cornucopia of noxious street drugs, including a particularly virulent mixture of Methedrine and LSD.

The motley and menacing Angels were followed by a half-dozen flatbed trucks, each hauling a load of portable toilets, some ninety in all for a crowd that, by the time high, gray clouds drifted in to hide the sun, had grown to 300,000.

As the rotgut liquor and mind-warping substances began to spread throughout the crowd, the serene sense of cosmic confluence gave way to a grim and gritty tableau. The Angels, tanked to the gills on bad acid and jug wine, began enforcing their authority with arbitrary displays of random violence. Nineteen medics, scattered in tents across the sprawling site, were quickly overwhelmed by the influx of hapless revelers, reeling from overdoses of every possible chemical combination. After a paltry supply of Thorazine was exhausted, bad trip casualties were corralled behind roped-off enclosures to keep them safe from a throng whose mood had gone, by stages, from euphoric to uncertain to ugly.

Which is not to say the Angels weren't maintaining order with an unseemly relish. By the time Santana hit the stage, late that afternoon, the bikers had formed a phalanx around the stage, keeping the crowd at bay with a variety of chains, knives, and blunt instruments, including the wicked weapon *du jour*, a sawed-off pool cue weighted with lead.

Santana's percolating Latin rock seemed, for a moment, to bring back the good vibes. "It was like being in the eye of a hurricane with energy and turmoil all around," reported Sol Stern of *Ramparts* magazine. "I thought everything was going to be all right—that the power of the music would keep it all in balance."

Questions of balance seem especially ironic considering the malevolent forces of chaos the Stones had been so assiduously whipping up across America. At Altamont, it wasn't only the chickens that had come home to roost. It was the vultures and the crows and all other ill omens portending the devil's due.

Even before the last notes of Santana's first number had rung out over the heads of the seething crowd, flashpoints of violence ignited along the scrim of the stage. A photographer, scrambling to record the incidents, was himself felled in a flurry of fists and boots.

But the day was still young. The Jefferson Airplane's arrival on stage was met by a barrage of half-empty beer cans and the sickening sound of flesh rent by whistling pool cues. By the time the band launched into "Revolution," the song's exhortation of "Up against the wall, motherfucker" had become moot. The mob around the stage was already up against a wall of acid-crazed Angels mercilessly flailing at anyone who ran, staggered, or was pushed into their perimeter.

The horrific violence began to spread away from the stage in concentric waves of brutality. The Airplane's diminutive lead singer, Marty Balin, jumped into the crowd to stop a three-on-one drubbing and was himself beaten unconscious. "I'd like to tell you all what's happened," shouted the group's distraught guitarist, Paul Kantner, over the PA. "The Hell's Angels have just smashed Marty Balin."

While the crush of people at the far edge of the speedway peered into the gathering dusk, Kantner's tremulous voice was suddenly interrupted by the snarl of an Angel who had grabbed a spare microphone. "Are you talking to me?" he demanded.

"I'm not talking to you," came the frightened reply, echoing out over the expanse. "I'm talking to these people."

"Fuck you," the Angel said as another flurry of pool cues arced over the heads of the packed and panicked mob.

The band played on, even as fingers pointed into the sky, tracing the descent of the Stones' helicopter, delivering the band into a maelstrom of their own creation. "I hate you, fucker! I want to kill you!" screamed a deranged teenager as Mick made his way toward the trailer where he and the rest of the band would await nightfall to make their grand entrance. Before anyone quite knew what was happening, the gibbering acid casualty lunged, landing a glancing blow to Mick's face.

While clearly shaken, Mick had no idea how far his dream of a utopian love feast had degenerated into insanity. He turned to his own phalanx of bodyguards, led by a hulking black man named Tony Fuchs, and ordered that his attacker be freed.

Fuchs and the others already had their hands full. Confronted by hostile Angels apparently intent on dismembering this mincing English fop, Fuchs landed two roundhouse punches with such force that both his wrists snapped.

On stage the Flying Burrito Brothers performed for a crowd clearly in no mood to be placated by their lilting country-flavored rock. The afternoon wore on as a cold wind blew in from the Pacific and people began to light garbage fires for warmth, spreading the stench of burning plastic over the landscape.

In the medical tents doctors struggled to cope with the flood of bad trips brought on by the toxic acid or simply the overwhelming angst that hung in the air like the putrid smoke from the bonfires. Richard Fine, the physician in charge of emergency services, would later comment, "The people running the thing . . . didn't realize what was crucial from a medical standpoint. . . . They wouldn't give us the authority to do such things as set up a workable evacuation procedure. It was just piss-poor planning. A lot of the bad trips were violent because there was so much violence in the air."

Under the circumstances the wisest choice would have been to end the whole deadly debacle as quickly as possible. The Stones however had no such intention. They waited for the sun to set and darkness to settle, the better to heighten the moment everyone had been waiting for: the appearance of the popularly acclaimed Greatest Rock 'n' Roll Band in the World.

In the blizzard of recriminations that followed Altamont, the Stones' unconscionable delay in taking the stage was among the more damning indictments. Mick would defend his actions by claiming that the organizers and the other groups had neglected to tell him exactly how dire the situation had become. It was a claim vehemently countered by those who insist the Stones were kept fully informed of the chaos that was sweeping the speedway. It's an unlikely claim: in a setting where the last vestiges of actual and effective authority had long ago been borne away on a surge of terror and violence, it seems unlikely that anyone would have had the presence of mind to make regular reports.

By sunset, as the last warbling notes of Crosby, Stills, Nash and Young croaked from the overloaded PA, an Angel, alarmed at the increasingly barbaric behavior of his cohorts, approached Mick and urged him to crank up the main event.

"Jagger's so vain with the whole scene," he would later recount. "We kept telling him, 'Hey, you know what? You've got a half-million fucking people out there that made you what you are and here you are stalling!' The man says, 'Well, my makeup looks better at night.' "

Delays were, in fact, a deliberate element of the Stones' show throughout the tour, a ploy to build expectation and energy that would often find them taking the stage two, three, or even four hours after their scheduled start.

The band's imminent arrival was announced by one of the concert organizers. Sam Cutler shouted into a microphone, "The Rolling Stones won't come out until everybody gets off the stage." Cutler hoped with this announcement to clear the stage of nearly a hundred Angels and roadies, along with the battered fans who had made it through the gauntlet.

A long moment passed. Nobody moved. Then in the distance through the rapidly gathering dark came the throaty roar of dozens of gleaming Harley hogs. Sonny Barger, notorious president of the Oakland Hell's Angels chapter, led a corps of bikers through the crowd, deploying in front of the stage to create an impenetrable barricade. Its strength was tested almost immediately when one of the motorcyles was accidentally kicked by a hapless bystander.

"I ain't no cop," Barger would later insist. "I ain't never gonna police nothing. I just went there to sit in front of the stage and drink beer and have a good time, like we was told. But when they started kicking our bikes, man, that started it. I ain't no peace creep, man."

Those injured in the subsequent melee were ferried back to the medical tents, but doctors were unable to see the wounds to treat them, given the strict injunction against any bright light that might distract from the Stones' entrance.

That entrance, when it came, was the trigger that finally released the brewing fury that had been leaking out over the course of that long, nightmarish day. "There were rumors flashing around everywhere," Keith recalls. " 'There's a bomb gone off and twenty people been blown to bits, man.' You say, 'I think you got it wrong, man. I'm sure you got it wrong. 'Cause you been hearing crazy rumors all day, that you're dead, as ridiculous as that.' "

As the group tore into a ragged rendition of "Jumpin' Jack Flash" and Mick pranced in and around the stolid, glaring Angels, a fat, naked woman leapt onto the stage. She was immediately brought down in a lashing hail of pool cues. Out in the darkness, men and women stripped off their clothes and inhibitions and danced demented jigs around the bonfires. Angels singled out victims, surrounding and pummeling them.

It was a spectacle only too clearly witnessed from the band's vantage point. But it was far too late for them to defuse all the malevolent energy brought to this moment. The only thing left to do was go on with the show. In what may well have been the most shocking act of irresponsibility in the entire catastrophic concert, the band stuck to their set list. "Please allow me to introduce myself," Mick intoned as the band leaned into the infernal samba rhythm that opened "Sympathy for the Devil."

The result was an instantaneous eruption. It was as if Beelzebub himself, angered by the mortal who had presumed on his name and power, let loose hell's full fury. Stunned by the carnage their music had unleashed, the band ground to a halt. "Brothers and sisters," entreated Mick in a wavering plea. "Brothers and sisters . . . come on, now. That means everybody. Just cool it. Just cool out now. We can cool out everybody."

Cooling out was a forlorn hope. The pool cues continued to rain indiscriminately. The band began "Sympathy for the Devil" again, but realizing at last the implications, let it go after another few bars. Keith, incensed over one particularly vicious attack, moved to jump into the crowd and had to be restrained by stage manager Sam Cutler. A large German Shepherd materialized from somewhere and hunkered down on the stage, staring balefully and growling at Stones drummer Charlie Watts.

"San Francisco," Mick pleaded, his voice cracking with fear and something close to despair, "this could be the most beautiful event. Don't fuck it up." No one paid the slightest attention. To one side of the stage a black man was spotted waving a gun. He was immediately set upon by an Oakland Angel in Nazi regalia. A knife blade flickered and Meredith Hunter, eighteen years old, fell to the dirt, mortally wounded.

"We need a doctor, now please," Mick implored, not quite certain what had just happened in front of his eyes. "Look, could you let the doctor through, please? Somebody's been hurt."

Horrified bystanders tried to wash away Hunter's blood with coffee, but by the time the teenager was carried back to the medics, it was too late. He had succumbed to multiple wounds from a seven-inch shiv.

On stage Mick continued to plead with the mob, his black and red silk outfit wilted over his slight shoulders. "All I can do is ask you— beg you to keep it together. It's within your power."

Wyman played the opening notes of "Under My Thumb" in a

deliberately soothing tempo. The group lurched through the rest of their set, barely stopping from one song to the next.

"We knew that if we stopped," Mick Taylor recalls, "there really would have been a riot." The headlong music churned toward the final number before anyone had a chance to think about it, and "Street Fighting Man" split the air with a crowning irony.

It was at this point that the last chopper pilot clamored onto the stage, telling Wyman that he was leaving, with or without the band. "We're gonna kiss you goodbye" were Mick's last words as he and the group ran from the stage, heading for the hovering helicopter. "It was like Vietnam," recalls Keith. "You had to jump and climb up this rope ladder. Gotta get away."

It was a very near thing. "We piled in there on top of each other," Wyman remembers, "and we took off going slantways." They left behind a scene of medieval bedlam. The crowd, slow to realize the show was over, roared their indignation as the chopper flew low over the lurid landscape. In sullen confusion those who could began to find their way back to the clogged freeway, while others too stoned or sated to leave simply hunched down for the evening.

By midnight the speedway looked like a battlefield, littered with inert bodies. But the carnage wasn't quite over. Early that morning, a car plowed into a cluster of campers sitting around a campfire, killing two, while in the distant hills, another victim lay drowned in an irrigation ditch.

"Mick kept saying it was his fault," recalls a witness in the band's hotel suite that night, "and that maybe he would quit rock 'n' roll forever." By the next morning he had clearly talked himself out of that notion. Early press accounts of Altamont hailed a crowning achievement of peace and love and world class rock 'n' roll. Mention of the four deaths was balanced with the news that four babies had been delivered during the concert, an outright lie of unknown origin. "Things went smoothly and people were happy," insisted one radio reporter. "When you have a big amount of people together, a couple of things happen." The DJ added with a flourish of political correctness, "After all, look what happens in Vietnam everyday."

The Stones welcomed the impression of general peace and harmony as they kissed the States goodbye and returned home. "The day after Altamont they couldn't get out of America fast enough," recalls Stu, and when the English press interviewed them about the aftermath of the concert, accounts had already changed dramatically. "It was basically well-organized," Keith blithely told reporters, "but people were tired and a few tempers got frayed."

But as the true story of murder and mayhem began to emerge, thanks largely to the investigative efforts of radio station KSAN, people began to see Altamont for what it was: the karmic comeuppance of the haughty, high-flying Rolling Stones. "To those who know," wrote one fan, "it's been obvious that the Stones, or at least some of them, have been involved in the practice of Magick ever since the *Satanic Majesties Request* album. But there at least the color was more white than black. . . . I don't know if they were truly aware of what they were doing or not . . . But an agonizing price has been paid for the lesson . . . and we are all guilty because we have all eaten of the cake the Stones baked."

Not everyone saw supernatural forces at work. David Crosby, who would struggle mightily with his own demons, chalked it up to overweening hubris. The Stones, he sniffed, "are into an ego game and a star trip. . . . I think they're on a grotesque, negative ego trip, essentially, especially the two leaders."

Bill Graham, the outspoken San Francisco rock promoter, couldn't have agreed more. "Every fucking gig he made the promoter and the people bleed," Graham railed against Mick. "What right does this god have to descend on this country this way? But you know what is a great tragedy to me? That cunt is a great entertainer."

As the true proportions of Altamont became clear, the Stones were increasingly confronted with questions of their own responsibility for the event. The clamor would grow with the release of *Gimme Shelter*, a documentary film of the American tour shot by the Maysles Brothers that contained searing images of the Altamont atrocities.

Keith, with a callousness that was becoming habitual, laid it off on America's ultraviolent aura. "People were just asking for it," he insisted. "They had those victims' faces. Really, the difference between the open-air show we held here in Hyde Park and the one there was amazing. I think it illustrates the difference between the two countries. You can put a half-million young English kids together and they won't start killing each other. That's the difference."

For Mick, tight-lipped and evasive, the moral of it all was obvious, yet another hard-earned lesson in maintaining control. "At the time it was a nightmare," he would later admit. "It was just one of those

'Here we go, we've gotta get through it somehow, because we can't just leave, because if we leave, what's going to happen?' It taught me a lot. It taught me never to do anything I wasn't on top of. As much as I could be organizationwise, I had to do it. Never, never trust anyone else to do it for you."

It was a conviction born from more than even the crucible of Altamont. For Mick, keeping it all under control was becoming a ruthless exercise in cutting losses and keeping a stiff upper lip. The trick was survival, and Mick was perfecting the knack of not looking back.

FIFTEEN

Goodbye, Marianne

Besides establishing irrefutable proof that the sixties were really over, Altamont also pointed to a cul-de-sac of intents and expectations into which the Stones had, for so long, been heading. For eight years they had maintained the mantle as rock 'n' roll's best and baddest, cultivating a relentless cool.

The group's disdain, expressed in everything from Mick's misogynistic lyrics to Keith's ever-more-blatant drug use, had been played out in the hills outside San Francisco. Having been elevated to the role of sinister spokesmen for the sixties' dark side, the group assumed the aura of demonic demigods. They discovered, having stepped to the precipice, that there was no road back. There would be inevitable consequences.

But such consequences spread far beyond the group's particular public relations problem. Altamont became known, in the phrase of one observer, as "the death of innocence in the Woodstock nation." The truth was more sobering. The Stones, and the cultural firestorm over which they presided, were an integral part of the sixties. There was no innocence to lose, only the self-deluding presumption that society could be remade in the image of eternal youth.

The countercultural consensus rested on a simple, subversive tenet: that no one—not parents, politicians, or preachers—could dictate values. Good and evil were not simply relative, they were irrelevant. Love and hate were two sides of an eternally evolving harmony that was sublimely indifferent to moral cause and effect. The Stones, of course, stood at one extreme of that cosmic polarity. The Beatles, the San Francisco youthquake, and the seductive notion that love was all we needed were balanced on the other. But both were equally intrinsic expressions of the age. "There was nothing about peace, love, and flowers in 'Jumpin' Jack Flash,'" Mick would say, and he was right.

If the sixties ended at Altamont, so too, in some undeniable way, did the Rolling Stones. "In the beginning there was rock 'n' roll," wrote George Paul Csicsery in his perceptive Altamont postmortem. "The Beatles came and made it good with love and the bluebird of paradise. But even while the children lifted their faces to the sun, Mick Jagger coiled himself around the tree of flesh, offering a sweet bite of chaos. Saturday, at Altamont, the children swallowed their bite, after chewing and tasting their alliance for nearly a decade. Until Saturday, evil was value-free, something to do for its own sake. A lot of people who thought they were children of chaos dropped out of their sugar-coated camp . . . to see the core of their religion at work."

The theme of that religion, and of the subtle spiritual deception it disguised, would be evoked over and over again by those grappling with the meaning of the Stones, their music, and the consequences of its message. Declared *San Francisco Chronicle* critic Ralph J. Gleason, "The gathering was religious, of course, but the high priests were as cynical as any Elmer Gantry."

"It took only four months to go from Woodstock to Altamont," wrote journalist Andy Gordon, "only four months to sell out the myth. The myths become shorter- and shorter-lived as history accelerates. . . . We fear that the terror of Altamont may be the wave of the future."

Mick, with his lifelong issues of control and the prohibitive cost of commitment, would deny his part in this seismic change in values. "Society has pushed me into this position of responsibility," he would assert, insisting elsewhere that, "I never spoke for my generation. I just spoke for myself. I did things that were taken to represent others just because I wanted to do them. People should speak for themselves."

But people preferred Mick to speak for them, at least until that humiliating moment on the Altamont stage when the devil departed his scared servant, leaving only a shivering English lad in an outlandish costume standing alone in the glare of the spotlight.

It was a light that continued to illuminate the tightest corners of his life, leaving him no choice but to play out his private traumas before the public. It was, in fact, getting increasingly hard to tell, by the waning days of 1969, where the private reality ended and the public persona began.

Mick's education in adulation had left him woefully unprepared for the maneuvering of his own heart. What had always been ordinary about him—that dyed-in-the-wool Dartford commonness—had faded and folded in on itself. There was nothing conventional, no ordinary yearnings that would serve as an anchor. In Mick's grotesquely magnified world, the smallest gesture took on the grandest overtones. His mission in life was simply to be the best Mick Jagger he could.

He was experiencing that particular, surreal side effect of fame that compressed time, obliterating the past, reducing the future to the next hit single, stadium stage, or limo ride. Mick and the Stones were existing in some eternal present, a reality so subjective that it became a trap, self-contained and self-perpetuating. What was unpleasant or unsettling—the greed and violence and varieties of excess and abuse that swirled around them—was simply sucked into the orbit of their stardom. A passive, numbing sensation set in, and through the ennui, things began to slip away.

Like Marianne. To suggest that Mick was simply unaware of his longtime lover's imminent flameout is to give him far less credit, or blame, than he deserves. Nothing so obvious could have have escaped his gaze, just as nothing so messy could be tolerated for long. Perhaps he could have brought her back through some extraordinary effort of love and sacrifice. But Mick wasn't up to extraordinary efforts. Unless it was on stage before millions.

At the same time, the pragmatic part of him realized the drag she exerted on his life. The key to survival was to keep moving forward, past all entanglements.

It was the same principle he applied to the total Rolling Stones enterprise, now under his complete control. In the early days of 1970 the first order of business was the ouster of Allen Klein. Klein, absorbed with the disintegration of the Beatles, seemed resigned to the dissolution of his plundering partnership. It was the measure of retribution for his misdeeds exacted by the Stones that shocked.

The end came when the band abruptly announced that they would sever their ties with the portly accountant and henceforth the Stones would be represented by Mick's longtime fiduciary counselor, Prince Rupert Lowenstein. Under Mick's direction, Lowenstein, as an agent for the merchant banking firm of Leopold Joseph, wasted no time in filing a twenty-nine-million-dollar suit against Klein, alleging gross fraud for indecent personal enrichment.

The news followed hard on word that the Stones would be ending their longtime and acrimonious association with Decca Records. With the Stones holding the most awesome earning power in rock 'n' roll, bidding for the band would be fierce. Every major label would eventually compete, including Decca. The company courted the band in a futile attempt to put the past behind them. The band's reply was best summed up by the final single they presented to the company to fulfill their contract: "Cocksucker Blues."

Klein's fall from grace, as Andrew Loog Oldham's before, provided another opportunity for Mick to consolidate his hold on the reins of the band. Keith, his only serious contender for control, had long ago abdicated his partnership role in favor of dazed exile in the heroin hinterlands. Anita, his seedy traveling companion, systematically contracted Keith's circle of human contact until their Cheyne Walk home became a fortress. The couple shared the sodden hours in the company of the loathsome Tony Sanchez, their resident connection.

"Obtaining enough drugs to keep the three of us happy wasn't easy," Sanchez would later write of the daily routine in the Richards household. "Through friends in Soho, I arranged to buy heroin and cocaine from registered drug addicts. . . . The trouble was that these kids tended to be extremely unreliable and sometimes Keith and Anita would be going through the agonies of cold turkey before I could get supplies to them."

For all the distance Mick and Keith had traveled together, a contemptuous distance had been growing between them. Mick's innate dread of drugs played a part, but there was more to it than paranoia. Caught up in marketing the band, Mick had stepped back from the music and from the close collaboration that kept the group honest. As his manipulation of the commodity—the Stones' image and legend—became more assured, his involvement in the music waned. His vested interest was less in a lifestyle now than in a career. Rock 'n' roll stardom was a full-time job.

For Keith, living the legend had taken its toll. Yet whatever junk was doing to his soul, there is little doubt from the evidence of the music, that it was, for now, fueling his art. "I felt I had to protect Keith," said Anita Pallenberg. "He was flying so high in the musical world. He'd sit for hours and hours on the toilet. He used to play guitar and write in the bathroom."

The explicit connection between drugs and creativity—the noble tradition of Bird and Burroughs—had long been the cornerstone of Keith's outlaw ethos. What real difference did it make if one could no longer distinguish knowing where one left off and the other began? The songs were taking on a life of their own.

Let It Bleed marked the beginning of a period of creative dominance for the guitarist. Reenergized by Mick Taylor's concise, surgical fills, Keith's flagrant energies were honed and targeted. His playing was precisely focused, the textures and timbres tasteful and spare.

"I don't think I like singing very much," Mick said with wistful regard for Keith's talent. "I'm not really a good enough singer to enjoy it. . . . I enjoy playing the guitar more than I enjoy singing, but I can't play the guitar either."

An album notable as much for the excellence of its guitar work as for the excesses of its conception, *Let It Bleed* would point the way to Keith's flourishing as a stylist and technician.

Exhausted and enervated by the bloody end of the US tour, Mick had hardly found his bearings back in London when the court case for his and Marianne's second drug bust came due. The couple's appearance at the Marlborough Street Magistrate's Court on December 19, 1969, was again marked by Mick's courtly behavior: he took sole responsibility for the infraction, allowing her to get off with an acquittal. Mick claimed, without much conviction, that the arresting officer had solicited a bribe. Mick's own punishment, by a legal system now clearly in sync with the larger interests of British commerce, was hardly more than a slap on the wrist: he was fined two hundred pounds.

Marianne, in no mood to tolerate the pace of the Stones' barn-storming American tour, had chosen to stay in the quiet environs of Cheyne Walk, where she lovingly tended her junk habit and nursed her neurosis.

Then in early November, just as the Stones charged into a Dallas concert date, one of the band's assistants broke the news to Mick: Marianne had lit out for Rome on the arm of Italian painter and movie director, Mario Schifano. He had once had a fling with Anita Pallen-berg, who had worked for Schifano as a model as far back as 1963, seven years earlier. Schifano was precisely the sort of somewhat unsavory Euro-trash playboy that increasingly orbited around the Stones. In that crowded game of musical beds, everyone sooner or later got around to everyone else.

When seen by reporters in the Rome airport, Marianne pro-claimed Schifano her "Prince Charming." The implications for her three-year affair with Mick were clear. The sixties' Most Beautiful Couple wouldn't survive the decade.

It was a provocation that could hardly be ignored, yet Mick was not in a position to reclaim either his girlfriend or the moral high ground. Hundreds of thousands of dollars rested on the final dates of the tour, including already sold-out stadium dates in Chicago, Los Angeles, and New York. There was simply no time to fly halfway around the world to fetch the errant Marianne.

Besides, even if he could have spared the time, what redeeming argument could he have offered? Certainly not accusations of infi-delity. The American tour established a high water mark for lascivious behavior, with groupies vying for favor by ever-more-audacious acts of sexual extravagance. It was itself a sort of golden age for the groupie calling, with the circuit boasting its own superstars, from the Plaster Casters to the G.T.O.'s to Susie Suck, with Mick, of course, as the supreme object of their affections.

It's doubtful that Marianne's precipitous flight with her Italian lover had much to do with evening the score on Mick. It is difficult to know, with any precision, *what* her real motivations might have been, so blurred and blunted were they by her heroin addiction. The junk not only killed her all-encompassing pain, it obliterated the lively, engaging, and intellectually curious creature that had, so long ago, stepped from the cloisters of high culture. What stood, or slumped, in her place was a dead-eyed, straw-haired zombie, who on more than one occasion would fall asleep at the dinner table, her face in a plate of pricey food.

In the end it was perhaps only a long overdue reaction to Mick's neglect that caused Marianne to bolt. "The only way I knew how to deal with my relationship with Mick was to go off with another man," she would say later. "I could never have sat down and explained to Mick why I had to. It was my way, that I simply had to remove myself."

For his part, stranded in the American wasteland, heading inexorably toward Altamont, Mick sought comfort where he could. The joyless encounters with the groupie corps were hardly enough to quench his conviction that he needed one woman by his side—however fanciful the urge might have been. Infuriated by her rejection, Mick made it his business on returning to London to be seen in the company of Marsha Hunt, the stately black actress he already had set up as his mistress within walking distance from his home on Cheyne Walk. Hunt, who had announced she wanted to bear his child, hardly fit the profile for a long-term relationship. She was, in her own words, around "to help him make the transition."

It was a transition he was, at first, unwilling to face. According to Marianne, he finally summoned his courage on Christmas Eve, when he flew to Rome, confronting both her and Schifano over his mortifying cuckoldry. "I suppose that his motivations were not so much to get me back but to overcome his public humiliation," she would say, with an anger clearly not overcome. "He had to do it to preserve his personal machismo."

A violent argument between Mick and Schifano ensued, verging, according to Marianne, on physical violence. In the early hours of Christmas morning she decided to let them fight it out between themselves and, swallowing a handful of pills, retired. She awoke the next morning to find Mick sleeping beside her.

"I felt happy that Mick cared about me enough to wage this fight for me," she would later admit, "but I knew in my heart that . . . once we were back in London we would settle back into that deadly routine that was slowly killing me."

Yesterday's Girl

The year 1970 became a kind of mopping-up operation for the twenty-seven-year-old Mick.

The long-overdue ouster of Klein and the dispute with Decca were only the beginning. The first year of the new decade also saw the long-delayed release of both *Ned Kelly* and a radically recut version of *Performance*. Mick and *Performance* director Cammell were incensed by the extensive editing performed on their movie by the studio to remove the more outrageous sex and drug use. They sent a telegram to Warner Brothers Pictures. "This film is about the perverted love affair between Homo Sapiens and Lady Violence. In common with its subject, it is necessarily horrifying, paradoxical, and absurd."

"If *Performance* does not upset audiences, it is nothing," the telegram scolded. "Your misguided censorship will ultimately diminish said audiences both in quality and quantity."

Performance's savage drubbing by critics and near-universal lack of interest from the paying public put the brakes on Mick's fledgling film career and required a good deal of furious backpedaling. "It isn't me really," Mick would insist in a rambling interview with *Time Out*. "You just get into the role—that's acting, isn't it?"

For his part Cammell was considerably more perspecacious on

Mick's performance and the mix of unease, outrage, and scorn it engendered. "There are a number of people who hate the film and all it represents," he would assert in an interview with the *Guardian*. It was an accurate assessment of the continuing fallout from Altamont. Accounts of the mayhem had just reached England, stirring a backlash against Mick's arrogant faux-satanic posturing.

"He got a lot of mileage out of playing the demonic character, the bisexual," Cammell would elsewhere assert. "He can be very sort of blank as a human being, like a lot of good artists are, like the best actors. It's a sort of emptiness, not quite being centered. It's got something to do with narcissism. It's thinking always in a mirror, living in too many worlds."

Another witness to the film's creation said, "It's not insincerity, it's a lot to do with self-protection. If he presents a well worked out, slightly overstated image, no one is going to get at the real Mick, whom he wants to protect." Given the public's surly mood, protection was hard to come by.

Ned Kelly, if possible, fared even more dismally. "As lethal as last week's lettuce," read one review of Mick's on-screen presence, while another derisively called attention to his "almost catatonic lack of expression, battling with an Irish accent in which he would seem to have been coached word for word without graduating to sentences."

"Someone asked me if I minded bad reviews," Mick remarked, trying to put the best face on the embarrassing debacles, "and I said no. As long as my picture is on the front page, I don't care what they say about me on page ninety-six."

"The thing is," he would sigh, "you never know until you do it whether a film will turn out to be a load of shit, and if it does, all you can say is, 'Well, that was a load of shit' and try to make sure you don't do anything like it again."

In fact, Mick was acutely more distressed by the outcome of the film and the damage it could wreak on his career than his calculated flippancy would suggest. After screening *Ned Kelly* for the first time, he burst into tears of rage and embarrassment. There was good reason for his anguish. It would be a long time before he appeared in a major motion picture.

Mick turned with renewed vigor to the future of the Stones. Even as the group announced a fourteen-city European tour and began recording tracks for a follow-up to *Let It Bleed*, Mick began intensive discussions with Lowenstein on the band's long-term financial future.

Despite the empty coffers left by Klein, long-term prospects looked bright indeed. *Let It Bleed* had continued to build on the Stones' spiraling sales record, and with the band freed from their former recording ties, the possibility of an enormously lucrative new contract promised an infusion of cash. Mick and Lowenstein had, in fact, already opened the bidding for a new recording contract at five million pounds.

"I'm interested in business," Mick would remark with a flair for the obvious. "I'm not interested in making more and more money. . . . It is an abstract. . . . I just don't want any trouble. When you do these deals, they are done once every four years. So I just want to make sure that they are done right. That's all."

Mick's grip on money matters and the band's epic earning power boded well for a precedent-breaking new arrangement with a new label. By late summer a report was floated by the group's publicist Les Perrin that the band would form their own label under the manufacturing and distribution auspices of a recording company to be named later. "We want to release the odd blues record and Charlie Watts wants to do some jazz," Mick said. "What we're not interested in is bubble gum music." Then, in a burst of leftover sixties altruism, he added, "We want to control prices, to stop the price of records going up. I'd like to find new ways of distribution."

In fact, the precedent had already been established, once again by the Beatles, with their bold, balmy, and ultimately doomed multimedia enterprise, Apple Corps, that included recording, publishing, and film divisions.

"I always sort of looked at Apple Records," Mick said. "And the whole thing about Apple Records was you got the feeling that was a new company with new ideas . . . running through the old structure."

Thanks in part to Klein's freewheeling accounting techniques, the group owed staggering sums to the Inland Revenue. The bad news came first to Stones bassist Bill Wyman, who was informed that he was 118,000 pounds in arrears. For Mick the news was no better.

"I just didn't think about it," he would later admit. "And no manager I ever had thought about it, even though they said they were going to make sure my taxes were paid. So after working for eight years, I discovered nothing had been paid and I owed a fortune." The exact sum of Mick's tax burden was never made public. As for the Inland Revenue's failure to detect the lost money for almost eight years, it was Allen Klein's clever bookkeeping that had kept them at bay.

In May of 1970 Mick and Lowenstein reached an inevitable conclusion. The group would have to become tax exiles, leaving England and the threat of bankruptcy behind.

They would now become a wandering tribe of rootless rockers. The long struggle to find some shred of permanence and stability had been abandoned. What had for so long been endured as a temporary lifestyle—the endless, enervating globe-trotting, the bleary mornings staring at the ceiling of yet another strange hotel room—would now become a permanent condition, as close to routine as the Rolling Stones could ever get.

With his decision to abandon London, where Dartford and the past were always in theory a train ride away, Mick had become a wanderer entrapped by fame. He would say, "When you reach it, you may not like it, which accounts for the way a lot of people behave. They work hard for it and when they finally achieve it, they don't like it or can't handle it."

He would be a man without a country and, at least for the moment, a man without a woman. The move had to be made by April of the following tax year in order to avoid more crushing levies. The group decided to relocate to the Côte d'Azur in France, with all its aura of privileged indolence and decadence, not to mention France's liberal currency exchange regulations.

The shift across the Channel was also the beginning of Mick's carefully stage-managed shift in the group's image, veering sharply away from the disastrous overkill of the sixties and toward a creation almost solely of his own making. The Soho rowdies of Edith Grove were dead and buried: the Luciferian princes had been exorcised. What would emerge in time was a canny composite of bad boys and jet-setters, a combination of rock 'n' roll outlaws and rock 'n' roll royalty.

Meanwhile, Marianne's arid affair with her lover of five dispiriting years continued to unravel in the months after the Schifano farce. Mick agreed to take her back less for love than for convenience. Even as he threw himself into his grand schemes for record labels and tax dodges, he made no attempt to disguise his philandering, often taking his one-night stands up to the gloomy confines of Stargroves, where he and Marianne's illusions of a hip Camelot had died a long time ago. Between groupies, he was seen ever more frequently in the company of Marsha Hunt, still intent on siring a pretender to Mick's rock 'n' roll throne.

Marianne responded to Mick's repertoire of slights and humiliations by rendering herself a pathetic junkie. Her once-pristine looks began to dissolve into a stuporous morphine mask. Her behavior was increasingly unpredictable, her will to obliteration ever more apparent.

Yet some essential instinct for survival, some bloody-minded determination not to flicker out in a faint whimper, would assert itself at the last possible moment. In August, as Mick readied to depart on the group's next European tour, Marianne announced that she would not be leaving with him on the planned exodus to France.

Her account of those final days, as told to A. E. Hotchner in his book *Blown Away*, is colored by the paranoia familiar to anyone who has ever strayed into that realm where drug demons and personal identity become indistinguishable.

"I realized that if I didn't get out quickly, Mick was going to get even with me for running away with Mario. But it was difficult for me to organize myself enough to act upon what my mind told me to do. The heroin kept me off balance."

She would rediscover her equilibrium on a muggy night in late May when she emerged from the abyss of her slowly unwinding devastation long enough to realize that it was now or never. "I did love Mick very much, and he loved me," she would say. "But I knew it was the end of an era. I knew nothing could ever be the same again."

Distractedly gathering a random armful of clothes, a spare Persian rug, and a bundled-up Nicholas, she simply walked out of her gilded cage, leaving behind Mick Jagger and the ruins of her life.

"That was a mistake," she would subsequently confess in the cold light of hindsight. "If I had it to do over . . . I would have stayed and I would have said to Mick, 'I'm staying in this house, you go. . . . I've given you five years of my life. I'll take the house and I'll take an allowance too, thank you.' It was insane that I went off the way I did. I just left the house with all the furniture that I had not only picked out, but some of it I had paid for."

Having finally made the decision to free herself from heroin, she was also free to let loose a surge of bitter resentment. "I didn't take my jewelry," she would sniff. "I didn't take anything. Out of pride. But in a way it was a good thing, because it gave me an edge on Mick. . . . He really feels women are a terrible sort of grasping, feral creature. But he can never accuse me of that."

Discovering that Marianne had moved in with her mother in Berkshire, he telephoned constantly over the next several weeks, pleading with her to come back. Whatever their relationship had been finally reduced to—that grim game of sexual and psychological brinksmanship—the prospect of losing her and the veneer of stability she lent to his life was more than he could bear. The loss of Marianne left him crushed, bewildered, and frightened. Without her he could no longer pretend that the best of both worlds was his to pick and choose.

In the end he would try to resolve the conflict in a song, as if reality and artifice had become one in the same, leaving what could not be said by the man to be sung by the minstrel.

"Mick couldn't talk in an ordinary way with the people he was involved with," Marianne explains. "But he used his songs to express his feelings. He wrote 'Wild Horses' when we were breaking up. He didn't want to break up and he wrote that to try and prevent it."

"I burst into tears," Marianne recalls. "I was terribly moved." In fact, much had already been made of the supposed connections between Mick's musical output and his personal life. Unremittingly nasty ditties such as "Under My Thumb" and "Yesterday's Papers" were alleged to be direct kiss-offs to Chrissie. They were, according to Marianne, "horrible public humiliations" for her predecessor.

"Rock 'n' roll is not a tender medium," Mick would later reply in faint defense of his lyrical content. "It's raunchy and macho. There's no such thing as a secure, family-oriented rock-'n'-roll song. I suppose I'm a bit hidebound by that tradition, but I don't actually think like that. In actual fact I love women; I'm absorbed by them and if you ask any of my women friends, not just the ones I've had affairs with, they'll tell you that I'm very nice."

As his most famous affair, Marianne's opinion would necessarily have to be excluded from the poll. Yet, of all Mick's "women friends," she seems best qualified to pass judgment. And it is a very harsh judgment, indeed. However moving the melancholy lament of "Wild Horses" might have been, it could hardly have healed the gaping wound in her soul. "It was a very effective way to accomplish what he wanted," she would say with brittle irony. "Much more effective than if he had sat down and had a long talk about it."

It was indicative of her hardened resolve, won at the cost of her innocence, that Marianne would not allow Mick the chance for talks, long or short. "Mick continued to phone every day, and I could tell he was on the verge of coming to get me, to induce me to go back with him."

She countered in the only way she knew how, instinctively grasping the single most effective tool at her disposal to dissuade a man whose own vanity had once been her principal rival. "The shape of a woman's body was of extreme importance to Mick," she recounts. "I let myself get fat . . . stuffed myself with gobs of fattening food. It was a conscious decision—I wanted to show I wasn't in the market anymore. When Mick walked in and saw me, his jaw dropped. I knew that it was really the finish."

SEVENTEEN

Nellcote

Despite Mick's best efforts to distance himself and the band from Altamont, the group's 1970 European tour was accompanied by the sort of violence and mayhem the Stones had for so long gleefully encouraged. The group could not convince the public that the anarchy and disaffection were just for dramatic effect.

Their Paris appearance was met by widespread street fighting that recalled the famous May uprisings of two years before, complete with flanking attacks by gendarmes wielding tear gas launchers and rampaging fans overturning and torching cars. The pattern was repeated with numbing regularity on virtually every stop of the fourteen-city itinerary, including one appearance in West Berlin which ended with sixty-five injured policemen. The frenzy became infectious. In Rome, an obviously undone Mick punched a reporter at a press conference for "asking stupid questions." His frustration at being unable to rein in the demons he had unleashed was obvious. What was less obvious was his desperation to fill the void left by Marianne.

Mick flitted from woman to willing woman, seeking someone who would bring together the loose ends of his life. Among them was Marsha Hunt, who announced she was pregnant prior to the violence-marred European tour. In November she gave birth to a girl, Karis. Though Hunt steadfastly refused to reveal the name of the

166

child's father, it was apparent from the horde of reporters gathered outside St. Mary's Hospital in Paddington that his identity was hardly a secret.

"We had the baby on purpose," she said. "Now he's no longer involved with us. At first I thought I cared for him a lot. When people said he was no good, I didn't believe them because I saw goodness in him, and I do forgive him because I don't think he understands what he's doing."

She went on, "The sad thing about our relationship was the attitude he assumed after the child was born. It is sad that we are not friends now. . . . The father felt a great deal of confusion, which I didn't have time for, so I told him to go solve his own mental and emotional problems and that I would take care of the child. I feel like I didn't really know him at all."

It had long since become a familiar refrain. Mick simply refused to comment until forced to do so by persistent reporters. His response was to deny paternity.

Soon after Hunt became pregnant, Mick widened his search for a new consort. High on the short list for a time was Janice Kenner, a vivacious, statuesque California model. Kenner was a friend of Stones producer Glyn Johns, who had recently completed work on *Get Your Ya Yas Out*, a frenetic live album recorded at Madison Square Garden two weeks before the Altamont debacle and, upon release, the latest number one in the Stones' unstoppable hit parade.

Kenner, anxious to linger in the glittering aura of the Stones, jumped on the suggestion by Johns that perhaps Mick, the newly minted bachelor, would require some live-in help around the Cheyne Walk digs.

Following the London premiere of *Ned Kelly*, which a surly Mick refused to attend, Janice Kenner was taken to meet Mick. She arrived at Olympic Studios, where the group was in the midst of recording new tracks. After a round of reefers, Janice was introduced to Mick, who barely acknowledged her until a rough cut of the track "Bitch" came over the studio speakers. Approaching the wide-eyed model, he began dancing lasciviously to the music. Janice joined him, recounting later how it felt like "passing some sort of test."

By early July Janice was ensconced in Cheyne Walk, where Marianne's clothes still hung in the closet. Over the next few months she became a confidant to the troubled star, listening to him late into the night. "She was always there to talk to him," recalls Tony Sanchez, "always around when he needed someone. . . . Jan would occasionally go to bed with Jagger when he was too lazy to bring one of his many women home."

Janice had recognized over the course of those long summer nights that "Mick didn't need a lover. He needed a friend." With Janice, he had both. Shortly after Janice had moved in, Eric Clapton introduced him to another American model, who serviced him sexually. The ménage à trois continued uneasily for a few months, with Janice eventually joining Mick on the European tour.

By early 1971, the long-gestating plans for the Stones' departure from Britain were finally complete. Trusted aide-de-camp Jo Bergman led an advance team on a search for suitably stately accommodations. Rumors abounded among Riviera real estate agents that among the primary specifications for the group's future estates were bathrooms large enough to accommodate "Roman-style orgies."

The announcement of their tax exile was, for Mick, a prickly public relations problem. It was compounded in early spring by persistent scuttlebutt that the group's personal fortune was in excess of two hundred million dollars.

"We do not know how or whence this figure originated," insisted a press release that bore Mick's signature, "but it is vastly in excess of the worldwide retail proceeds of sale of all our recordings."

The fact that a denial of so absurd a figure was necessary at all points up the extreme sensitivity Mick had about the band's image. Uncertain how news of the imminent departure would sit with their thousands of British followers, he was taking pains to plead something short of fabulous wealth, if not poverty.

The Stones certainly did not have eighty-three million quid squirreled away, even if they acted like they did by moving to the Mediterranean Gold Coast. But what was important was to maintain some sense of street-level authenticity, at least for the time being. Mick joshed with the press, after the move was finally made public on March 1, "If you know me, you know I'll be back in Britain more times than I have been in the past."

Looming financial disaster at the hands of Inland Revenue had forced the rest of the group to join Mick in exile. Wyman and Watts left their country estates with the same spirit of stoic resignation with which they had always greeted life in the fast lane. Newcomer Mick Taylor was given no choice.

Keith, on the other hand, was different. His crash course in substance abuse had continued since the end of the European tour, even as the ever-calculating Anita began to realize that enough was quickly becoming too much. It was only a matter of time before the endless concoctions of coke, smack, cannabis, and Jack Daniels would drag them all down. She quietly began readying herself for the inevitable detox, with Keith following her lead and submitting to a grueling apomorphine cure at the Redlands estate.

It didn't take. "You sweat, you scream, you hallucinate," he recalls with deadpan calm. "In seventy-two hours, if you can get through it, you're clean. But that's never the problem. The problem is when you go back to your social circle, who are all drug pushers and junkies. In five minutes you can be on the stuff again."

Whether fueled by his drug daze, his dim-lit stubbornness, or his growing resistance to the image Mick was engineering for the band, Keith fiercely resisted the move to France. "I think the reason we were forced out in seventy, seventy-one was they realized it was pointless," he would assert in retrospect. "They were showing their own weakness, a country that's been running a thousand years, worried about two Herberts with guitars and a singer. . . . To me there was no choice: I'd rather fuck off. Why not? I mean, I love England and it's my country."

Whatever, precisely, Keith was talking about, his actions left no doubt where he stood. While the others glumly packed, he hunkered down at Cheyne Walk, steadfastly refusing to budge even as the April deadline drew near. He had set the stage for what would become in time, a famous feud with his Dartford bandmate.

"It's not a case of running from the tax man. The Stones like France tremendously." So ran the official line as promulgated by their veteran publicist Les Perrin. Uncertain whether anyone was buying the notion that the band was still the same lovable hell-raisers they had always been, they announced a nine-date "farewell" tour up and down the island.

Initial response was reassuringly ecstatic. Under the headline "Jagger the Superbaddie," the influential *New Musical Express* described the early shows as "a spectacular aura of sheer, outrageous campery. . . . Jumpin' Jack Flash has this week been a-thumpin' and a-bumpin' and a-humpin' his way through ninety-five action packed minutes of revived British rock, the likes of which we haven't seen since the days of the first coming."

Yet a distinctly sour note had sounded by the tour's final stop, a ballyhooed appearance at their old stomping grounds, the Marquee Club, on March 27. With cameras rolling for a proposed TV broadcast, Keith's surly mood had hardened into rebellion. Arriving late and shoeless for the performance, he proceeded to assault the promoter and had to be dragged off the stage backwards. It was vintage Stones, as evidenced by the following morning's banner headlines, summed up by *NME*'s "Stones—Out With a Bang."

Wrote veteran music journalist Roy Carr, evoking Mick's wispy, lisping character in *Performance*, "Looking like a shorn version of Turner, Michael Phillip Jagger went through his overtly camp 'Performance.' . . . The epitome of magnified bisexuality, Jagger pranced about in heavy makeup and a minuscule silver sequined bolero jacket, which only helped to emphasize his skinny blanched body and bony hips."

The guest list for the Stones' send-off included John Lennon, Yoko Ono, and Eric Clapton. Their departure was celebrated by an unusually sedate affair at Skindles Hotel in Maidenhead on March 30. A mixture of melancholy, dazed enervation, and the final realization of their expatriate status seemed to have knocked the wind from their collective sails.

The next morning, the group's corps of moving men arrived at Keith's Cheyne Walk den and carefully removed every trinket and artifact, packing it away to be carefully replaced in approximate position in his new home. It was a voluminous villa called Nellcote overlooking the pristine blue bay of Villefranche-sur-Mer, with Errol Flynn's yacht docked in the harbor below. The estate had been built by an eccentric nineteenth-century British naval man, who had eventually killed himself by jumping from the roof. By virtue of its sheer size, Nellcote would serve as the group's de facto headquarters during their French exile.

The home selected for Mick was somewhat less grand, but with no less impressive a pedigree. An exquisite example of French country architecture, it was located in the village of Mougins and had once served as a refuge for Pablo Picasso. The rest of the group had been moved into residences designed to soften the fact that they were no longer in England, Wyman in a comfortable estate near La Bastide Saint-Antoine, Watts in his Cévennes farmhouse, and Mick Taylor in considerably more modest accommodations near Grasse.

The band, with their assorted entourages, barely had time to settle in before Mick and Prince Rupert Lowenstein made the long-awaited announcement of a new recording contract, the next step in Mick's plans for a revitalized Stones empire.

The publicity pump had been primed earlier in the month with the news that the new Rolling Stones label—the group's version of the Beatles now-floundering Apple Corps—would be headed by Marshall Chess, son of Chess Records founder Leonard. Leonard Chess had discovered and recorded many of the artists, from Chuck Berry to Bo Diddley to the leading lights of Chicago blues, who had initially inspired the Stones.

It was a nice touch, calculated to reconnect the group to their roots, at least in the permeable minds of their fans, but in reality it was all a stunt. Having secured the reins of the group's financial future, Mick and his advisers were hardly about to relinquish them. Chess was quickly relegated to figurehead status.

On April 7, 1971, the true dimensions of Mick's ambitious new undertaking became clear. At a sumptuous ceremony at Cannes, followed by a blowout bash at St. Tropez's Canto Club House, the band signed a distribution deal with the Kinney Group, a faceless American conglomerate that got its start in parking lots and had recently swallowed Atlantic Records. Like Chess, Atlantic was home to some of the very artists who had sparked the Stones' early music, including Otis Redding, Ray Charles, and dozens of other soul masters.

It was Atlantic's president—the urbane, inscrutable Turk Ahmet Ertegun—who had brokered the deal, negotiating an astronomical advance with Prince Rupert and wooing Mick with a campaign designed to emphasize Ertegun's impeccable credentials among the monied elite of Europe and the States.

An exquisite clotheshorse, Ertegun boasted of diplomatic connections stretching back to his childhood as the son of Turkey's American ambassador. He was precisely the sort of high roller to whom Mick had become drawn.

The deal called for the group's future output—both Stones albums and various projected solo numbers—to be released under their own Rolling Stones Records moniker. The label's emblem, designed by Andy Warhol, depicted a tongue thrusting out from between a pair of plump red lips—another shift in the Stones' image, from a coequal musical partnership to a band backing its charismatic lead singer.

The group's deal with Ertegun and the megacorporation behind him represented the highest bid from among no fewer than twenty-one suitors. The contract's fine print called for six albums over the next four years. The band already had the debut outing for Rolling Stones Records ready to roll.

Recorded in fits and starts throughout 1969 and 1970, the new album, *Sticky Fingers*, further demonstrated Keith's musical dominance, expanding and enhancing advances signaled on *Let It Bleed*. Cuts like "Bitch," "Let It Rock," and "Can't You Hear Me Knockin' " were fueled by the guitarist's increasingly concise playing. At its frequent best, *Sticky Fingers* seemed to encompass the band's entire musical history, revealing the nerves and muscle of their music.

"Brown Sugar," with its clattering castanet and smoky horn charts, was the album's first single, recorded back in Muscle Shoals, Alabama, a few weeks before Altamont. Depending on who was listening, it was either a paean to miscegenation, Mexican heroin, or Marsha Hunt. Whatever the case, it shot to the top of the charts, pulling the album along with it. *Sticky Fingers* became the group's first American million-seller, a feat repeated virtually around the world.

It was also an album that marked a new level of sophistication in Mick's manipulation of the by-now rote controversy surrounding the band. The ten cuts making up *Sticky Fingers* bristled with explicit drug references, from the languid reverie of "Sister Morphine," a track cocredited to Marianne, to the "cocaine eyes" evoked in "Can't You Hear Me Knockin'."

"I don't think *Sticky Fingers* is a heavy drug album any more than the world is a heavy world," Keith would disingenuously declare.

Although ascribed to the platinum-minting team of Jagger/ Richards, the bulk of the material had, in fact, been assembled by Keith. Mick cannily realized that the chic aura of unfettered drug use was a valuable facet to the band's notoriety as long as it didn't directly impact his life.

Incitements to violence like "Street Fighting Man" and "Midnight Rambler," however, would have to go. In comparison to what had come before, *Sticky Fingers* was positively pacific, with the blood and mayhem being replaced by a much more marketable commodity— sex.

The album's cover, again designed by Warhol and among the most famous of the time, depicted a male lower torso, replete with bulging crotch, all tightly sheathed in denim. The jean's real zipper invited buyers to take a peek beneath, where the tongue-and-lips logo leered. The message was unmistakable. Simply by laying hold of the zipper pull, fans were invited to partake in the band's titillating tawdriness. The geriatric fascist government in Spain quickly obliged the attention-getting gambit by banning the album.

Yet for all its oh-so-clever conceits and razor-sharp riffs, *Sticky Fingers* seemed, finally, a work without a center, lacking the principle of passion that had ignited the group's earlier, more ragged and uncertain output. It was as if the band, while not precisely crossing the line between calling and careerism, were beginning to forget, exactly, what all the excitement was about. The music, for all the prodigious effort that went into it—Keith spent entire, junk-fogged evenings capturing the right inflection for a bridge or chorus— sounded effortless, almost offhanded. It was getting too easy, and while a band with the collective talents of the Stones had never exactly phoned it in, they were, with *Sticky Fingers*, substituting craft for commitment.

It was a hardly surprising development, considering the distractions they were facing. Not the least was the persistent rumor that, record-breaking record deals notwithstanding, the band's move to France was the prelude to retirement.

"The band is not retiring just because we're going away," Mick insisted with barely concealed petulance. "We're not going to stay in the South of France for a whole year, we're going on the road. I couldn't live in France for a whole year. I hope to visit Japan, Bangkok, Ceylon, Persia and hope to be touring Britain some time next year. We'll remain a functioning group, a touring group, and a happy group."

At twenty-nine Keith found his short-lived flirtation with sobriety followed by an equally halfhearted effort by Anita. By the spring of

1972 they had returned to their old ways with a vengeance, taking along a large and disreputable troupe of hard cases, hangers-on, and heroin adepts for the ride.

The endless lost weekend begun at Cheyne Walk continued at Nellcote. Unable to buy Errol Flynn's yacht, Keith found another and named it Mandrax after the potent barbiturate. Tony Sanchez, the drug procurer, was in constant attendance, servicing a retinue that often exceeded thirty people.

Gourmet banquets were mounted every evening, employing the culinary skills of the region's best chef enhanced by frequent raids on its best wine cellars. Life at the estate became an immobile feast of rich sauces, expensive drugs, and indiscriminate fornicating.

"Anita was always running Keith down for not having fucked her properly," recalls one friend. It is questionable how well Anita herself could have performed in bed. Her mainlining continued unabated despite the fact that she was by now three months pregnant.

The couple's son Marlon, meanwhile, became his father's soul mate and sole nonchemical comfort. The child's first words, according to the inside joke circulating at the time, were "room service," and when not being carried about like some living good luck charm by Keith, Marlon slept in a room next to a toy piano where Sanchez stored his stash of smack.

The excesses funded by Keith would have given even the most determined friend pause, and Mick was hardly disposed to let friendship stand in the way of self-preservation. In truth, there was little anyone could have done to slow Keith's plunge into addiction. Given his inability to anticipate even the most obvious consequences of his lethal lifestyle, backing off seemed to be the best policy.

Unfortunately, that option was out of reach for Mick. His fate, and that of the band whose course he now charted, depended in ominous measure on the whims of this hollow-eyed and snaggle-toothed rock-'n'-roll outlaw.

It was a point driven home as the band prepared to record a follow-up to the high-flying *Sticky Fingers*. Excluded from England, with its familiar recording haunts, the group decided to import their own state-of-the-art recording truck, dubbed the Mighty Mobile, and cut their new album, as it were, "on location."

The location selected, less from choice than necessity, was Nellcote, as the only one of the Stones' abodes large enough to accommodate the personnel and equipment necessary for what had become the epic-scaled enterprise of a Rolling Stones recording session.

The rambling mansion now became not only the site of Keith and Anita's ghastly domestic routines, but also ground zero for an absurd, latter-day version of Edith Grove. Scattered too far afield to make the commute, the other members of the band were obliged to move in, sharing space with all of the rest of Keith's felonious lodgers. The only difference between the rock stars and the rest of the raunchy encampment was the 250 pounds a week Keith charged his bandmates for room and board. In short order the sweeping marble expanses were littered with filthy laundry, empty bottles, overflowing ashtrays, and all the disgusting detritus of the rock 'n' roll high life.

It was an irony that apparently escaped the group, who labored throughout the sweltering summer in the dank and insufferably muggy confines of Nellcote's basement, where the jury-rigged studio had been erected. "We had opened the gates," recalls Anita. "The doors were open because basically everyone was coming and going— the musicians, everybody—so it was open house. . . . It was a marathon of music, but it was also a nightmare."

No one had to tell Mick, for whom the ordeal was pure torture. "It looked like a prison," he says, recalling the basement with a shudder. "The humidity was incredible. I couldn't stand it. As soon as I opened my mouth to sing, my voice was gone. It was so humid that all the guitars were out of tune by the time we got to the end of each number."

Yet Mick's acute discomfort had less to do with his proximity to Keith, or even the surreal reminders of Soho squalor, than to a whole new development driving him to distraction. Her name was Bianca.

EIGHTEEN

Bianca

The acute sense of abandonment that settled over Mick in the wake of Marianne's sudden departure grew in the ensuing months to something akin to existential panic. He had, after all, not been without a steady girlfriend—if only in idealized illusion—since before Chrissie Shrimpton, and the sensation of singleness gnawed at him. This was not how it was supposed to be, and the ministrations of Janice Kenner and a host of other willing, rotating partners could not bring him peace.

It was, of course, the orthodoxy of his upbringing asserting itself once again. Keith had lost himself completely in the cartoon epic of his own legend. He believed totally that rock 'n' roll wealth and privilege put him above mortal men.

"The Stones, they always have to be so trustworthy," says Anita. "They trust everybody until something happens, and then, when it's already happened, it's too late."

It seemed that Mick, at twenty-nine, hadn't learned how to love and be loved and that such lessons might forever elude him. That sense of desperation explains the haste in which he fell into his next serious relationship. And the truth he sensed about himself—the frightened feeling of time slipping away—was revealed in the disaster that followed.

There was, of course, more to his instant and unseemly infatuation with Bianca Perez Mora Macias than the need to salve his bruised heart and battered ego after Marianne. There was the startling, almost spooky resemblance between the new couple—the same large, soulful eyes, the same high, imperial cheekbones and delicately carved jaw, and—most uncanny of all—the same wide, voluptuous, and infinitely expressive mouth. But for her obvious Latin bloodline they could well have been brother and sister. It was that mirror image they shared that made their relationship seem somehow incestuous, as if they were in love not so much with each other, but both, instead, with reflections of themselves.

Bianca was born to privilege in the vicious and corrupt domain of General Anastasio Somoza's Nicaragua. Daughter of the nation's ambassador to another ruthless Latin American regime—Cuba under Batista—Bianca grew up surrounded by high walls, the scent of mimosa, and silent, watchful servants in one of Managua's most exclusive neighborhoods. After her parents' divorce she lived with her mother, who, discarded by the grim mandates of machismo, ran a small cafe and nursed resentments against her ex-husband and the dictator he served. It was a hatred that would, in time, infect Bianca's brother Carlos, who would join the opposition to Somoza and thus jeopardize the safety of his mother and sister.

Bianca exuded an aristocratic aura which, with her native intelligence and exotic appearance, gave her the weapons she need to accomplish her aims, and what she meant to accomplish was a very ambitious agenda indeed. In 1960, at age seventeen, she won a scholarship sponsored by the French government and was invited to attend the Institute of Political Science at the Sorbonne. In the world of Paris's glittering social ramble, she found little time for her studies and after two years returned home, where she was offered, through her father's connections, a job in the Nicaraguan foreign office. Paris and the world that it spread before her made the decision easy: she turned down the job and within a week had returned to France. For a year she lived in a cheap apartment, working a series of odd jobs, including a brief stint as a hostess at the Paris Meat Fair.

Escorting prosperous merchants around sausage displays was hardly the future she had envisioned for herself, and it wasn't long before she prevailed upon her father to intervene again on her behalf—this time getting her a job in the office of Nicaragua's ambassador to France.

The position was one of high visibility and Bianca was quick to capitalize. She made it a point to be seen regularly on the glittering Paris diplomatic circuit, impressing more than one embassy functionary with her cool beauty and fluent command of French, Spanish, and English. She was also a regular on the city's rough-and-tumble underground club scene, where the impression she left was considerably seedier, one of dancing, drugs, and anonymous sex.

British actor Michael Caine, with a roving eye toward the exotic, fell under her spell and began showing her off to the London show business crowd. She would later move on to Eddie Barclay, head of France's biggest record label, married and thirty years older than Bianca. It was in his adulterous embrace that she would linger for a time, keeping her large brown eyes peeled for the next opportunity.

What happened next was less an opportunity than a quantum leap straight onto the international stage. She would handle it all as if born to the part, becoming the symbol of what Mick himself hoped to become, regal and removed, jet-set royalty with a purple past.

They were introduced by Donald Cammell in Paris during the 1971 European tour. The twenty-eight-year-old Bianca had been one of Cammell's many girlfriends, and he initially had reservations about putting her together with his most famous friend. "She was an old-style courtesan," he explains, "the sort who was always basically saying to herself, 'Well, who's going to pay my rent five years from now?' But she had set her cap on him and was determined, so I engineered a meeting. I procured Mick for Bianca."

Mick was instantly mesmerized, seeing all the connections in their looks, their attitude, and their ambition. They were, indeed, made for each other.

Mick had always idealized the women he favored—Chrissie as the girl next door, Marianne as Guinevere in his Carnaby Camelot, and now, best of all, Bianca as his own bewitching alter ego. Cammell had suggested the two join him in bed with the director's girlfriend. They declined, barely able to take their eyes off each other, and by the next morning had become virtually inseparable.

"I split as soon as she showed up," Janice Kenner would recall. "She made it obvious from the beginning that she was getting what she wanted and that no one was going to stand in her way."

Least of all Mick, who was only too happy to surrender himself to Bianca's charms. He took her with him on the remainder of the tour and gallantly attacked a hapless paparazzo, one of a horde that descended on the couple. In Vienna Mick was obliged to jump over a garden wall to escape a reporter's pursuit, and by the time they returned to England, Bianca insisted that she could not speak English to keep the press at bay.

Overnight they had become an international sensation, the press, of course, making all the same connections as had Mick. Their separated-at-birth looks were one thing. What would prove an even more enticing angle was the sheen of high culture Bianca conferred.

After the disillusionment of life with Marianne, Bianca seemed like an act of divine intervention. She was practiced in the art of making a man feel singularly lucky; she turned her attention solely to him and fulfilled him with her favors. Mick had to have her.

In contrast to Mick's obsession, the rest of the Stones' inner circle greeted Bianca's arrival with a mix of fear, mistrust, and dark intrigue. Following the tour, when the group returned to England and Mick began planning their move to France, he had Bianca installed at Stargroves. To his friends, Mick's obvious fixation was unsettling; they had never seen him quite so completely under a woman's sway before.

That influence in turn upset the balance of power within the group, as Bianca was perceived to be a pretender to the power Mick wielded. "They could hardly get any work done, with Mick the way he was about Bianca," Stones office manager Shirley Arnold reports. "She especially threatened Anita." As the band's de facto den mother for almost a decade, Anita knew a rival when she saw one and dispatched Tony Sanchez to dig up any dirt from Bianca's past— including confirmation of the rumor that she had had a sex change operation.

Bianca's checkered past slowly began to emerge. Shortly after their return to England, Mick arranged for a session with Stones court photographer David Bailey. Bianca was difficult and temperamental. At one point when the photographer irritated her, she let loose with a string of Nicaraguan-inflected swearing that was recognized immediately by Bailey's Brazilian housekeeper. "The only women who speak like that are tarts," he later told his employer. Marshall Chess, in town for the impending record label announcement, lost twelve thousand dollars to her playing gin rummy. Bianca had certainly been around the block.

It was a fact not entirely lost on Mick. When one friend was looking for love, Mick suggested a good Paris whorehouse. "I don't want some old scrubber," the friend said. "Watch what you're saying," grinned Mick. "That's where I got my wife."

Matrimony was Mick's intent almost from the beginning. The courtship continued as the group redeployed to France. Those first days on the sunny grounds in Mougins were the prelude to the decision Mick had shied away from his whole life. It had been barely six months since Marianne had walked out. Bianca had turned his world around. What mattered now was to make it last.

On May 7, 1971, the *Daily Mail* reported, "Pop star Mick Jagger and his beautiful South American girlfriend are planning a secret wedding in France. They have applied for a special dispensation to marry without having their banns posted—which would allow the ceremony to go ahead without anyone but local officials knowing. Jagger called the senior magistrate yesterday in Draguignan in Southern France to make his application."

Only two days before, the paper went on, Bianca had said, "There's not going to be a wedding this week, next week, or ever. Mick and I are happy together. We don't need to get married. Why should we?"

One reason might well have been the fact that Bianca was four months pregnant. The news only strengthened Mick's resolve. Bianca, by contrast, was in no particular hurry. She had Mick's baby, after all, but something in his eagerness seemed a little unsettling. Things were moving too fast.

Mick telephoned Shirley Arnold in London and announced that on May 12, a mere two days away, he would marry Bianca in St. Tropez. The guest list would include some seventy people, flown to France on a chartered plane. Those who made the cut included Paul and Linda McCartney, Ringo Starr, and Eric Clapton, among an assortment of other British rock regulars and London friends along with, significantly, Joe and Eva, Mick's parents.

For Mick the line between a private moment and a public spectacle was almost impossible to distinguish. He insisted that the timing of the announcement, so close to the event, was to keep it from becoming a "media circus." However, Mick himself had summoned the glittering guest list and thus ensured the circuslike atmosphere of the event.

Mick was required to take instruction in the rudiments of Catholicism to conform to his bride's religious upbringing. He had been tutored by a local friar, who found him "very receptive." In keeping with this aura of humble and heartfelt surrender, Mick had selected Ste. Anne's, a small, charming fisherman's chapel overlooking St. Tropez bay.

The flip side of Mick's spiritual bliss was expressed in his reflexive instinct for publicity. The phone call to Shirley was only the beginning. By the time the chartered jet landed in France with its elite cargo, a steady stream of reporters, photographers, and scene makers had already arrived to witness the celebrity wedding of the year. While one part of Mick may have fancied a tastefully discreet affair, another demanded maximum media exposure. In the end it was no contest.

The French civil functionaries enforced a stipulation that required the marrying couple to declare beforehand whether their property was to be held separately or jointly. It was not the kind of choice Mick was comfortable making. It wasn't until the morning of their wedding that he managed to summon his courage and insist that Bianca sign away her rights to his considerable assets in the event of a divorce. Tense and cornered, Bianca insisted otherwise. The impasse continued for hours, past the time when the wedding was scheduled to take place. Now aware of how much he had jeopardized with his precipitous proposal, Mick simply dug in his heels, refusing to yield. Bianca, sniffing disaster, pleaded with him to cancel the wedding, at least until the legal niceties could be settled.

He refused, angrily accusing her of "trying to make a fool of me in front of all these people." At last Bianca relented, signing the wedding contract and relinquishing her claim to his fortune.

Across town at the Hotel de Ville, where the civic ceremony was now well behind schedule, reporters and TV crews jostled with guests and bystanders in a council chamber made stifling and sweaty by the glaring lights and crush of bodies. Apprised of the escalating chaos, Mick sent word that he and Bianca would not make their entrance until the room was cleared of everyone but invited guests.

Already upset by the delay, Mayor Marius Estezan, who was to conduct the nuptials, replied that in the Stones' adopted country civil weddings were open to the public. The carnival Mick had summoned would stay, a decision confirmed by the chief of police, who had his hands full trying to keep the increasingly unruly crowd at bay. It was another standoff and, after considerably more foot tapping, the mayor announced that if Mick and Bianca failed to appear in ten minutes there would be no wedding.

The ultimatum was passed on to the couple and Mick said sullenly, "Then I'm not going through with it. It's all off. I am not a goldfish bowl and I am not the King of France."

His panic-stricken publicist Les Perrin pleaded with him to reconsider and, with prospects of a headline-splashed debacle looming, Mick relented. The couple arrived at the chamber to the accompaniment of photographers jostling for position, the better to catch sight of Bianca's nipples, periodically peeking through a blouse cut nearly to her navel, which itself was beginning to protrude.

At the sight of the waiting crowd Mick again balked. Perrin persisted, however, shoving Mick and Bianca into the crowd. Meanwhile, Keith, the only Stone invited to the affair, had arrived, stoned and disheveled and in the midst of a furious spat with Anita. Unable to gain entrance to the hotel through the swarm of reporters, he took out his frustration on a hapless photographer and security guard who stood in his way. "They didn't know me from Adam," he would later explain. "I had to get in somehow."

The ceremony, officially witnessed by French film director Roger Vadim and actress Nathalie Delon, was conducted over the incessant noise of flashing cameras and the battle between Keith and Anita, now being carried out in furious whispers. The combined noise level was so shrill, the mayor had to shout out his instructions to the couple.

The next stop was Ste. Anne's, where Abbé Baud, Mick's Catholic tutor, would conduct the sacred segment of the wedding. The route up the hill to the chapel was clogged by eager fans, befuddled townsfolk, and a contingent of left-wing students protesting the decadent excess of the event. They vented their spleen by screaming at the wedding party's passing Bentley, occasionally rushing forward to kick and claw at the fenders.

Inside Mick was pale with fear and outrage. Arriving at last at the chapel gate, he and Bianca were obliged to run full-speed to the portals, their clothes pawed at and ripped by the mob along the way.

At the steps of the chapel, they discovered they couldn't get in. Trying to head off a repeat of the civil ceremony, Perrin had locked the doors after the guests were safely inside. The couple pounded futilely while the rabble closed in. At the last moment the doors opened a crack, and sweat-drenched, terrified, and utterly undone, the couple tumbled into the hushed confines of the church to face their guests and the music, chosen by the bride from the soundtrack to the movie *Love Story*.

"You have told me that youth seeks happiness and a certain ideal and faith," ran Abbé Baud's remarks to the couple, adding, with no apparent irony, "I hope it arrives today at your wedding."

It was a forlorn hope. Apparently for no other reason than publicity, Bianca was given away by the Queen's cousin, photographer Lord Litchfield. Bianca seemed to sense for the first time the true dimensions of the chaos and cross-purposes swirling around her new husband. She would later remark to a friend that her marriage ended the day of the wedding.

The reception, held in a small theater in the village, continued the air of frantic confusion, simmering violence, and wildly inappropriate behavior that had marked the entire, exhausting day. Bianca, having set an unbecoming standard with her wedding dress, appeared that afternoon wearing a completely transparent blouse along with a turban. Underneath the provocative getup, however, was a badly shaken bride.

Marrying Mick was more than she had bargained for. It would take a while for her to regain both her equilibrium and her agenda. After her appearance she retreated to the honeymoon suite, leaving her new husband to preside over the frenetic festivities. Mick took to the stage for the obligatory impromptu jam, backed by wedding guests Stephen Stills and Doris Troy. Keith had also been scheduled to join the combo, but after hurling an ashtray through a window, he had passed out on the floor, where he would lie, insensate, for the rest of the evening.

"Girls kissed and cuddled each other," one guest recalled. "Men in hot pants with short, hairy legs did the same. Couples lay about the floor on cushions. And if a girl wasn't showing at least one nipple, she was out of fashion."

Joe and Eva, meanwhile, wandered forlornly through the star-studded crush, trying to get close enough to their son to deliver their wedding present. "I hope my other son doesn't become a superstar," Eva said with a sigh to reporters. By the next morning the newlyweds were gone, leaving St. Tropez by yacht and heading for a château accessible only by sea. The honeymoon continued with stops in Venice and Ireland, where the couple picked up a flock of paparazzi who would follow them virtually without interruption for the rest of their married lives.

NINETEEN

Exiles on Main Street

However ill-fated his wedding day, Mick remained deeply devoted to his new bride, and to the promise of a domestic Eden she offered as her dowry. In the weeks following their nuptials he was to spend every available moment at her side, as they took their preeminent place among the international jet set.

Mick and Bianca's effortless ascension was helped by Lowenstein, Ertegun, and a host of others who smoothed the way. With her natural-born haughtiness and instinctive presumption of privilege, Bianca set precisely the proper tone in those circles to which Mick was now so welcome. Her aristocratic bearing him Mick a measure of dignity and decorum that hitherto had eluded his raunchy rock persona. With Bianca by his side he artfully dodged the inevitable irrelevance of pop stardom. The Rolling Stones, and the music they made, had become an ancillary spin-off of a much more important enterprise, Mick Jagger, Inc.

It was a remarkable transformation, masterfully executed. But not everyone was buying the package. Wrote British journalist Richard Neville, "The wedding was stark confirmation that Mick Jagger has firmly repudiated the possibilities of a counterculture to which his music is a part."

American rock writer Dave Dalton used the same brush to tar the whole band: "To many, the Rolling Stones have become the very people they had once warned us against. Their image as jaded socialites parading an entourage of jet-set hangers-on seems to trivialize them."

Following their high-profile honeymoon, Bianca had accompanied Mick to Nellcote, where the group was still locked in their feverish recording sessions in Keith's basement. In close proximity to the group's shared madness, Bianca quickly drew back, declaring her allegiance to Mick alone. "She was incredibly aloof and never gave out nothing," Anita recalls. "Nobody in the group liked her and I'm sure it was hard for her to try and fit in with that way of life."

That way of life by now had descended to a freewheeling, full-court drug festival sucking into its orbit dealers, desperadoes, and elegant deceivers from across the continent. As the sweltering summer days unfolded with vapid regularity, the potential for a calamitous breakdown increased. An addled chef had exploded the kitchen; Keith and Anita had set their bed on fire after nodding out one evening. The prodigious abandon that spilled out of Nellcote had attracted the attention of French police, who set up an elaborate surveillance operation around the estate, waiting for the right moment to maximize their haul.

"We've got to get out of this place quick," Keith told Tony Sanchez, with a practiced instinct for the limits of official tolerance. "They're going to sling us inside and throw away the key."

Bianca responded to the disintegration at Nellcote by pulling Mick even further into the orbit of Lowenstein and his associates. "They were the kind of people we sneered at," Anita says. "Mick had changed—he was responsible for her. . . . There was this huge gap."

There were also dark mutterings about Bianca threatening the future of the group by coming between its creative mainstays and upsetting the band's always precarious balance. With the atmosphere at Nellcote growing more hostile by the day, Mick eventually moved Bianca to Paris, putting her up in L'Hôtel while he made mad dashes to Keith's estate to continue recording.

On October 21, 1971, Bianca was rushed to the Belvedere Nursing Home, where she gave birth to a daughter. The couple named her

Jade. For the twenty-eight-year-old Mick, glowing with paternal pride, the infant reinforced his impetuous decision to marry Bianca. Aside from the palpable sense of class she lent him, she now had bestowed respectability on him as well.

"She is very precious, and quite, quite perfect," Mick gushed as he described his daughter to the press, before inexplicably adding, "I've always been a good father and this kid makes it easy to be."

Back in the basement at Nellcote, Keith could hardly contain his ire. For him it was the music that mattered. Despite his own fondness for his son, Marlon, and the dim awareness that the pregnant Anita, now on an uncontrolled junk binge, threatened the life of his second, unborn child, he would let nothing deter him from the task at hand. Shortly after the birth of Jade, Mick phoned to say he would be staying in Paris for three more weeks. Keith was then heard to mutter that the baby was a plot by Bianca to derail the new album.

That this recording is one of the most accomplished and ambitious offerings in the group's entire oeuvre testifies both to the durability of their talent and their ability to fashion great music under the most chaotic circumstances. The long, slow flameout of Brian Jones had resulted in such incisive, inventive albums as *Aftermath* and *Beggar's Banquet*. Now, with the group teetering on the edge of oblivion, they would call upon their collective resources once again, emerging from the depths of the Nellcote basement with music as galvanizing, generous, and highly charged as anything they had ever done.

The album's title was itself a stroke of self-revelatory genius. *Exile on Main Street* perfectly summed up the harrowing, high-profile consequences of the Stones' banishment from the relative sanity of their British home. Produced again by Jimmy Miller, who had overseen both *Let It Bleed* and *Sticky Fingers*, the album's bumper crop of eighteen cuts, spread over two discs, can again be seen as the product of Keith's ongoing musical ascendance. Certainly his trademark guitar work—tense, trebly riffing, and showing a masterful instinct for the cut-and-dried hook—was *Exile*'s linchpin.

"It was not until the seventies that he really came into his own," remarked British critic Michael Watts, on the subject of Keith's role in the group. "It was all Jagger in the sixties. And before he died, it was all Brian Jones. . . . I don't think that up until then Richards's abilities were properly adjudicated."

Exile on Main Street is a consistent marvel of economy, emotional resonance, and—most extraordinary of all, considering the birth pangs—infectious exuberance. Its simple, unaffected joy of making music, although bristling through the album's many high points, is best summed up by the track "Happy," sporting a rare Keith Richards vocal solo.

" 'Happy' was cut in one afternoon," he would later recount. "We were basically doing a sound check, making sure everything was being set up for the session and the track just popped out. It was just because, for a change, people weren't laying down on the beach or at a local bar in Nice."

"Happy" would eventually become Keith's signature song, delivered at times with intense irony, on other occasions with authentic elation. The fact that this spontaneous rock-'n'-roll rhapsody could have emerged from the Nellcote nightmare is a measure of the touching faith the guitarist had in his band and their music. When it shone, the Stones' brilliance—vigorous and indomitable—was unsurpassed. On such classic tracks as the turbo-charged "Rip this Joint," the stately and somber "Shine a Light," the furious "All Down the Line," and the majestic hit single "Tumbling Dice," *Exile on Main Street* was the Stones' last rousing hurrah.

The personal, emotional, and spiritual malaise that had infected the creative core of the band would soon take its toll. The price of overweening egos and overblown pretensions, the sucking undertow of animosity and addiction would finally render their survivors' status a hollow triumph. But for the near hour of explosive music that made up *Exile on Main Street*, the Rolling Stones forever earned their immortality. When it was hardest of all to do right, they made it look easy. It was a diehard professionalism, a clearheaded commitment that made each note and every world-weary word matter one more time.

Released in May of 1972, *Exile on Main Street* followed both the group's escalating estrangement and the inexorable advance of Mick's ambitious agenda. Despite the painfully apparent rents in the band's personal ties, and the crying need for an extended vacation from one another, Mick announced in late November a barnstorming forty-date tour of the United States, their first live appearance in America since Altamont.

The band in general, and Keith in particular, were in no shape to embark on such a grueling undertaking. The final months of 1971 had been filled with a string of haphazard events that saw the eventual dissolution of his Riviera reverie.

In November the group had left Nellcote, with Mick and Keith heading to Los Angeles to remix the new album. Mick's state of mind can best be summed up by a mid-air incident in which he allegedly attacked a stewardess who had the temerity to point out that they were sitting in the wrong seats. "I asked him not to use bad language," reported the luckless attendant. "He came up behind me and grabbed me by the arm and swung me around roughly."

Mick denied the charge, adding that "I'd like to give her a good slap in the face because she deserves it."

Within days of their departure, French narcotics police, belatedly realizing that the Stones had departed, raided Nellcote, turning up prodigious quantities of illicit substances.

Meanwhile, well into her second trimester, Anita again submitted herself for heroin detox, this time in a pricey Swiss clinic in Montreux with Keith settling in nearby at the Montreux Metropole. It was in Montreux that rehearsals for the upcoming tour would take place, interrupted only by the birth on April 17 of Keith and Anita's second child. A daughter named Dandelion, she appeared none the worse for being the victim of her mother's callous abuse, suffering only a hairlip at birth.

As for Mick and Bianca, the ill omens of their wedding day seemed, in the first flush of married life, to have all been just a bad dream. "I've settled down, well, almost to domestic bliss," Mick grinned to reporters as he toted Jade through customs on his way to California, where he and Bianca had decided to alight until the start of the scheduled spring tour.

Yet for the Jaggers, domestic bliss had an enviable international flair. They made conspicuous appearances in every fashionable watering hole, invariably dressed in the height of the era's decidedly frilly and flouncy fashion. A brief fling back in St. Tropez featured the pair motoring through the cobbled streets on a scooter, both in matching newsboy caps. In Los Angeles Bianca took to Rodeo Drive in the bloomers and puffy blouse of a vintage Gibson girl. Flitting briefly back to England, they were captured by former Third Reich photographer Leni Riefenstahl on the roof garden of the ultrachic boutique Biba, he in a lemon yellow silk suit, she in a virginal white lace gown and parasol. Descending on New York's burgeoning disco scene, they were seen emerging from one or another fabulous nightspot, he in an impeccably tailored houndstooth suit or pale pastel ensemble, she in a Geneviere tunic or Napoleon tricornered hat or one of a seemingly endless selection of peek-a-boo blouses.

Mick had always relished his role as a hip fashion plate, appearing regularly on various best dressed lists, and Bianca was quick to follow suit. A model in her younger days, she returned to the runway now for a variety of glittering charity events, modeling wigs at Grosvenor House for Oxfam or preening in the latest creations of St. Laurent and Zandra Rhodes.

As intended, their world had become a fairy-tale existence. Yet it was only a matter of time before their marriage would be subject to the same dislocations and disenchantments that had drained the life from Marianne. Initially enamored of their own brother-and-sister lookalike appearance, they quickly realized that, no matter what they might share in good bones and generous lips, they were two distinct individuals, each accustomed to having his or her way.

"I don't want to be a rock 'n' roll wife," Bianca said in an interview shortly after their marriage. "I don't want to be Mick's wife—I want to be myself. If I were him I wouldn't want to be merely Bianca's husband."

It was an early indication that both were aware, however dimly, of upstaging tendencies.

"Perhaps the public thinks of me that way," she continued, "but to my friends I am a person in my own right. Mick's achievements and his accomplishments are his own. . . . The people who surround the Stones bathe in the reflected light. I refuse to. Since I've had the baby, I feel a change in myself. I feel life is just beginning. I need to concentrate on something. Mick's just starting to notice."

Mick had begun to notice that Bianca was hardly the sort of girl to meekly play the role of royal consort. She had set her sights on establishing her own celebrity, quite apart from her rock star mate. In fact, an unspoken suggestion lingered, despite his best efforts to establish credentials among the glitterati, that there was still something distinctly disreputable about Mick's profession.

Without ever quite stepping over the rigid line of outright gaucherie, Mick still tip-toed uneasily around the sort of people with whom Bianca seemed to connect—with Gore Vidal in his Italian villa, with Andy Warhol in his Factory loft, with J. Paul Getty II in any one of his lavish retreats. With scant exception, they seemed to regard him with a faint air of bemusement, as a novelty from another world, an upstart with awkward pretensions.

Mick did his best to compensate. "In the early days Mick defended himself with bad manners," remarked one friend. "Later on he used a kind of detachment. He found a way of looking at the camera which made it clear that he was keeping his distance."

It was the sort of studied disdain that, to Mick's class-conscious criteria, bespoke high breeding and old money. What lay behind the facade was an insecurity as deeply rooted and naggingly unreachable as ever.

The dilemma came to a head during the Stones' 1972 US tour, the first in rock history to be mounted as a military-style campaign, every detail prearranged from seat assignments to dressing room decor. "I feel a bit like Montgomery before Alamein," remarked tour manager Peter Rudge. "It's not like a rock 'n' roll tour. It's more like the Normandy landing."

A memo to American promoters spelled out precisely the back-stage accommodations the group expected at each stop:

Two bottles per show of Chivas Regal, Dewar's, or Teacher's scotch
Two bottles per show Johnnie Walker Black Label
Two bottles per show tequila (lemon quarters and salt to accom-
pany)
Three bottles iced liebfraumilch
One bottle per show Courvoisier or Hine brandy
Fresh fruit, cheese (preferably not plastic), brown bread, butter,
chicken legs, roast beef, tomatoes, pickles, etc.

The staging for the extravaganza was another first, the sort of in-your-face spectacle that would set a standard for all arena rock con-certs in the future. Backed by a towering forty-by-sixteen-foot mirror and flanked by two writhing sea serpents, the stage was nightly doused with a blend of water and 7-Up to enhance Mick's slipping, sliding dance routine.

With Mick as the commander-in-chief, nothing was left to chance. There would be no repeat of the rout at Altamont. Security became a prime obsession, with Keith toting a .38 everywhere he went and Mick admitting to reporters he was "scared shitless" at the prospect of confronting North America and the demons he had left behind there.

The demons, it developed, were still afoot. The opening show of their seventh North American tour—in Vancouver on June 3—was occasioned by a sold-out house of seventeen thousand along with a few thousand more without tickets churning at the gates. Storming the front entrance, hurling rocks and bottles, the mob managed to bring down thirty policemen before a contingent of Mounties charged in and restored order.

In San Diego sixteen people were arrested as they set fire to police barricades, and in Tucson three hundred arrests were made in a choking fog of tear gas.

In Montreal one of the group's equipment vans was blown up by fanatic, if not precisely focused, French separatists, while in Rhode Island, after a fracas with a photographer, Mick and Keith were arrested and thrown into jail. As the hour for their Boston concert drew near, the city's mayor, fearing wholesale carnage, intervened and had them released.

All the while the group seemed to hover above the fray, jetting from city to city in a private Lockheed DC-7 dubbed S.T.P. after "Stones Touring Party" or, as some suggested, a potent psychedelic then in vogue. Its fuselage festooned with Mick's lips-and-tongue logo, the plane became the airborne setting for many of the tour's most infamous incidents, as described by a famously erudite witness.

In keeping with the grandiose scale of the tour, several publications vied for high-profile coverage by assigning world-class authors as on-the-spot reporters. It was an impulse actively encouraged by Mick, who immediately saw the cachet of having his every move chronicled by the best available writers. *Saturday Review* initially enlisted William Burroughs—no doubt for the sympathetic junkie angle with Keith—but was forced to substitute novelist Terry Southern. But it was *Rolling Stone* magazine that landed the real literary coup by signing up Truman Capote.

It's hard to imagine what, precisely, Capote saw in the assignment, aside from the undisclosed advance. Hardly a rock-'n'-roll connoisseur, Capote was far too accustomed to his own star status to be either impressed by the Stones' fawning minions or sympathetic in his reportage. Mick, on the other hand, was happy to welcome the legendary writer aboard at the group's Kansas City stop on June 22. He was happier still to discover who Truman had brought along as a traveling companion, Jackie Onassis's sister, Princess Lee Radziwell.

The following two days endured by Capote and Radziwell as part of the Stones' entourage—much of it spent aboard S.T.P.—pointed up with graphic clarity the distance between Mick's glossy class conceits and the grungy reality of a life in a rock-'n'-roll band.

Capote, as persnickety as he was perspicacious, witnessed a mid-air incident that became the locus for all the loathing he would later vent at the group and their unsavory behavior. It occurred on a jaunt between Pittsburgh and Washington, D.C., when the group's "tour doctor" passed through the plane, "with a great big plate of pills, everything from Vitamin C to vitamin coke." The fun-loving physician, according to Capote, had gathered a gaggle of groupies at various stopovers along the way.

"He would walk around and say, 'You know, I'm Mick Jagger's personal physician. How would you like to see the show from back-stage?' He would get quite a collection of them and every now and then he would bring one of them back to the plane. The one I remember most was a girl who said she'd come to get a story for her high school newspaper. . . . She sure got a story all right.

"They fitted up the back of the plane for this," continued Capote, who went on to describe how filmmaker Robert Frank, another prestige addition to Mick's fleet of chroniclers, shot footage of "Dr. Feelgood, fucking this girl in every conceivable position."

Frank later confirmed the account. "The Stones improvised some bongo music to go with it," he recounted. "But they got bored after a few minutes and returned to their seats. When the plane started coming in, the couple was still at it. The doctor took the girl, still naked, on his lap and fastened the seat belt around them both."

"Dr. Feelgood had a terribly hard time getting his trousers on when the plane landed," concluded Capote's account, "and in the end he had to come off the plane holding his trousers in his hand."

The whole sordid little interlude would hardly have caused a ripple in the Stones' camp. Such indiscretions were part of the daily routine for everyone involved. "When thirty-five chicks come to seduce the Stones," remarked Rolling Stones Records head Marshall Chess, "and there are only five Stones, that leaves thirty, so everyone close to the tour gets one. It's part of the ritual."

Indeed, Capote himself was said to be only "mildly amused" by the episode, but it was clear enough what the term meant when conveyed by a personage of his impeccable credentials. Mick and company were, finally, guilty of the most egregious sin of them all, bad taste.

It was an impression driven home later that night when Keith, drunk on one or another combination of complimentary backstage bottles, pounded on Capote's hotel room door to invite him to a postconcert party.

"Wake up, you old queen!" he shouted. "Come up to the party and find out what rock 'n' roll's all about!"

When Capote declined to respond, Keith moved down the hall to Princess Radziwell's suite, where he continued his drunken rant. "Princess Radish! Come on, you old tart! There's a party downstairs!" He then proceeded to smear a bottle of ketchup over Capote's door. Possibly it was Keith's way of commenting on Capote's best-known work, *In Cold Blood*.

It was hardly surprising that relations between Mick and Capote quickly disintegrated, with the author and the princess leaving the tour after only forty-eight hours of "mild amusement." They would, however, carry the cat fight into the press, with Capote describing Mick as "a scared little boy" and "about as sexy as a pissing toad."

For his part Mick dismissed Capote with his usual flair for loss cutting. "That whole business was very exaggerated," he would sniff. "After all, they were only two people on the tour and they were only there for a couple of days. I mean, really."

Others, however, were not so quick to dismiss the implications of this unlikely cohabitation between high society and rock lowlife. "If the Rolling Stones are the newest mind fuck for the Truman Capote crowd," asked Grace Lichtenstein in the *New York Times*, "what does that say about the Stones?"

The final concert of the tour happened to coincide with Mick's twenty-ninth birthday. At a sold-out appearance at Madison Square Garden, which would bring the tour's final tally to something in excess of two million dollars, seventy thousand fans joined in the singing of "Happy Birthday" while the group gleefully hurled custard pies at each other.

Following the concert, Mick was joined by Bianca at a lavish celebration at the St. Regis Hotel. In keeping with her media campaign for independent identity, Bianca had been conspicuously absent to this point. She had made only a brief stopover in New Orleans, leaving Mick to conjure up a convincing excuse. "I find it very difficult to travel with anyone on tour" was the best he could do. "Bianca's easier than some people, but I'm better alone on the tour. I have to be on my own."

There was no way, however, that Mrs. Jagger would miss the star-studded fete staged in honor of her husband. Among those in attendance were Tennessee Williams, Bob Dylan, and Andy Warhol, who was rapidly becoming one of Mick and Bianca's trusted confidants.

Also on the guest list was a young singer named Carly Simon, who immediately caught Mick's eye. Rumors of a subsequent affair spread quickly, based less on hard evidence than on the notion that the two full-lipped singers made an even better couple than Mick and Bianca. One family friend recalled, "Carly was awfully innocent compared to Jagger. He was one of the most worldly men she had ever met, and one of the most exciting. He'd fly all over the world at the drop of a hat; he seemed to know everybody, to have slept with everybody." Simon would eventually memorialize her fling with Mick in the hit song, "You're So Vain," which featured Mick singing backing vocals.

Even Truman and Princess Lee deigned to appear at Mick's birthday celebration, along with pugnacious promoter Bill Graham, whose last public pronouncement on the band, following Altamont, had dismissed them as a bunch of "cunts." His tune had changed this time, although an edge of cynicism still cut through. "They are the biggest draw in the history of mankind," Graham remarked. "Only one other guy ever came close—Gandhi."

It's Only
Rock 'n' Roll

What neither Bill Graham, seventy thousand singing fans, nor even Truman Capote had any way of knowing was that by the end of 1972, the Rolling Stones had shot their wad. The group's epic surfeit of scandal, self-destruction, and salacious behavior would have long ago done in a dozen lesser rock-'n'-roll hellions. The Stones' ability to hang on, and in the process continue to create important and innovative music, was certainly the cornerstone of their mind-boggling ten-year run.

But the glue that held the band together—the sense of common creative purpose, the bloody-minded camaraderie forged from so much harassment and repression—had weakened the band, pulling it apart even as they continued, from force of habit, to play their parts. No one, it seemed, really noticed that the play itself had become something of a tired farce, repeating the same scenes with ever-diminishing impact.

No one, perhaps, but Mick. In the middle of the American tour, he was quoted as saying, "When I'm thirty-three, I'll quit. That's the time when a man has to do something else. I can't say what it will

196

definitely be—it's still in the back of my head—but it won't be in show business. I don't want to be a rock star all my life. I couldn't bear to end up as an Elvis Presley and sing in Las Vegas with all those housewives and old ladies coming in with their handbags. It's really sick."

One thing was clear. At twenty-nine, Mick found it was already too late to change the game. Rumors of bisexual affairs only lent fuel to the decadent fires that lit Mick's international stature. Tabloid talk show host Geraldo Rivera relates an unlikely story of seduction involving himself, Mick, and ballet superstar Rudolf Nureyev, after whose moves Mick had patterned his own stage antics. "If I were ever going to have a homosexual experience," quipped the publicity-hungry muckraker, "it would have been that night, with Rudolf Nureyev and Mick Jagger."

Everyone, it seemed, wanted a piece of Mick's world-class celebrity. Angie Bowie, wife of androgynous rock star David Bowie, got her name in the papers with an account of a love affair between Mick and Bowie in late 1973. After catching them in bed in Bowie's home, not far from Cheyne Walk, Angie reportedly fixed the pair breakfast. "Even though I cared," she said, "there really wasn't much I was going to do about it. I wish it had been me and Mick. I always thought that Mick must be a wild man in bed. He was a very sexy guy."

One theory suggests that a decade's defining characteristics only emerge well into any ten-year cycle: thus the forties lingered until 1955 and the sixties really only began in 1964. If it's true, then the seventies, with all the garish trappings of the Me Generation, really kicked in midway through the decade, when disco began its popular rise and the dreamy nonchalance of hippie fashion yielded to the formal foppery of *Saturday Night Fever*.

For the Stones, the seventies could also be seen as one long hangover from all that had come before. And nowhere was the group's lack of focus more evident than in their music. From the dizzying high water mark of *Exile on Main Street* and the subsequent tour, which one critic called "the one in which the group exulted in the pure professionalism of their own style of rock 'n' roll," they were left with no clear direction or sustaining creative momentum. What had always bailed them out in the past—the ever-fertile songwriting team of Jagger/Richards—was the first casualty of their dissipating lifestyles.

Following the North American tour, Keith and Anita would return to Montreux, where they would spend the next three years alternately coddling or battling their monstrous heroin addictions. With Mick and Bianca lost in a permanent world of no fixed address, Mick and Keith's songwriting partnership began a rapid and irreversible decline.

"Suddenly we were scattered halfway around the globe," Keith would remark, "instead of 'See you in half an hour.' We'd been working nonstop and then suddenly had to deal with a backlog of problems that had built up because nobody'd had the time to deal with them. . . . Throughout most of the seventies I was living in a different world from him."

The boredom and barely contained contempt that each felt for the other made for some of the most dispiriting music of the group's career. The slide began in late 1973 with the release of *Goat's Head Soup*, recorded, with more luck than foresight, in Jamaica at the inception of the short-lived reggae craze. Cut over five months, beginning soon after the North American tour, the album's ten colorless tracks lacked the focus and whip-cracking discipline of producer Jimmy Miller, who had enough of the band's endless tribulations during the Nellcote sojourn.

Although it yielded the obligatory hit single with the desultory ballad "Angie," *Goat's Head Soup* found the band repeating, for lack of a fresh tack, the same tired, Luciferian shuffle that once sparked *Beggar's Banquet* and ignited Altamont. "Dancing With Mr. D," the album's opening track, was a pale and preposterous reworking of "Sympathy for the Devil," with neither Mick nor Keith able to summon the requisite venom to give the song the slightest hint of menace. The best the boys could call up by way of controversy was a pallid rocker initially titled "Star Fucker." When a no-nonsense memo arrived from Ahmet Ertegun demanding a name change, such was the band's apathy that they went along without protest.

The group descended further still into the slough of sloppy music with *It's Only Rock 'n' Roll*, released in October of 1974. The first album produced by Mick and Keith under the name the Glimmer Twins, the album's title said it all. 'What was the big deal?' On each of the album's ten moribund cuts, including a particularly embarrassing rendition of the Temptations classic "Ain't Too Proud to Beg," they seemed to be declaring, "It's only rock 'n' roll. Another session, another album, another hit—we can do this in our sleep."

With *It's Only Rock 'n' Roll*, however, the fans started to wake up. The album not only failed to yield a hit single, it sank virtually without a trace within a month of its release.

It was clear by now that the Stones were in an agonizing free-fall, exacerbated in part by the departure of Mick Taylor, who had finally tired of his perpetual status as the group's innocent bystander. He was purportedly incensed over Mick and Keith's reluctance to give him songwriting credit for material he had written, though it's hard to imagine why exactly he would care. *It's Only Rock 'n' Roll* was in fact, a convenient nadir for the retreat of a musician whose retirement press release stated only that he "needed a change of scene." Indeed he did. During Taylor's stint with the band he had acquired his own heroin habit.

The final installment of this dreary triad was 1976's *Black and Blue*, an offering so inert that the group itself delayed release for nearly a year. Recorded in Munich, Germany, in late 1974 and early 1975, *Black and Blue* managed to arouse interest only with an inflammatory billboard on Hollywood's Sunset Strip, depicting a bruised and battered woman, trussed and spread-eagled. The group's knack for generating controversy had been reduced to a base pandering that seemed beneath even them. The Top Ten charting of the cut "A Fool to Cry" seemed more an act of kindness by the group's fans, now nearly as drained as their heroes by their long and painful decay.

The by-product of that degeneration was music that sounded increasingly like self-parody. As long as Mick and the Stones were on the cutting edge of the rock revolution, the grotesque embellishment of their personal characteristics and performance style seemed in keeping with their legendary status. But once the group began, through inertia and simple indifference, to fall behind the curve, they left themselves open to mockery and disdain. It was a fatal flaw in Mick's master plan. His transformation from streetwise rock delinquent to gentrified dilettante had gone smoothly as long as the tough, steel-tempered music was there to back it up. With the solid underpinning of the Stones' sound turned flabby and ineffectual, Mick's changeover began to backfire. His grip on fame had begun to slip as the essential core of the band's appeal shrank further with each abysmal album.

The release of *Black and Blue* marked not only a low point in the band's songwriting and recording history. It coincided with Keith's long-delayed collision with fate. His further destruction had been temporarily postponed by his discovery of a Swiss clinic where, for a hefty fee, he could undergo a three-day treatment to cleanse his blood of heroin residue, thus largely avoiding the horrors of cold turkey withdrawal.

He would repeat this process many times in the ensuing years, staving off a final reckoning with the drug and its devastating effects on his life. "He looked very wasted, very frail," reported journalist Michael Watts, visiting the group in Jamaica during the recording of *Goat's Head Soup.* "He looked as if you could blow him over."

Which was exactly what the authorities, in virtually every place Keith and his bedraggled family tried to find haven, attempted to do. The fallout from the raid at Nellcote resulted in warrants for Keith and Anita's arrest in France, which effectively banned him from the very place he had sought exile.

The following summer, in late July, the couple was arrested at the Cheyne Walk hideout, once again for possession of cannabis. Keith was additionally charged with possessing an illegal firearm, the .38 he had carried through the American tour. A month later, back at Redlands, the couple awoke to a fire of unknown origin that virtually gutted the guitarist's country estate.

Hounded, homeless, utterly helpless in the grip of the high-grade heroin supplied by Sanchez and a far-flung network of connections, Keith's deterioration by 1974 was almost complete. "I only ever get ill when I give up drugs," he would explain with humor that was more bleak than black. He was gaunt, prematurely wrinkling; his once-infectious smile had given way to a gap-toothed grimace. His skull-and-bones appearance brought him the title of the World's Most Elegantly Wasted Human Being, awarded by *New Music Express.*

Seeming at last to realize the difference between a becoming pallor and a death mask, Keith would announce, "I'm changing my image. I've arranged for a whole series of dental appointments in Switzerland."

For once Mick's loss-cutting instincts were undermined by a genuine concern for one of the few enduring friends he had ever made. "He was . . . very protective of Richards," Michael Watts reported. "Jagger came up and put his arms around him and talked to him, and you knew that he was looking after his welfare. I think it became a terrific strain for Jagger to hold this guy up."

Mirroring Keith's physical decline at the time was the disintegration of his tortuous relationship with Anita. "Our communication was pretty low," she said. "I mean, we hardly even talked to each other if it wasn't about drugs or 'Have you got anything?' or 'Let's go get something.' It was so very sad."

The couple fought often, the meaningless spats of junkies irritated by some or another imagined slight. They would drift apart only to find themselves together again. Keith had a brief fling with a stunning German model, Uschi Obermeier, but the sickness he shared with Anita had forged a bond he had no will to break.

By early 1976 the pair found themselves back in Switzerland, where Anita, whose rampant addictions now encompassed cocaine, settled in to await the birth of their third child. Born March 26, he was named Tara, with the improbable middle name of Jo Jo Gunne, from a line in a Chuck Berry song.

For a time it seemed as if Keith had once again found his center. He announced that he would marry Anita and began grandiose plans for an onstage wedding. Two weeks later, after an English concert in Stafford, he plowed his Bentley into a divider on the M-1. With him in the car were Anita, six-year-old Marlon, and several friends, all of whom escaped serious injury. When the police arrived, the by-now customary search of Keith began, and although he had the foresight to dump the bulk of his stash, he neglected the coke spoon and snorting tube that hung around his neck. He was charged with possession of a controlled substance.

"With all this weight over our heads," Anita recalls, "and all this pressure, we just got even more into drugs, basically. We were completely embittered."

Returning to Geneva with her ten-week-old infant while Keith was on the road, Anita awoke on the morning of June 6 to find the child dead. The official cause was later listed as "a flu virus."

Keith insisted the news be kept out of the press until the group finished the final night of a Paris concert series, during which his playing, according to biographer Victor Bokris, "was unusually intense."

After returning to Switzerland for a day, Keith Richards was back on the road. "Keith was very calm and very protective and very normal and loving," Anita says. "He just said 'Forget it.' But as Tony Sanchez would write, "Death seemed to be shuffling out of the mist toward Keith, coming into sharper perspective. . . . There was a desperation about him in those days—a feeling that the drugs that had rotted his teeth were blackening and rotting his skeleton."

The work, meanwhile, continued with deadening regularity. The American tour was followed in early 1973 by a violence-ridden swing through Down Under. The release of *Goat's Head Soup* occasioned still another European tour later that year. After laboring to bring some spark of life to *It's Only Rock 'n' Roll*, Mick and Keith had set on a frantic search for Mick Taylor's replacement following the album's release.

After exhaustive auditions and endless press speculation, Ron Wood, former guitarist for British mod rock staples the Faces, was recruited. The addition was at first provisional, but given Wood's habitually complaisant nature and the London street roots he shared with the band, he was eventually handed the job full-time. "I can sort of tell a good guitar player, but Keith can probably tell better than me," Mick remarked at the time, underscoring the band's creative impasse with the added comment, "Remember, Keith used to be the lead guitarist of the Rolling Stones."

"Ronnie's very stupid but nice," observed writer Nick Kent, who traveled with the band intermittently during the seventies. "When Ronnie came in, Keith Richards had a real buddy. . . . And he was also, I hope you understand, exactly what Jagger wanted. Jagger was worried about Keith. Ron was brought in as much as a mediator between Keith and Mick as he was a guitar partner for Keith."

In the spring of 1975 the group announced an eighth American tour. Like troupers gamely shuffling long after the house lights had come up, the band would attempt to conquer the hemisphere one more time with the longest, most exhausting itinerary of their career: forty-two dates in the United States and Canada with an additional sixteen south of the border.

The new tour would bring forth another attempt at the Stones' outrageous showmanship. It took the form of a forty-foot inflatable penis that Mick would ride with calculated abandon around the stage. With no compelling music to galvanize the proceeding, the wormy latex appendage became both the object of press attention and a symbol of the band's impoverished sense of theater.

A sampling of critical opinion tells the tale: "What all this ceremonious cakewalk finally disclosed," wrote Jonathan Cott, "was simply that behind the incantation, the gesture, the charm, lay . . . nothing."

"Here was rock royalty gone cynical," concurred Jim Miller in *Newsweek*. "They could coast on their past and titillate new fans by flaunting their celebrity—fabulously monied superstars with . . . nasty habits and jet-set sidekicks."

By spring of 1976 the band undertook a thirty-nine-date European swing to promote the lamentable *Black and Blue*. It was a measure of the rote, secondhand feel of the Stones' once-celebrated concert experience that this time around no one even bothered to riot. It was, indeed, "only rock 'n' roll."

Yet even as the group and its fleet of accountants tallied up the take from the perpetual road show—something over three million dollars for the American leg alone—the band's music was beginning to feel dated. On the London underground, a contingent of hollow-eyed, fork-headed musicians were beginning a new musical revolution, dubbed by the press as punk rock. The banner they waved read, "No Beatles, Elvis, or the Rolling Stones."

"I thought they were pretty good," Mick would remark after seeing the movement's prime exponents, the Sex Pistols, adding, "Well, not really good but . . . they could be."

With rock 'n' roll's imminent changing of the guards, the Rolling Stones were in danger of becoming not only irrelevant, but—by their music and manners—the very enemy they had for so long railed against.

If Mick picked up on the rumblings, he didn't let on. He was in Montauk, Long Island, celebrating his thirty-third birthday with a few close friends, including Andy Warhol.

TWENTY-ONE

Exposure

Under Mick's watchful eye and famous attention to detail, the group had become a hugely profitable enterprise by the late seventies, thanks primarily to their near-constant touring schedule. While the music may have been lackluster, and album sales less than sensational, there was still, in the minds of most maturing baby boomers, nothing like the flash and thrill of a Rolling Stones concert. Somewhere along the line they had become, by popular acclamation, the Greatest Rock 'n' Roll Band in the World, and on stage at least, they played the role to the hilt. Critical slights aside, the group could fill any stadium, anywhere in the world, as often as they chose.

For a time it seemed that Mick and Bianca's married life would be an unending photo opportunity, punctuated by vacations in various scenic wonderlands. The company they kept in those early days included Princess Margaret, Roddy Llewellyn, Lord Hesketh, Colin Tennat, and innumerable other glittering illuminati. They were sighted, early on, attending the Test Match at the Oval in the members' stand in England, sightseeing with baby Jade in Bora Bora, or ducking through the portals of Lord Gowrie's fabled Irish estate near the Curragh, where they tucked themselves away for a holiday in the summer of 1972.

A month later they were back in London, on hand for a farewell bash for longtime Stones secretary Shirley Arnold, who, after starting the Stones fan club nine years earlier, was at last ready to reclaim her life. Arnold, in her role as the band's nursemaid, majordomo, and mother superior, had come to dread Mick's new wife and her imperious, arrogant assumption of privilege in the Stones' inner circle.

According to Arnold, Bianca was infamous for railing against inadequate limousine service, once dismissing a chauffeur for neglecting to tip his hat to her. While in London Bianca spent her mornings at Ricci's, the expensive hair salon, and her afternoons on furious shopping binges. She ignored the rest of the Stones, privately referring to the whole organization as "the Nazi state," and complained bitterly at her inevitable ostracism.

Shirley Arnold's party, attended by Mick and Bianca, Charlie Watts, Mick Taylor, and special guest Elton John, provided a glimpse into the increasing estrangement that had begun to undermine the marriage. Mick had given Arnold an expensive topaz necklace from Phillip's of Bond Street, presenting it as a gift from both himself and Bianca. Arriving late, Bianca handed over a bottle of perfume, announcing that it also was from the two of them. A fight occurred on the spot as they accused each other of negligence and the embarrassed guests looked on.

Arnold recalls, "It used to get us down at the office the way they were always arguing, right from the beginning. They just seemed to want to hurt each other. . . . There was never a time when they seemed happy. Mick didn't ever seem to us to love her, not the way he loved Marianne. . . . She was very difficult."

Refusing the role of consort, Bianca was at a loss to consolidate her standing as Mick's wife. In turn, Mick did not want an equal partner. Vanity and necessity had allowed an army of sycophants and enablers to form buffer zones between him and the rest of the world. Bianca soon discovered her desire for intimacy and exclusivity was seen as a nagging demand on his precious time. In the presence of the group and its extended circle of intimates, she found herself competing for his attention, his affection, and most importantly, his allegiance.

Mick's panic-stricken need for the rudiments of domestic tranquillity had driven him to this precipitous marriage. For all her often preposterous airs, Bianca too yearned for conventional comforts and the equilibrium to nurture them. But even the most rudimentary sense of balance and perspective did not exist within Mick's orbit. "I try to be in control of my ego," Mick once admitted. "I see myself go off the rails . . . I get really difficult to deal with. The media and going on the road makes you immodest as well. It does, because you're getting all this attention, and that's when I start going around the bend. . . . My personality changes, warps."

In December of 1972 Mick and Bianca, with Jade in tow, had returned to London from recording in Jamaica. It was a period of relentless globe-trotting, which allowed Mick to keep one step ahead of the tax man while fulfilling his and Bianca's haute monde obligations. This particular stopover was particularly unnerving to Bianca. Because they had returned to England, the Jaggers were, in fact, subject to taxation. They were thus reduced to a clandestine existence at Cheyne Walk, where they kept away from the town house windows.

Bianca's sense of rootlessness was interrupted on December 23 when a massive earthquake demolished large portions of Managua, the Nicaraguan capital. Early reports indicated a death toll upward of six thousand—a figure impossible to confirm since all communication with the country had been severed. Despite frantic inquiries, Bianca was unable to make contact with her parents. After an agonizing three-day wait, she and Mick flew to Kingston, Jamaica. Two days later they had chartered a plane to fly them into Managua, bringing with them two thousand vials of typhoid serum and other medical supplies.

The city was an almost total ruin, For three days they searched futilely for Bianca's family. It was only after Mick put together a radio appeal that they were finally found, safe in the nearby suburb of León.

It was the kind of crisis that invariably brings people together, and for those few days, Mick and Bianca presented an admirable portrait of compassion and concern. Leaving Bianca behind to help with relief efforts, Mick flew to Los Angeles, where he organized a benefit concert to aid the homeless of Managua.

The concert, one of the only charity events the Stones had ever played, was held on January 18 and was followed the next day by a charity auction, in which Stones memorabilia, including instruments and costumes, were auctioned. All together, nearly $600,000 was raised, but Mick, at Bianca's urging, didn't stop there. Realizing that the money would likely get no further than President Somoza's corrupt minions, the pair used their diplomatic connections to assure direct distribution, with eventual assistance from U.S. Senator Jacob Javits of New York, a longtime friend of the Moreno family.

The glow, however, would not last long. The Stones' scheduled Australian tour would begin shortly afterward. Bianca was once again left alone to pursue her costly diversions. In late spring and early summer of 1973 the couple attended a round of New York parties hosted by Bette Midler and Liza Minelli; in Washington D.C., they presented the Pan American Development Fund with the proceeds from the Managua benefit concerts; in London, they dropped by a party celebrating the signing of Mick's brother Chris to a recording deal and later graced a postconcert reception for Paul McCartney's new band, Wings.

On June 18, an unpleasant reminder of the past surfaced to mar an Italian holiday the Jaggers had planned. Marsha Hunt, the purported inspiration for "Brown Sugar" and the willing mother of Mick's love child, filed an application order at Marleybone Magistrates Court in London, claiming what had long been known to everyone involved, that Karis was indeed Mick's daughter.

Her request for maintenance from her famous former lover irked Mick, who promptly responded by denying any connection with Hunt or the child. "None of the allegations are admitted," insisted a stonewalling Stones legal spokesman. Hunt allowed herself to be photographed with Karis for the next day's tabloids. Whatever lingering doubt there may have been about the child's paternity was quickly dispelled by her uncanny resemblance to Mick, right down to the wide mouth and generous lips. The accompanying story suggested the child had recently injured herself and needed medical attention.

Despite his grand gestures on behalf of his wife's homeland, Mick was in no mood to render more personal aid. He demanded a blood test to prove he was not responsible nor financially accountable. Willing enough, privately, to admit the obvious and even pay child support, he balked at the public humiliation brought about by Hunt's impulsive lawsuit.

"There are discussions between the parties about the merits of the allegations," Mick's lawyer would eventually announce. Those discussions dragged on for nearly two years until, in March of 1975, Hunt finally settled the suit for an undisclosed sum.

Everything now seemed to provide grist for a mill that regularly ground out its bile and petty grievances. Director Donald Cammell chronicled a typical, tempestuous interlude with the couple during a holiday in Spain. "It just rained all the time," he recounted to author Carey Schofield. "We were holed up in this huge old house, an incredibly beautiful Spanish ruin. . . . Bianca and he were just at the torrid part of the romance. . . . They got into fights all the time and threw mud at each other. Most of the time Mick just sheltered in his room. He was like a little monk, living away in his cell, playing the guitar."

There was hardly anything monastic, however, about Mick's habitual need for the kind of international attention that was, in its way, as addictive as anything Keith and Anita were pumping into their arms. For Mick, publicity—expressed in its purest form by the maxim "there's no such thing as bad press"—had become a form of discourse. Painfully inarticulate in expressing his private thoughts and emotions, he had become a master at sending messages between the lines of his public pronouncements. It was a skill Bianca too quickly learned, and the result was a bizarre playing-out of their personal hell on a very public stage.

It was a game of escalating confrontations and devious dares and double dares that made for one of the more convoluted melodramas in the history of tabloid trash. "It's what I call my fictional life," Mick would disingenuously declare. "Someone called it the 'longest-running rock-'n'-roll soap opera' and they're probably right. I get into trouble with journalists when I tell them the media are just a joke, especially in England. But they'd know what I meant if they had to live what I go through. I'll be sitting in New York and read about what I was supposed to be doing the night before in London or someplace. You just try to ignore it."

He would insist, "I don't put out wild pictures of me and whoever I'm going out with. Even before I was married, with girls I was seeing or living with—most of the stories were completely untrue and it's hopeless to try and tell people that it's not true. I don't tell them anything I'm doing, what I'm reading, where I'm going. They don't know anything about my private life. I have no respect for people who earn their money peeking through keyholes. This takes in most journalists."

Coming from Mick Jagger, the claim had a hollow ring. Mick and the keyhole press had long ago established a mutually seductive relationship and, as much as he may have whined about the intrusions, he knew as well as any celebrity that he was, finally, their property.

The press could exaggerate, embellish, and lie, but wasn't that Mick's stock in trade? Romping before millions on the back of an inflatable phallus, living a life of conspicuous, sometimes obscene opulence, flirting openly with the camera before flitting away like a shameless tease, Mick knew the dance better than anyone.

"He was uncommunicative, unforthcoming, uncooperative," wrote Maureen Cleave of Mick's early career. "No one knew anything about him; all he had to do was stand there for the theories to form."

By the midway point of the decade the theories were abetted by the couple themselves. Mick and by proximity Bianca had no private life. From the beginning, their marriage existed to make headlines. Accordingly, it was through sound bites and snapshots and column snippets that it came to its bitter conclusion.

Some Girls

As early as the summer of 1973 Mick found himself fending off queries of a troubled marriage. When asked why Bianca would not be accompanying him on the group's forthcoming European tour, he snapped, "There's really no reason to have a woman on the tour unless they've got a job to do. The only other reason is to screw. Otherwise they get bored. . . . They just sit around and moan. You wouldn't take your wife to the office, would you?"

Certainly not. A wife's place was at home, minding the baby. The only problem was, the Jaggers had no place they could settle long enough to call home. But they did have a baby, and Mick's devotion to Jade increasingly took the place of his interest in and attention to Bianca. Innocent baggage in the family's constant trans-Atlantic shuffle, Jade suffered the obligatory neglect of many children of privilege, being left in the care of innumerable nannies when her parents were off on their various and increasingly separate adventures.

Mick, sensing that one of the few bright spots in his personal life was becoming tarnished by his transient lifestyle, deposited Jade whenever possible with his own parents, who now lived in a home he had bought for them in the seaside resort of Westgate. It was here— or at the Garden House School in London or down the street from their temporary digs on East Seventy-third Street in New York—

where he would come whenever he could find the time, surprising her at the schoolyard gate, bearing gifts and guilt and trying his best to play the role of dutiful parent. He would occasionally buttonhole Jade's bedazzled teachers to discuss her academic achievements, and when one remarked that she sang off-key, he laughed and attributed the trait to Bianca.

While bright and certainly well traveled, Jade was a difficult child, pitching wild classroom tantrums in a classic bid to be noticed and nurtured. Bianca had only intermittent interest in child rearing.

"Bianca has no glimmer about looking after Jade," remarked one confidant to British writer Cary Schofield. "It is all very Mommy Dearest, the whole carry-on. Suddenly Jade's got to be dressed up in some wonderful new dress and brought down and shown to whoever it is that's come to tea. It's awful, she's completely ignored for days and then Bianca starts trying to impose her ridiculous ideas."

"I think it's bad for her to be with me too much," Bianca would insist. "She is too grown-up. When she sees another little girl, she just goes mad; she wants to play but she really doesn't know how to."

Her parents, however, were thoroughly practiced in the art of play and the attendant illusion of life as an endless diversion. The summer of 1974 was a high point in this hallucinatory social swirl. With Mick in Los Angeles, putting the finishing touches to *It's Only Rock 'n' Roll*, Bianca was spotted at the trashy birthday party of Austrian actor Helmut Berger. The theme was "bad taste," and she played it to the hilt, arriving on the arm of the Aryan-visaged actor wearing a sequined skirt slit to the waist to reveal black stockings and garter belt.

It was one of the first instances in which she appeared alone at a high-profile event without her husband, and her outrageous attire— matched only by Berger's own tie-dyed hot pants and studded leather bracelet—seemed to suggest more than simply conflicting schedules.

"I married her because I looked like her," Mick was quoted as quipping that autumn after he and Bianca moved into a Montauk estate next to Andy Warhol.

"I know that people theorize that Mick thought it would be amusing to marry his twin," Bianca countered. "But actually he wanted to achieve the ultimate in sexual experience by making love to himself."

The remarks were typical of the barbed comments that the couple increasingly indulged in to the delight of the world's gossip columnists. While the tabloid press certainly were not above fabricating stories and comments, they were often given all they could handle, straight from the mouths of Mick and Bianca.

The couple continued to sharpen their talons, even as they made splashy entrances at an Eric Clapton concert at New York's Nassau Coliseum; at a film premiere for the animated feature *Sgt. Pepper's Lonely Hearts Club Band* at a sumptuous Gotham nightspot, the Hippopotamus Club; and at an Elton John bash at the Grand Ballroom of the Pierre Hotel.

Meanwhile, Bianca forged ahead with her plans for a freestanding career. She would eventually sign with two high-powered agents, the ubiquitous Swifty Lazar and Harry Ufland, who represented, among others, Jody Foster and Robert De Niro. She continued her modeling career as well, often charging exorbitant fees just for the privilege of using her charmed name. "Sure, I charge for things that I don't want to do," she boasted. "They always come back on the phone and say, 'Yes, we will pay the money.'

"It's hard being beautiful," she would insist. "I don't like people who have this false modesty. I know I am beautiful. I know that when I go out into the street, people will take notice of me."

It was that same supreme self-confidence that would eventually land her roles in a string of ill-fated films, mirroring Mick's own stillborn movie career. The first, an Italian soft-core quickie called *Trick or Treat*, was aborted after she refused to do the nude scenes.

She had no such compunction about her role in another forgettable flick called *The Ringer*, in which she appeared as the lover of American actor Jeff Bridges. "I make her a different kind of whore than you usually see on the screen," Bianca insisted of her film character. It was an analysis that at times veered perilously close to describing what many saw as her own predicament.

"I make her sympathetic—a good, high-class whore. . . . She's simpatico, you know? She moves you. She is not used to this, being a whore . . . not used to getting close to her tricks. But this man comes to her and asks her to teach him to be a better lover. And they establish a relationship that grows. And in the end she falls. People think that prostitutes have no feelings. This is wrong. Prostitutes are human."

In a third film, a French-English coproduction, *Flesh Color*, which ultimately failed to find distribution, she costarred with Dennis Hopper and leonine model Verushka. Bianca was an on-location prima donna, who, according to one observer, "just got incredibly pretentious and silly."

As foolish and indulgent as her professional aspirations may have seemed, there was a powerful driving force underlying her efforts.

"I've never been Mrs. Jagger," she insisted. "Never. Always Bianca Jagger. We are two very strong-willed people. Maybe each of us should have married someone different, somebody quiet and easygoing. But maybe that would have been boring. I should tell you that Mick is very critical of me. He is always watching me, saying if he thinks I look wrong or something."

Bianca's fierce, inchoate need to assert and establish herself was in direct opposition to Mick's demand for the facade of homespun harmony. The charade continued into 1975. It was reported that the Jaggers would take a lengthy family vacation in Ireland as guests of the Guinness family at Leixlip Castle. Mick made the journey alone and spent six lonely weeks in the company of old friend Maldwin Thomas, who later recalled that he was "going through an emotional upheaval." Mick did manage to corral Bianca and Jade for a Christmas trip to Rio, but even there the pair was rarely together.

By the following year, however, the pretexts were simply too hard to uphold. A getaway on the island of Mustique following the completion of *Black and Blue* marked one of the few times the couple had been photographed together for months. Bianca was seen ever more frequently in the company of a glamorous assortment of escorts: *Love Story* star Ryan O'Neal, photographer Helmut Newton, and for a brief time Jack Ford, son of the President of the United States. Ford, a recent forestry school graduate, seemed the most unlikely of the lot.

"I was used by the White House to turn him into a glamour boy," Bianca sniffed. "He was very simple, very shy and naive."

As it had in Marianne's well-publicized liaison with Mario Schifano, Mick's injured pride quickly got the better of him. When he lashed out, it was on the couple's mutually agreed-upon battlefield—the pages of the tabloid press.

"I got married for something to do," he told a *Woman's Own* interviewer. "I thought it was a good idea. I've never been madly, deeply in love. I wouldn't know what it feels like. I'm not an emotional person."

Bianca replied, "As far as marriage is concerned, I was frightened by the whole idea. Actually, it is Mick who is the bourgeois sort about this. He insisted on having a proper ceremony and becoming man and wife in the conventional sense.

"I hated my pregnancy," she continued. "It was horrible. I was three months pregnant when we married. Mick was quite difficult about the whole thing."

Did having a child change her? reporters asked, echoing Bianca's own assertion of a few short years before. "I don't have stretch marks," she said, perhaps not quite understanding the question. "I'm not marked in any way by the birth. And I don't carry any pictures around of Jade."

By late 1976 the checkout counter racks offered the latest barbs between Mick and his defiant wife. "So we had an affair?" Bianca joked to Warren Beatty even as rumors of a torrid encounter between the two made its way through the grapevine. "You must be pretty bad. I don't even remember."

Also forgotten were the inconvenient vows of faithfulness the two had taken on their wedding day.

"Mick screws many," Bianca would say with a toss of her raven tresses, "but has few affairs."

"I follow a gentleman's pursuits," was Mick's offhanded rejoinder, and he added, "Domesticity is the enemy of the artist."

As Mick and Bianca's seventh anniversary approached, Bianca would reveal, "In the first years of our marriage I played the wife. I was docile and subservient . . . but groupies weren't an easy thing to get used to. Mick is in some way misogynist because there are too many women available to him. . . . He distrusts women because they are all trying to use him—they are nobodies becoming somebodies."

As a former nobody herself, Bianca had assiduously cultivated the perks of style and status, even as her relationship with Mick grew progressively more chilly. She personally oversaw the decor and maintenance of no fewer than five homes: a villa in St. Tropez, a London flat, the Stargroves country estate, a four-story Manhattan town house, and a Malibu beach bungalow. Each was decorated with Bianca's impressive collection of African art and Indian painting along with constantly replenished supplies of her favorite flower, jungle orchids.

East Coast stopovers were usually spent at a charming five-bedroom "cottage" on Long Island, rented for five thousand dollars a month from friend and confessor Andy Warhol. Lending an all-too-willing ear to both Mick and Bianca, Warhol was privy to most of their fleeting peccadilloes in the final months of their marriage. His diary bristles with frequent references to casual encounters and cozy afternoons spent with one or the other and offers a fascinating portrait of the frantic pace of Mick and Bianca's unmoored lives during the period.

For example, at a 1976 Christmas dinner at the Jaggers', attended by, among others, fashion designer Halston and publisher Bob Colacello, Warhol provides a glimpse into holiday cheer among the jet set, including the liberal use of the quintessential seventies libation, cocaine:

"Mick sat down next to Bob Colacello and put his arm around him and offered him a pick-me-up, and Bob said, 'Why yes, I'm rather tired,' and just as he was about to get it, Yoko and John Lennon walk in and Mick was so excited to see them that he ran over with the spoon he was about to put under Bob's nose and put it under John Lennon's."

A few weeks later Warhol makes the casual observation that Bianca and scene maker Tony Portago "look really in love. This started over the holidays." In early February 1977 on a visit to Los Angeles he notes that Bianca was in the midst of "a fight with Mick and he'd left that morning for New York—she'd accused him of an affair with Linda Ronstadt." The singer, in fact, lived a few doors down from the Jaggers' Malibu address.

While Warhol was in Paris on a promotional tour, a May entry sums up the air of languorous detachment that had settled over Mick and Bianca, even as they glided effortlessly through one opulent stage setting after another: "Dead in Paris, it was Pentecost," writes, or rather dictates, Warhol. "Got up to meet Bianca to go to the tennis matches. . . . She said she was running late, so we ran late but we were still there early when we got to the Plaza-Athenee (taxi $4). James Mason was in the lobby.

"Then Bianca appeared in white slacks, white halter top with an amethyst pinned to it. She said she had been up until 5 A.M. just talking to the tennis player who never makes it with anyone but his wife. She said he wanted to make it with her but she hates affairs because they get 'too complicated.' Who's she trying to kid?"

Certainly not Mick who, according to Bianca, was duly apprised of her various indulgences. "It's unhealthy to do everything you want," she insisted. "You shouldn't for the sake of discipline. Basically I'm conservative and a good Catholic girl at heart. I have had very few affairs. I could never have one without telling Mick. He will say go ahead, but he knows I won't do it."

It was obvious by the spring of 1977 that things simply could not continue to drift. Bianca's public pronouncements were, for one, getting increasingly sharp and unruly. "Perhaps Mick isn't attracted to me anymore," she said. "When I first met him I knew who he was. But I don't know now. He has changed."

She too had gone through some startling changes. "I like men's company and Mick is not always with me," she would blithely assert. "But I never really fall in love for a long time with anybody. However, I am not saying that men do not play a big part in my life. Men play a big part always in every woman's life. I mean, what else are you supposed to relate to?"

The baiting continued. "He's a very conservative Englishman who thinks his wife should take care of the children," Bianca said in a *People* magazine puff piece, poignantly tagged, "Bianca Is Tired of Playing Zelda to Jagger's Scott."

Bitterly, she went on to make the connection explicit, likening herself to Fitzgerald's star-crossed spouse. "I don't approve of what Scott did to Zelda. He used her through all his books, and when she started to write herself, he said it was all his work and then he got her locked up."

She hammered home the comparison by relating an incident in which she had announced plans to write a book on one of her favorite topics, nutrition. "I thought he would say, 'That's wonderful.' Instead he said, 'Why do you need to write a book? Why throw away a year of your life?'"

The truth was they had both thrown away considerably more of their lives in a relationship that had begun in a narcissistic swoon and was now careening toward an ugly and acrimonious finale. By the summer of 1977 Mick, belatedly realizing that his third romance was about to fail, made a halfhearted attempt to patch things up. At a birthday bash for Bianca, hosted by Halston at the just-opened New York disco Studio 54 (soon to become Bianca's de facto residence), Mick presented her with a pure white stallion as a token of, if not his love, then certainly his flair for the grand gesture.

But it was too late for lavish gifts. In late August Mick and Bianca took to the Greek island of Hydra for one last attempt to save their floundering marriage. They were spotted by photographers at a local disco, sitting at separate tables. "They both seemed very unhappy," reported a friend, Nick Karantilion. "Mick was in a very distressed mood. After spending the evening with them I am convinced they are busting up."

Mick still clung to the pretense. "So many people have been nasty and tried to divorce and divide us," he complained in a *Daily Mail* interview. "I am very thick-skinned but it affects me a bit and affects Bianca an awful lot. She gets very upset about it. We have no intention of splitting up."

Trouble in Toronto

The moribund state of Mick and Bianca's marriage was matched, in the early weeks of 1977, by the appalling condition of the Stones as a continuing musical entity. Even as the group wound down from their *Black and Blue* European tour, it was obvious that they could not continue to churn out the same lackluster music of their last three albums.

At the same time neither Mick nor Keith would try to breathe life into their songwriting efforts. The two were barely on speaking terms, so wide was the divide between their respective lifestyles.

As with his wife, Mick had begun to engage in a sniping campaign with Keith in the music press, letting slip his displeasure over his bandmate's mounting legal difficulties and grousing about the school-boy antics of Keith and Ron Wood, which included one on-the-road episode in which they had burst into his hotel room and, announcing that they were the "Trampolini Twins," bounced wildly on his bed while the unamused Mick glowered. Keith responded with barely coherent monologues about Mick's blatant social climbing and the overblown artifice he had affected on stage during the last tour. It was all "theatrical shit," he had muttered.

Regardless of their bitchy sparring, the group had to stage some kind of comeback. Their only course was a live album, with material taken from their three-night Paris stand the previous June, when Keith had managed to turn in one of his better performances despite news of the death of his infant son.

In order to give the projected in-concert package an additional marketing lift, the group hit upon the novel and instantly appealing idea of returning to a small club to recapture the excitement and immediacy of their glorious early days. The set would then be added to the Paris material already in the can.

The venue selected was the El Mocambo Club in Toronto, Canada, and the news spread like lightning down the rock 'n' roll network. The Stones' up-close-and-personal Mocambo dates, set for March 4 and 5, quickly became the hottest ticket in the world. An audience of three hundred actual fans would be selected from among contestants of a local radio promotion, inviting listeners to answer the musical question, "Why I Would Like to Go to a Party With the Rolling Stones."

"They're nervous," a spokesman said of the group as news of the Mocambo date spread. "They've been rehearsing and are wondering what people will think of them when they hear them this close."

Preparations for the shows were laid amidst the usual chaos of the Stones' daily routine. Mick and Lowenstein were deep into negotiations for a new worldwide record deal which would kick in with the upcoming live album. In late January 1977 they announced their choice, British giant EMI, which had weighed in with a million-pound advance. "In this Jubilee Year," said a gleeful Mick, "I think it is only fitting that we sign with a British company."

Keith's numerous drug busts were making their way through the various halls of justice. In early January he appeared at Aylesbury Crown Court, where he was found guilty of possession for the roadside rousting of the previous September. While the fine, dubbed by Mick as "a good old British compromise," was only a thousand pounds, Keith was warned, in no uncertain terms, that were he arrested in good old Britain again, he would most certainly do time.

That warning, like every other flashing light, apparently went unheeded. Even as the rest of the group jetted to Toronto in anticipation of one of the more significant gigs of their career, Keith dazedly returned to Redlands, steadfastly refusing to budge even as the rehearsal dates came and went. Dawdling with Marlon, shooting up in the bathroom, and enduring Anita's by now constant harping was about all he could handle. The band, frustrated, angry, and increasingly concerned over Keith's reckless disregard, sent him a telegram on February 20, two weeks before the El Mocambo dates. It tersely inquired: "We want to play. You want to play. Where are you?"

Finally pulling himself together four days later, Keith, with Anita and Marlon and trailing twenty-eight pieces of luggage, left London for Toronto. It was the beginning of the end of Keith Richards's long slide into the void of junk and jaded nihilism.

Waiting the arrival of the World's Most Eloquently Wasted Human Being was a sizable contingent of Canadian customs officials, who immediately set about searching every last piece of luggage. Keith, who had shot up in the toilet of the plane halfway across the Atlantic, had neglected to tell Anita of the scorched cooking spoon he had deposited in her handbag. When it was discovered at the airport, along with a small piece of hash, Keith hardly noticed. He was still under the impression that the customs men were simply helpful Stones personnel.

The spoon and the hunk of hash were confiscated and the guitarist and his family were sent on to their hotel, the Harbour Castle Hilton in the heart of Toronto. Although Keith and Anita still had over two grams of undetected heroin and cocaine between them, they set about securing a more substantial supply for the stay. A day later they had laid in over an ounce of smack and five grams of cocaine.

This was the sizable stash that fifteen members of the Royal Canadian Mounted Police found in their hotel room on the evening of February 27. "What disappointed me," Keith would later joke, "was that none of them was wearing a proper Mounties uniform. . . . They were all in anoraks with droopy moustaches and bald heads . . . fifteen of them round my bed, trying to wake me up. I'd have woken up a lot quicker if I'd seen the red tunic and Smokey Bear hat."

The arrest—the fifth and last of Keith's checkered career—was, in light of its probable consequences, hardly a joking matter. The amount seized would make not only a charge of possession stick— Keith was now facing a maximum penalty of life imprisonment for intent to traffic.

"They are out to make rock 'n' roll illegal," Keith was to declare with befuddled outrage as news of the bust made headlines worldwide. "That's the basic drive behind the whole thing." The notion that he was being made a martyr for the backbeat may have appealed to that portion of Keith's brain not entirely embalmed in drugs, but for Mick, this latest scandal was at last too much. As rumors flew of the Stones' impending demise, he retreated to New York under the pretense that his daughter Jade was suffering from appendicitis. Predictably, Bianca was not in town to handle the emergency.

His disgust was compounded by still another high-profile wrinkle in the Toronto saga. Among the obligatory flock of celebrities and hip hangers-on descending on the group was Margaret Trudeau, the flighty wife of Canadian Prime Minister Pierre Trudeau. Margaret had previously elbowed her way onto the tabloid pages by a spate of conspicuous jet-set frolickings with many of the same characters familiar in Mick and Bianca's circles. Dubbed "Madcap Margaret," she had already earned her countrymen's ire by her flagrant disregard of her husband's dignity and office.

Nothing, however, could have quite prepared Canadians for the exhibition she staged when the Stones blew into town. Immediately moving herself into the Hilton, she hung out in the hallways at all hours, reportedly dressed only in a bathrobe and shamelessly sucking up to any- and everyone who even looked like a rock star. She made vague promises to Keith and Anita about smoothing over their recent difficulties with the authorities, but the real object of her attention was Ron Wood, whom she followed to New York when he too lit out to escape the barrage of press coverage.

Margaret Trudeau's behavior set off still another feeding frenzy in the press, now speculating that Mick and the prime minister's wife had had a go in Toronto. It was a ludicrous claim under the circumstances and one that Margaret did little to disavow.

"I'm very fond of him," she quipped, "and I like to think he's a friend." Then, with a blink of her saucer-sized blue eyes, she added, "But after all, I'm a married lady."

Stones drummer Charlie Watts didn't help matters by drily remarking for attribution, "I wouldn't want my wife associating with us."

"Margaret Trudeau is a very nice and attractive person," Mick explained, "but we are not having an affair. I never met her before and I haven't seen her since I got to New York."

Privately, he would adopt a more catty tone: "It would have been difficult to kick her out," he said snidely. "She had six security men with two guns each. No, thank you. . . . I think she was just a very sick girl in search of something. She found it, but not with me. I wouldn't go near her with a barge pole."

With a stoic resignation that was, by now, as much a Stones trademark as Mick's patented lips logo, the El Mocambo dates went on as scheduled, to general critical acclaim. "The Stones went back to their roots," wrote John Rockwell in the *New York Times*, "knocking out raunchy British rhythm and blues in a smoking club."

Speculation about Keith's future, however, marred what was calculated to be a triumphant return to form for the Stones. "The Rolling Stones would be inconceivable without Mr. Richards," Rockwell continued. "Should he wind up in jail, it might mean the end of the band."

The issue was still very much in doubt when, two days after the El Mocambo shows, Keith appeared in court, where he was formally charged with heroin possession, a charge that carried the possibility of twenty years in prison. In a fractious encounter with outraged Canadians outside the chambers, Keith was peppered with shouts of "limey bastard" and "evil cocksucker" before he was attacked by a photographer who wrestled him to the ground.

Remanded on bail and forbidden to leave the country, Keith for the first time in years was stopped dead in his lurching path. It was, he at last realized, now or never.

"I never considered myself a junkie," he would later say, in an astonishing admission of his own drug-drenched delusions. "My particular situation was so different from ninety percent of the people hung up on the stuff. Nothing on earth will make you go through coming off it, short of a lightning bolt of logic. I had reached the point of no return. I realized I was endangering myself and everything I wanted to do and what people around me wanted to do. I just knew I had to finish with dope."

In June of 1977, three months after the El Mocambo show, Keith was allowed to leave Canada after a special visa had been issued by the American government, allowing him to enter a drug treatment program at New York's Stevens Psychiatric Center. It was there that he and Anita submitted themselves to a new technique called neuro-electric acupuncture that relieved the worst effects of withdrawal through mild electric shocks.

Restricted to a thirty-mile radius of the clinic, Keith received a visitor halfway through his course of treatment. It was Mick, who, realizing his old friend's new resolve, had come to lend moral support. The pair spent the night drinking, remembering the dear dead days and wondering what the future might bring.

Like some horrendous hangover, the past, however, refused to be dispelled quite so easily. Keith's future would hang in the balance for the better part of the next two years until, in October of 1978, he would finally have his day in court.

Taking into account his newfound sobriety and a promise to contribute $100,000 toward a Canadian drug rehabilitation clinic, the judge allowed his plea to be bargained down to the lesser charge of simple possession. "If you want to get off it, you will," Keith was to say in his own defense, "and this time I really want it to work."

But the judge was not quite finished, sternly questioning him about the glorification of drugs in the Stones' music.

"That is a misconception," Keith replied with all due respect. "I mean, about one percent of our songs glorify the use of drugs, and Mick Jagger wrote them anyway, not me."

Anyone who had listened to *Between the Buttons* or *Sticky Fingers* might have argued with Keith's percentage figure, but the judge, satisfied, delivered a one-year suspended sentence along with an order for Keith and his band to perform a special concert to benefit the Canadian National Institute for the Blind.

A palpable sigh of relief could be heard in the Stones' camp. The group had just released a new studio album, *Some Girls*, and completed a highly successful American tour to support what many were calling their best album since *Beggar's Banquet*. With Keith's freedom, futilely contested by the Canadian government, the Stones were free to roll on.

Some Girls was, in fact, a potent reminder of the flash and sass that had for so long sustained the group in the past. Written primarily in the summer of 1977, it was also among their most commercially calculated. Capitalizing on the dance music vogue that had set the entire seventies to a disco beat, the album's first single, "Miss You," was an out-of-the-box smash and the group's first chart topper since 1974's pallid "Angie."

There was also a spontaneous crackle of renewed creative energy that sparked such tracks as "Respectable," "Beast of Burden," and the wry, razor-sharp "Shattered," with an autobiographical subtext that summed up much of the group's travails over the previous decade. Fans responded enthusiastically to *Some Girls*, which would eventually sell upward of five million copies worldwide, making it by far the most successful Stones album to that date.

While *Some Girls* banished the ghosts of lethargy that had clung to the Stones since *Goat's Head Soup*, Keith was busy exorcising heroin, which had served as the silent, dominating partner in what amounted to an oppressive ménage à trois with Anita. Freed from its grip, he began to also loosen her hold on him. It was a process compounded by a string of ghastly events and dark rumors that signaled Anita's own karmic comeuppance.

Increasingly estranged throughout 1978 during Keith's long recovery, Anita by the summer of the following year had taken up residence in a Westchester, New York, home Keith had purchased. No longer the svelte gamine who had insinuated herself successively into the lives of each significant Stone, Anita had begun to take on the dimensions of a corpulent Swedish hausfrau.

On the evening of July 20, Scott Cantrell, a seventeen-year-old friend of Anita's from nearby Norwalk, Connecticut, with whom she was rumored to be having an affair, shot himself fatally in the head with a .38. Arrested that night for possessing an unregistered gun, which was later discovered to have been stolen, Anita gave a garbled account of a troubled youth who had talked of playing Russian roulette that evening.

As news of the story broke, so too did accounts of the horrendous condition of the Westchester estate. "There was a powerful unpleasant smell in the room," one detective revealed, "as if there was a dead cat somewhere."

"The house was filthy, really dirty," a fifteen-year-old neighbor, Steve Levoie, was quoted as saying. "And Anita was dirty herself. She's a sick person, she should be put away. She even asked my sister if she wanted some coke. . . . She had a lot of young boys who would come to the house all the time. She would ask for sex and talk of sex quite often. She'd never ask me, but who'd want a dirty old woman like that?"

After reports surfaced linking Anita and Cantrell to a witches' coven in South Salem, local officials came forward with tales of being attacked by "a flock of black-hooded, caped people" on the grounds of the house. Keith backed away with an alacrity surprising for a former junkie. "That boy of seventeen who shot himself in my house really ended it for us," Anita would admit years later. "And although we occasionally saw each other for the sake of the children, it was the end of our personal relationship."

So concluded Keith and Anita's life of libertine indulgence and wretched excess. If the demise of Mick and Marianne marked the end of one flowery version of the sixties dream, then the dissolution of Keith and Anita symbolized the extinguishing of another.

On December 18, a month after Anita was cleared by a Westchester Grand Jury of involvement in the death of Scott Cantrell, Keith celebrated his birthday at the Roxy Roller Disco in New York. One of his guests was Patti Hansen, a perky, vivacious model from Staten Island. From that moment on they were virtually inseparable. Recalls this daughter of a deeply religious Lutheran family, "When I first met Keith, all I could think was, 'This is a guy who really needs a friend.' I gave him the keys to my apartment after only knowing him two weeks."

An ebullient, fresh-scrubbed blonde with a dazzling smile, Patti would prove to be the support Keith needed to carry him into middle age and beyond. At thirty-six he looked as if he had passed from irrepressible youth to premature old age in the space of a few hard-lived and barely remembered years. Clean and sober, with a beautiful young girl to love and care for him, Keith sadly would still never quite make up for all that lost time.

TWENTY-FOUR

Texas Two-Step

While Keith grappled at last with his addiction, Mick too was engaged in a struggle with demons of his own devising. After his failed attempt at reconciliation on Hydra, he and Bianca offered only the most cursory denials of their impending dissolution.

In the first days of 1978 Bianca was seen on the arm of tennis star Bjorn Borg, entering Studio 54 for another night of glamorous elbow-rubbing and ear-splitting disco. A few weeks later, amidst almost daily press speculation, she issued a statement through her agent: "There is no disagreement between us and we are tired of the harassment and falsely attributed statements."

It was quite a change from the coy charm she had once exuded. "The press," she had giggled, back at the height of her war of innuendo with Mick, "they are nice but they do not leave me alone. The press chases me, they try to catch me in embarrassing positions. They are always there, when I step off an airplane, step into a hotel, when I'm dancing at a disco or at a party. Flashbulbs, flashbulbs! They even post themselves constantly outside my home. Around the clock. I know they are merely doing a job and I tell them I realize that. I go out to them on cold nights and bring them coffee. . . . I say to them, 'I know boys, I know. It's merely your job to follow Bianca wherever she goes.'"

And the place she would go, almost nightly, was the glitzy Studio 54, Manhattan's *ne plus ultra* haven for dancing, drinking, and coke snorting. The place was ground zero for seventies cool. One eye-popping shot appeared on tabloid front pages around the world. It summed up Bianca's sweet revenge on her errant husband. In a spaghetti-strap gown, eyes closed and mouth agape, she was seen dancing with a black stud in denim who bore the unlikely name of Sterling St. Jacques. Her legs thrown around his waist, her fashionably thin shanks locked around his pelvis, Mrs. Jagger let one picture tell a thousand whispered words.

By 1978, however, she had retreated from the limelight, primly chastising the press for their outrageous incursions into her private life. It was the opening gambit of a campaign to win public sympathy for her next move.

In early spring of 1978, the couple were insisting that their marriage rested serenely on a solid foundation of love and respect. On May 2, Bianca celebrated her thirty-fourth birthday at Studio 54, with a guest list that included Ryan O'Neal, Liza Minnelli, Truman Capote, and David Frost.

Conspicuous in his absence, Mick had flown to Los Angeles to announce the new American tour that took place that summer following the release of *Some Girls*. It was there, during an interview for the magazine *Hit Parader*, that Mick remarked, "If you are with a woman and the sexual relationship is working like a Rolls-Royce or Mercedes Benz, everything smooths out. The other things don't become important. They're trivia."

What automotive metaphor he might have applied to Bianca was left unsaid: like his wife, Mick had become a master of snide suggestion.

Nine days later Bianca dropped her bombshell, while Mick and the band were in Woodstock, New York, rehearsing for the upcoming tour. Through her lawyer, "palimony" attorney Marvin Mitchelson, who had recently won a fortune for the ex-mistress of Lee Marvin, Bianca announced her intent to file for divorce, on grounds of "irreconcilable differences." The news broke two days after their seventh wedding anniversary.

Details of the suit quickly surfaced, thanks to leaks from the publicity-hungry Mitchelson. Bianca sought $12.5 million, a figure she claimed to be half of her husband's estimated earnings during their marriage. Thrown in for good measure: a $50,000 advance against legal fees and a $13,400 a month living allowance while waiting for the settlement. The stipend included:

Rent and mortgage payments - $4,000
Food and household supplies - $1,200
Clothes - $2,000
Utilities - $200
Telephone - $300
Transportation - $2,000
Entertainment - $1,000
Laundry & cleaning - $200
Child care, chauffeur, nanny, and live-in maid - $1,500
Auto expenses - $500
Incidentals - $500

Key to the success of her claim, of course, was the court's venue: Mitchelson fought doggedly to have it heard in California, where community property laws would make her designs on half Mick's fortune legally feasible. It was the issue Mick had foreseen seven years earlier on the maddening morning of his wedding, when he insisted that Bianca sign a prenuptual agreement forgoing any rights to his fortune. The battle was joined.

In late 1977, four months after Mick and Bianca's failed Greek getaway, reporters had first begun to notice a new, sensational traveling companion for rock's most eligible married man. She was seen first in Morocco, where Mick had flitted during a recording session break for Keith's Toronto trial date. She turned up again in London on Christmas Eve and two days later on Barbados, where she and Mick flew under the names Jagger Beaton and J. Hall Beaton.

"Well," replied a British Airways official, surrounded by reporters, "It's a new name for Mr. Jagger. He usually flies under the name of Phillips, and Bianca used that name only two weeks ago when she flew on the Concorde to New York."

She turned up again in late January, on Mick's arm outside the Elysée Matignon Club in Paris. When an eager paparazzo rushed them, Mick punched him in the mouth. The photographer responded by knocking him to the pavement. Two months later, and only a week after the Jaggers' joint denial of impending dissolution,

Mick made news by offering a reward for the bracelet and earrings he had given his mysterious new friend as a Christmas present and which she had promptly lost on the Paris Metro. Of course there was no mystery. This tall, gorgeous blonde from Texas went under the name Jerry Hall.

She was born to a truck-farming family in Gonzalez, in southwest Texas. She was one of five gangly, giggling girls: older sisters Linda, Cyndy, and Rosey, and the twins, named Terry Jaye and Jerry Faye. The Halls relocated to the one-stop-sign hamlet of Mesquite, outside Dallas, after the family farm failed.

Hardworking, tightly knit, the clan flourished despite her father's occasional bouts with booze. Jerry's early years are replete with archetypal memories of Barbie dolls, Dairy Queens, Frederick's of Hollywood catalogs, and the annual Rodeo Cowboy Association Girls' Championship, where sister Cyndy won bull-riding trophies and handsome boys drank beer and listened to Lefty Frizzell. Jerry herself won local renown as a leg wrestler and for good reason: her limbs, even then, seemed to go on forever.

What became apparent, as Jerry blossomed into her teen years, was an unaffected, blindingly wholesome beauty. With her long, oval face, corn silk blond hair, and cheekbones riding high over a generous and forgiving smile, Jerry was quick to realize that her radiance was her ticket to something altogether more enticing than life on the Lone Star flatlands.

In 1973, at age seventeen, she arrived in Paris with a knapsack full of Frederick's-inspired clothing sewn by her mother. A brief modeling stint in Dallas had inspired lavish dreams, and she followed her elegantly upturned nose down a road that Bianca Jagger and other dewy young things had taken before her.

By virtue of her drawling Texas charm and drop-dead beauty she quickly came to the attention of salacious fashion photographer Helmut Newton, who wasted no time decking her out in S & M attire for a whip-cracking photo session. "Jerry was the closest thing to a real grand horizontal ever to hit town," one observer would later recall. "If she was English, she wouldn't even have been a starter. She was hopeless socially: she hasn't any idea how to get on with people. But because it's done in Texan, it's cute."

Jerry Hall had considerably more than "cute" in her corner. Tall, lithe, pale-skinned, she arrived at the fashion capital of the world at precisely the moment when the waiflike ideal of the sixties was giving way to something altogether more robust and assertive. That package, which Jerry offered, was quickly bought by the city's prowling trendsetters, including fashion illustrator Antonio, who provided Jerry's first big break by including her in his haute monde compendium *Antonio's Girls.*

"Antonio taught me the word 'camp,' " Jerry told Christopher Hemphill in her breathless biography, *Jerry Hall's Tall Tales.* "There were always a lot of gay guys in and out of the apartment and they always used to say that I was camp. You see, I still thought these Frederick's of Hollywood get-ups were actually chic. And then from working in fashion I realized that they were really badly made and cheap. . . . But everyone loved them. And then I realized that camp was something that had a sense of humor in it and was fun. I realized I'd been campin' all along without knowin' it!"

By 1974 Jerry had become one of the hottest new models in Paris, photographed for a future-of-fashion feature in *Newsweek* and selected for a worldwide Opium perfume campaign. A regular on the Left Bank disco scene, she fell in for a time with Grace Jones, the ferocious omnisexual black model and aspiring vocalist. The two put together a racy cabaret act that made the most of their towering height and chocolate and vanilla skin tones.

At that same time she met Bryan Ferry, the moody, mercurial lead singer for a group of vaguely avant-garde English glam rockers called Roxy Music. Ferry's warbling tenor propelled the band, which also included Brian Eno, to modest cult success with such brooding originals as "Virginia Plane" and "The Stand." He had selected Jerry from an English *Vogue* spread to be the jacket model for the group's album *Siren.*

Ferry fancied himself a romantic in the urbane vein of thirties movie idols like Roman Novarro and John Gilbert. At first he was put off by Jerry's corn-fed insouciance, but soon found himself drawn to her irresistible high spirits, good nature, and astonishing looks.

For her part she said, "I was so impressed. He picked me up at Heathrow Airport in this big old Daimler limousine. . . . He was charming. He was a real gentleman and handsome and beautifully dressed and his hair was all black and shiny and slicked back and he smelled of Floris."

Over Christmas 1975, on vacation in Mustique, Ferry proposed marriage on an impulse worthy of one of his matinee heroes. Engaged, the couple relocated to the crooner's stately home in London, where Jerry immediately made as big a splash as she had in Paris. She would subsequently accompany him on two American tours with Roxy Music. Occasionally joining the band on stage, she would lend the singer's dour performances an electrifying tingle by appearing in a tacky, leopard-skin sarong, tossing her waist-length hair.

The blush, however, quickly faded from the rose. "It's hard to say when things started to go wrong with Bryan," Jerry says. "Maybe it was when I took him home to meet the family." The son of a Newcastle coal miner, Ferry was acutely class conscious, like Mick, which gave him an aloof, arrogant air.

"I think a cockroach crawled across the wall," Jerry recalls. "That can happen, you know . . . and Bryan sort of freaked out about it and everyone was embarrassed. Plus, I don't think he liked my mother's cooking too much—you know, real down-home cookin'. He made faces and sort of picked at his food. He wasn't exactly what you'd call a sport."

By summer 1976 it was clear that the twenty-year-old Jerry had begun to seek a way out. That was when she first met Mick, now thirty-three, backstage at a Rolling Stones concert. "He looked really small and slim and fragile and feminine," she recalls. "He sort of scared me. . . . It was definitely a sexual feeling."

Mick, clearly intrigued, engineered a few more meetings that year, prompting jealous fits from Ferry, who soon became aware of Jerry's growing dissatisfaction as well as his new rival's predatory instincts.

In the spring of 1977 Ferry departed for a tour of the Far East, leaving Jerry to her own devices. Flying to New York to visit her sister, she was invited to a dinner by Ara Gallant, photographer Richard Avedon's hairdresser.

"I didn't know who was going to be there," she recounts. "So I get to the restaurant and it's Penelope Tree, the great model of the sixties . . . and Warren Beatty . . . and Mick! It was May 21, 1977. I'll never forget that date."

Jerry later learned Mick had arranged the encounter, which continued that evening with stops at various Gotham clubs and, inevitably, Studio 54. "The next day," she continues in *Tall Tales*, "he called up and he was really calling up and calling up, from the studio, from here, from there, and always sending flowers. And I thought, 'God, this guy is really keen.' "

At this point Jerry received news of her father's death. "Mick was there when I needed someone," she explains, "and that somehow made a change. It made me close to him. It was like our relationship speeded up somehow."

Still officially engaged to Ferry, she made certain that she and Mick, as she puts it, "never got caught seen together. We'd go to those out-of-the-way places. We'd go to Coney Island . . . or we'd go to these small bars way up in Harlem. . . . I always wore jeans and sneakers and a T-shirt and Mick never dressed up either and it was fun, like sneakin' around."

The couple would rendezvous again in Paris, where Mick insisted that she break the news of their burgeoning love affair to Ferry. Before she could summon the courage, however, Ferry left for Switzerland to cut a new album. It was then she agreed to accompany Mick on a Moroccan getaway.

What Jerry had been unable to face, the press quickly accomplished for her. "News of Jerry Doesn't Find Ferry Very Merry" read one headline after reports appeared describing the Moroccan interlude and the subsequent Barbados holiday of "Mr. and Mrs. Beaton."

Incensed, his working-class roots surfacing, Ferry threatened to find Jagger and give him a good thrashing. Instead, when it became clear that he could not compete, he spread nasty rumors that Jerry, prior to their engagement, was the occasional plaything of the Shah of Iran.

His class pretensions and stuffy bearing notwithstanding, Ferry was genuinely crushed by the loss of the ebullient American beauty. He would eventually express his heartache, as well as vent his spleen, on a solo album titled *The Bride Stripped Bare*, featuring a cover that depicted him mooning in an empty cinema beneath a wide-screen image of his lost love.

Emotional Rescue

Initially, little love was lost between Mick's latest conquest and the Stones' inner circle. Jerry was regarded, in fact, with a mix of sullen suspicion and outright hostility.

"Very fashion crazy, this new one, Miss Hall," remarked one intimate. "She's terribly pretty. She's got this ruthless streak—she obviously started off without too many advantages and glimpsed the possibilities. . . . So Jerry wanted to get on in the world and she is frightfully keen on money and almost seems to equate it with sanctity and sex and worse. Everything that's wonderful has got dollar signs in front of it."

Said another insider, "Jerry hasn't the faintest idea about how to do anything except how to look after her own interests and career. There's no reason why she should know how to look after a big house and so forth, and she certainly doesn't. Jerry's great failing is she's a great sort of bullshitter, she pretends to be doing things and knows how they should be done when nobody would mind if she just came off it and was a nice dumb model girl from Texas."

As dumb and as Texan as she might have been, she offered Mick something he had never encountered before, a love and devotion that, while it may have had its strings attached, was fundamentally lacking in the neurosis, self-destruction, and selfish scheming that had characterized all his other serious relationships.

As Patti Hansen did for Keith, Jerry Hall provided something sunny, sanguine, and stabilizing for Mick. It's significant to note that, for both rock-'n'-roll veterans, the closest they had come to happiness was in the arms of American women. It was their optimism, their can-do brand of romance, and relative lack of pretension that set Jerry and Patti in such sharp contrast to the glum and grasping tendencies of those who had come before. In time, Jerry Hall would give Mick the confidence and sense of connection vital to his seriously pursuing that long-delayed dream of domesticity.

Which is not to say that Mick saw the error of his own profligate ways or, at least initially, any reason to mend them. Even as Mick began a globe-trotting romance with Jerry, he continued to play the field. "It was strange at the beginning," Jerry admits. "For one thing, there were all the girls—the groupies—chasing after Mick."

Adds a friend, "Mick's girls have always tended to come in two sorts. There are the international model and actress types, very glamorous, and the smart young English or American girls, most of whom are not at all glamorous. He's always found grand families as seductive as long legs."

During this period Mick enjoyed a brief coupling with a highly regarded British journalist, followed by a somewhat more protracted pursuit of Nina Eberstadt, the pubescent granddaughter of Ogden Nash.

But in the first flush of their affair, Mick was drawn steadily back into Jerry's nurturing orbit. "He loves to tease her," says costume designer Ossie Clark, "but she never, never gives into it. She's willing to give and take. . . . She just knows how to handle him, she knows when to act a certain way and she's a very good balance for him. It's not manipulative, though."

In sharp contrast, Mick and Bianca's skirmishes turned into a bloody battle. Immediately after she filed for divorce, Mick retaliated by cutting off Bianca's New York charge accounts while removing all the furniture from Cheyne Walk before she could take possession of it. When a puzzled Jade asked where all the sofas and tapestries had gone, Mick muttered that he had taken them out for "repair."

What followed was a nerve-racking bout of bare-knuckle legal maneuvering, beginning with Mick's nimble evasion of the actual divorce papers. In late October he departed their London house just before he was due to be served by Bianca's legal representative. "I think Mick Jagger left as soon as he heard they were after him," said a Stones spokesman. "He has a feeling about these sorts of things."

He also had the feeling, confirmed by his own battery of barristers, that if the inevitable proceedings were not kept out of California, he would eventually be several million pounds lighter.

In early May 1979, after finally being served in New York in April, Mick appeared at London's High Court for a three-hour session to determine where, exactly, the case would be heard. Five days later his spokesman issued a statement asserting that, while Mick had made love to Bianca as recently as October of 1977, their marriage had effectively been over "in every true sense since 1973." It was a tactic designed to thwart Bianca's claim on half his fortune for the entire span of their marriage, with Mick insisting that his total assets amounted to a mere two million pounds.

By the middle of the month the scene had shifted back to Los Angeles, where Judge Harry Shafer heard Bianca's lament that her monthly living allowance had been cut from eight thousand pounds a month to one thousand pounds. A sympathetic Shafer ordered Mick to up the ante, observing that Bianca should not be "starved into submission." Mick was summarily told to give Bianca fifteen hundred pounds a week until the case could be decided.

Traveling to Nicaragua in early June to bring out friends and relatives caught up in the country's bloody civil war, Bianca returned to London and announced, "I can do nothing to help them financially at present because I have no money. Although Mick was told by a judge in the United States to pay me money, he hasn't done so. After the divorce hearing, I intend to fly back to Nicaragua to work for the Red Cross, although it will be a very stiff task to raise my fare."

The plight of Bianca's country had left her genuinely moved, and in future years she would lend herself to the cause of Central American relief, occasionally putting herself at risk by visiting active battle zones. Tied as it was to the fate of war orphans, her plea, however, did nothing to hurt her standing in the escalating legal battle. Seen leaving the London court sporting a beard, Mick was asked by one tongue-in-cheek reporter how Bianca was doing. "Terrible," he snarled as he ducked into the waiting limo.

Finally, on July 16 a ruling on the venue was handed down, with little satisfaction to either party. Justice Eastman of the High Court announced that the divorce should, indeed, proceed in Britain but also ruled that Bianca's California petition would be allowed to proceed, on grounds that it would be "discourteous" to the American judiciary not to do so.

Meanwhile, Mick kept busy stamping out two other legal flare-ups, both also having to do with former romances. Earlier in 1978 a Los Angeles court had ordered him to pay fifteen hundred dollars a month to Marsha Hunt, who had reappeared with renewed claims of Mick's paternal responsibility for the nine-year-old Karis. Hunt was represented by the ubiquitous Marvin Mitchelson. The court's ruling was the first step in a process that would finally lead Mick to legally adopt the child, owning up at last to what had so obviously been his from the beginning.

The second difficulty reached even further back into his past. Chrissie Shrimpton had resurfaced, announcing plans to publish love letters written to her by Mick in the first flush of their adolescent affair. Mick indignantly claimed that his old flame's proposed sale to *News of the World* constituted copyright infringement. Chrissie backed down.

So too, eventually, did Bianca. Mick's stalling ploy, coupled with his haughty disregard of Judge Shafer's order, had finally worn her out. "Mick has put the financial squeeze on her," explained a forlorn Mitchelson, sensing the quick evaporation of a hefty contingency fee. "He's closed her bank accounts and returned her bills unpaid."

"He bragged that he'd never given any woman anything," sighed Bianca, "and never would, no matter what the circumstances."

At last, in November 1980, nearly two and a half years after Bianca announced her intention to divorce, a settlement was made. In every particular it was as Mick had wanted it. Heard in England, behind closed doors, his one-time mirror image was awarded the humiliating sum of a million pounds. One decision still had to be made, arrangements for the joint custody terms for nine-year-old Jade.

Whatever Mick may have gained, financially or in terms of some dark retribution against the one woman he had ever called his wife, the story of Mick and Bianca can only be described as a personal tragedy. So anxious to fulfill his fanciful notions of old-fashioned love, he had instead made a pact with a woman he neither knew nor understood, nor for whom, in the end, he could find a kind word to say.

"Since the divorce we're not even friends," he would remark shortly after the settlement, with the offhanded cruelty of a man already justified to himself. "She has been so difficult and devious that I'll never be friends with her again. I've tried to be friendly until quite recently, but every time I've tried, she has done something which shows she doesn't want to be my friend at all.

"The divorce went on and on, and yet it could have been settled ages ago. I think she just wanted it to last so long so she could get her name in the papers. All those pictures you saw of her going into court where there was nothing she could possibly say. She never had to go to any of those things. She went to every one she could—because she's got nothing else to do. That is the trouble. Her credibility is a bit blown, but I wish she'd succeed, then I wouldn't have to pay her so much money."

In June 1980 in Paris, Mick and Bianca would meet once again at a party given by South American millionaire Pre Catalan, for which the guests were requested to dress all in red. Mick arrived with Jerry, followed a short time later by Bianca, escorted by the deathly pale Warhol. The evening was spent in a minuet of circumvention, amidst a sea of crimson frivolity. It was a shabby final act that nearly matched, in vacuous splendor, the play's opening scene.

For the Rolling Stones, however, there was no end in sight. There were, to be sure, occasional grumblings, especially from bassist Bill Wyman and drummer Charlie Watts, about packing it in.

"I can't keep up being a Rolling Stone all the time," Watts said. "Plus the fact that I hate rock 'n' roll. Rock 'n' roll is a load of rubbish, isn't it?"

On the group's twentieth anniversary, in February of 1980, bassist Bill would make the first of several retirement announcements. "That's it for me, mate," he would tell David Wigg of the *Daily Express*. "I want to do other things. I only got into rock 'n' roll to have a bit of fun and to see the world for a couple of years. It ended up being such a part of me. But I refuse to let it dominate my life."

Mick himself would echo the sentiments in the first summer of the new decade, by proclaiming, "There is no future in rock 'n' roll. It's only recycled past."

Considering the generational shift that had occurred since the emergence of punk rock in the late seventies, it was an understandable sentiment. The term *dinosaur rock* had only recently been coined, and the Stones, as the sixties' most tenacious survivors, were held up as the final egregious example. "No matter what Johnny Rotten and Sid Vicious do," Mick would say on the subject of the Sex Pistols and their oft-stated contempt for their musical forefathers, "they can't do anything more disgusting than the Rolling Stones."

But it was all just bluster and bluff. The Stones' reign of outrage had ended long ago, as far back as Altamont or even the death of Brian Jones, and all that was left was a reputation that with each successive year seemed somehow less provocative. Jagger was a rich, sophisticated bon vivant. Keith had cleaned up his act. What was the point of carrying on?

Yet the band's momentum seemed to carry them forward when all other means of propulsion had failed. The renewed vitality signaled on *Some Girls* would slowly flounder over the course of the group's eighties output, beginning in 1980 with *Emotional Rescue*. The album would yield its standard harvest of hits, the title track and "She's So Cold." But Mick's instinctive grasp of the black idioms that had underpinned the group's early appeal sounded increasingly more affected or worse, simply ripped off. Keith's guitar work, in tandem with Ron Wood's, would on occasion elevate the proceedings but on halfhearted efforts like 1981's *Tattoo You*, '83's *Undercover*, and '86's *Dirty Work*, the conviction slowly settled that the parade had indeed passed.

Not that the group's fans, conditioned more to the spectacle of the Stones than their sound, really seemed to mind. Between 1980 and 1986, the band would mount their tenth American tour and still another sold-out European itinerary. Both would rack up record-breaking tallies; the US dates alone, over fifty in all, grossed a million dollars per performance, along with ten million in merchandising concessions and an additional four million dollars from the Jovan perfume company which, in a rock 'n' roll first, had underwritten the tour costs for the privilege of commercial tie-ins with the group. It was an enriching agreement that only accentuated the group's growing sense of sold-out futility.

Of the band members, only Keith kept the flame of true belief burning: "Rock 'n' roll is as healthy as ever," he would doggedly insist. "We all tend to forget that it's ninety percent crap anyway. But the ten percent is good."

To keep his stake in that ten percent, Keith would periodically dabble in musical projects outside the Stones, including such free-wheeling experiments as the New Barbarians and the X-Pensive Winos. For all the media attention these short-lived musical concoctions generated, they were, in the end, nothing more than diversions from the increasingly dispiriting business of being a Rolling Stone.

As the third decade of the group's existence wore on, as the purses grew fatter and the lines of age began to deepen, the code of secrecy that had kept all the turmoil and dementia hidden behind a stony facade began to crumble. "The band has done what it set out to do," Mick would say. "I don't know what goals are left."

And without those goals, more than just their raison d'être was open to question. They were beginning to wonder if they even liked each other anymore.

"We don't see each other so much anymore," Wyman would confess. "We tend to come together only when there's work. It really is like Christmas with the family. You get on all right, but you know you wouldn't be able to stand it if they were living with you for a month."

It was an atmosphere in which long-festering animosities were opened and aired. The hostilities naturally centered around Mick and Keith, who began to indulge in a protracted round of public bickering that left many in doubt as to the band's future, despite their re-signing in the summer of 1983 with CBS Records for the staggering sum of twenty-eight million dollars. It was by far the most lucrative contract in record business history to that point.

As it had with Anita, Keith's hard-won battle with heroin had thrown his relationship with Mick into a whole new light. While he continued to consume prodigious quantities of marijuana, nicotine, even cocaine and especially booze, he was nevertheless a changed man. The junk had left him permanently stunned, but he was no longer the loose cannon for whom Mick—for his own well-being and that of the group—was responsible.

At the same time Keith seriously questioned Mick's allegiance to the founding principle of the band: essentially, that the music mattered, that rock 'n' roll was something sacred, worth giving away one's life for. Mick wasn't fooled for a minute by Keith's worn clichés; he'd been through too much, and more often than not in close proximity to Keith.

Keith had good reason to be suspicious of his partner. Not only had Mick long ago backed away from the outlaw ethos, he was beginning to look for ways to break clean. "It will disintegrate very slowly," Mick predicted of the band, and he himself was far from resigned to some slow fade.

In the summer of 1984 Mick announced that he would begin work on a solo album. "He wants the new album to be totally different from anything he's done with the Stones," reported a source near the group. "He's going to take his career in a whole new direction."

Another insider was less generous: "He wants the ego trip. He wants to show everyone just what he's capable of without the support of the rest of the group."

The prospect of Mick's setting himself aside from the rest of the band undermined not only their future but his unquestioned authority. "I've lost touch with whoever Mick is now," said the increasingly voluble Wyman. "I'm not worried about what I say about Mick. He's not my boss. We're a band, you know, and Keith Richards runs the Rolling Stones really."

The notion that Keith was actually in charge of anything more than his guitar strap seemed dubious, but Wyman's assertion that Mick "just has his share of five votes" clearly sounded like mutiny.

It was a rebellion that burst into the open in Amsterdam in an unlikely brawl at a group meeting between a drunken Mick and a disgusted Charlie Watts. Arriving at the hotel, the sodden Mick crashed Charlie's room at five in the morning with cries of "Is that my drummer boy?"

Watts arose, shaved himself, put on a suit and tie, and proceeded to deck Mick with a wicked right hook. "Don't you ever call me your drummer boy again," Watts told him. "You're my fucking singer."

But it wasn't just Mick's singing solo that brought out the fight in the band. In 1981 his interest in a film career revived when he landed a part in *Fitzcarraldo*, a grandiose jungle epic made by German new wave director Werner Herzog. Filming was to begin in January of 1981 in a blighted Peruvian jungle town called Iquito. Mick, with Jerry by his side, was to be on location for the next four months.

The film chronicled the story of a madman building an opera house in the jungle. It was luckless from the beginning. Mick's costar, Jason Robards, dropped out early with jungle fever, followed in turn by actress Claudia Cardinale. A local revolution put a periodic stop to shooting, until in February the production was halted. Returning to New York, Mick decided to pass entirely when told that *Fitzcarraldo* would resume shooting in May. Herzog, a visionary, if slightly daffy, director, was generous. "Mick is a great actor and nobody has seen that," he told Jonathan Cott in *Rolling Stone.*

Whether his early return did much to assuage the band's discontent is doubtful. Headline warfare, at times reminiscent of Mick and Bianca's squalid squabbles, continued off and on for years. "Mick is the guilty one," said Wyman, who, once he got the hang of letting it all hang out, found it difficult to stop. "He wanted to do his own thing and be famous in his own right. . . . It's a pity we didn't go out with a big bang. Instead we went out on a whimper."

Wyman talked as if the group had already split, as if Mick's solo success was all but assured. They were all in for a surprise, sobering or satisfying, depending on the point of view.

Mick's debut solo album, *She's the Boss*, was released in March 1985 with much fanfare. Far from coming into his own with *She's the Boss*, Mick had managed to accentuate all that had become mannered, arch, and antiquated in his music. The strained, artificial feel of the material might have been the result of overproduction brought on by Mick's nervous jitters over the career move. But there was a vapidness that was harder to dismiss, by trying to update himself, by himself, he had lost touch with the primal drive of the band that had always kept him focused. Without it he was all over the place.

A second solo effort, 1987's *Primitive Cool*, also sank, reducing Mick to dredge up one of the oldest music industry chestnuts. After a six-date sold-out solo tour in Osaka and Toyko he could at least say he was "huge in Japan."

Mick was, in fact, leaving no stone unturned in his quest to establish himself as an independent entity. In 1982 he had signed a book deal with Lord Weidenfield, head of the venerable British firm of Weidenfield & Nicolson, to put his life on paper.

Two years later, in 1989, shortly after Mick's forty-sixth birthday, reports appeared that the project was running into "trouble." The autobiography, ghostwritten by John Ryle, a literary editor of the

London Sunday Times and sold for a rumored two million pounds, was deadly dull.

"No sex. No rock 'n' roll," sniffed a spokesman for Futura, a paperback house that was offered the manuscript. "It's just boring stuff about his ordinary parents and his ordinary upbringing. I was surprised at its poor quality."

Mick had even tried his hand at film producing, but ultimately failed to mount a movie version of Gore Vidal's *Kalki* despite commitments from Alec Guinness and director Hal Ashby. Breaking away from his past, his mates, and his musical legacy was proving harder than he had anticipated.

It was easy to see why. Mick's context within the Stones was what gave him an essential validity he didn't enjoy on his own, when what he was selling was less the music than his own flash, sizzle, and smoldering sexuality. Or at least his version of those qualities, familiar now to a thousand garage band frontmen.

"I can't believe how weird and dirty Mick Jagger is," Jerry would squeal in the tabloids. "Mick is one of the sexiest men in the world and the best lover I've ever had. . . . When I have to be sexy in front of the camera, I think of him and it always does the trick." Of course she would say that, echoing the dreams of those for whom Mick represented the ideal kinky lover.

But the times had caught up with Mick. He had passed forty back in 1983, on a birthday where he promised to punch out the next guest who brought up the subject. The competition was half his age now, prancing and preening like they'd invented the rock-'n'-roll tease all by themselves.

He lifted weights and jogged seven miles a day, but there was a big difference between being healthy and being sexy, especially for a star whose appeal was based initially on his pub crawl pallor and scruffy slouch.

"When you get to be my age, you really have to work at being young," he would say. "You've got to be fit because rock requires a tremendous amount of energy, and I find that if your body is alive, your mind becomes alive. When I'm on tour, I never touch hard liquor and I try to get as much sleep as I possibly can. I like to get as much as ten hours a night."

He sounded like nothing so much as his own father, the physical education, teacher, and in fact, for most of rock's new fans, hearing Mick was like listening to your dad singing rock 'n' roll.

Keith, who looked twice his age, was defiant about his impending irrelevance in rock's cult of eternal youth. "There's no good reason why the Rolling Stones can't grow old gracefully," he growled, even when his own face proved him wrong. "I'll be playing rock in a wheelchair."

His impatience with Mick spilled over into a lengthy interview in *Rolling Stone* in late 1988. "Mick and my battles are not exactly as perceived through the press or other people," he said. "They're far more convoluted, because we've known each other for most of our lives—I mean since we were four or five. . . . But I think there is on Mick's part a bit of a Peter Pan complex. It's a hard job being the frontman. In order to do it, you've got to think in a way that you're semi-divine. . . .

"I tip my hat to Mick," Keith continued, dredging up the strange mixture of friendship and almost sibling rivalry that had always marked their long partnership. "Most of my efforts with Mick go to trying to open his eyes: 'You don't need to do this, you have no problem, all you need is to grow up to it.' "

While the notion of Keith lecturing Mick on maturity was filled with irony, there was no question that he had found a measure of contentment outside the Stones that had eluded his partner. Keith had married his Staten Island sweetheart, and together they became one of rock's fun couples, clearly enjoying each other and the life they led.

"On top of the fact that I love the bitch to death," said Keith, moved to eloquence by Patti's sunny gifts, "she keeps up with me, she keeps me going."

There wasn't much, however, to keep Keith and Mick's relationship going. "I admire the guy enormously," Keith told *Rolling Stone*. "In the seventies, when I was on dope . . . Mick took all that work on his shoulders and did it all and covered my ass. . . . I mean, he did exactly what a friend should do. When I cleaned up and *Emotional Rescue* time came around—'Hey, I'm back. I'm clean, I'm ready; I'm back to help take some of the weight off your shoulders'— immediately I got a sense of resentment. . . . And that's when I first sensed the discontent, shall we say."

It was a discontent that by the close of the decade had kept the band off the road for seven years. In September 1988 Mick, shaken from the failure of his solo records and the future of his life beyond the Stones, proposed a new tour—effectively reuniting the band one more time—for the gate and the glory. Keith, then working on his own solo album, appeared cool to Mick's scheme.

"Mick suddenly called up," he explained, "and the rest of them: 'Let's put the Stones back together.' I'm thinking, 'I'm just in the middle of an album. Now what are you trying to do? Screw me up? Just now you want to talk about putting it back together?' "

But Keith couldn't conceal his delight for long. He had hoped Mick would eventually come around. On January 18, 1989, a very public reconciliation was held at the Rock 'n' Roll Hall of Fame dinner at the Waldorf Astoria in New York, when Mick and Keith, along with Ron Wood and Mick Taylor, were there to accept the Stones' induction into the hallowed, if as yet unbuilt, halls of rock history.

"It's slightly ironic that you see us here tonight on our best behavior," Mick grinned. "But we're being awarded for twenty-five years of bad behavior. . . . We're not quite ready to hang up the number yet."

Not quite. The 1989–90 Steel Wheels world tour, along with the album and the flood of merchandising that went with the event, was the most lucrative in the band's career. Although the new music did not elevate them to the top, the concert itself was a dazzling retrospective—a pastiche of oldies served up in a high-tech package of light, sound, spectacle, and nostalgia.

Ticket sales for the first four shows, offered in mid-July, immediately broke all existing sales records, with 120,000 bought in Toronto in under four hours. The fans were obviously happy to have them back. And so, it seemed, were the critics, for the first time in a long while.

Yet predictably, the rave reviews focused on the simple fact of their survival and not the band's fabled edge, nor any clear and present danger they might represent to the status quo.

"Mick . . . looked incredibly fit," observed Jonathan Takiff in the *Philadelphia Daily News*, "and still moves with agility."

"Five middle-aged English dudes led 64,000 Yanks to a fantastic two-and-a-half hour party sing-along," said Tom Moon of the *Philadelphia Inquirer*, describing the concert.

It was like old times, in more ways than one. In Philadelphia, where the tour opened on August 31, there were twenty-eight arrests and fifty-two injuries as drunken fans charged police barricades outside the stadium.

But as the Stones rolled on into a fourth decade, the end of the road also seemed to be winding near. The staggering take from Steel Wheels, a renewed recording deal with Virgin Records for forty-five million dollars, the petty quarrels put aside—for all that, time still felt short. The ride would soon be over. Only the victory lap was left. In 1993 Bill Wyman, whose hooded eyes had seen so much and revealed so little, announced his retirement, this time with a ring of finality. His scandalous marriage to and quick divorce from an underage Lolita named Mandy Smith had finally knocked the wind out of him.

Wyman took with him that granite-solid rhythm section that had kept the band going for so long. The Stones would write, record, perhaps even tour again. But it could never be the same.

EPILOGUE

Wandering Spirit

For Mick too the eighties became a time of summing up and laying to rest, resolving at last the conflicting desires and clashing agendas that had torn his life into so many pieces. The relationship with Jerry, which had started so promisingly, sputtered in the early years of the decade, as Mick stubbornly clung to his macho mandate, flagrantly stepping out on her when- and wherever he felt the urge.

Jerry, for her part, held on in hopes that eventually the two could find a life together. There was much to make the wait easier. Stargroves became a regular stop for the couple until Mick eventually sold the memory-haunted manse. Cheyne Walk and Mick's Manhattan town house were kept active by the couple's frequent trips in and out of London and New York. In 1980 Mick had bought the stunning Château de la Fourchette in the French hamlet of Poce-sur-Cisse, near Amboise in the Loire Valley, for a rumored two million francs. He would subsequently build, to his exacting specifications, a spacious vacation home on the island of Mustique. In their first years together, Mick and Jerry would visit Bali and Kashmir and take in Carnival at Trinidad.

Mick also seemed to be accustoming himself to the role and rigors of fatherhood. "I think I'm a pretty good father," he told writer Cordell Marks in late 1981. "I have a nice affinity with children, not

246

just my own. I like taking bunches of kids out for the day. Kids keep you young and they keep you laughing. Last time I went on holiday I took four kids to some beach somewhere or the other . . . including Jade. I let them run free to a certain extent and then get cross with them occasionally, especially when it's four little girls, because they're always bitching about what they're going to wear."

Although Mick's de facto family now included Karis and—on a shared basis with Bianca—Jade, he refused to entertain the idea of a second marriage.

"I wouldn't marry again," he told *Woman's World Magazine* in 1982. "If you're not successful at it, it's not a case of try, try again. In our society there is no reason to get married. . . . It's a near miracle that we have even survived in this business. It's because I know where to draw the line when the others are going over the edge. This, I think, is primarily due to my background. It takes a conventional upbringing in the English style to produce a normal human being. It gives you equilibrium, a balanced view."

Whether Mick saw himself as the product of "a conventional upbringing," he was certainly, after Bianca, risk-averse to commitment. By 1982, with his sexual exploits still numerous, Jerry's patience began to wear thin.

"It's hard being with someone like Mick because girls can be so pushy," she writes. "They have no sort of modesty. They'll throw themselves at him in restaurants, in front of people, and say the most outrageous things. They'll do anything to spend just one night with him, or just to get in the papers. I'm up against this every day. I'm not just talking about groupies. There's one girl, a famous singer—I won't say her name in print—who said to Mick when she met him, 'Should I put my diaphragm in? Or should we rap first?' Can you believe that?"

Mick was only too happy to believe it. "He decided to start taking advantage of the way girls are" is Jerry's quaint way of putting the situation of late 1982. "He wanted to go back to living the image of a famous rock star. . . . It was a very difficult period in my life. . . . I'd go to work, come home—and there'd be things from other girls lying around. It was so seedy. . . . And then I started finding things next to the bed, like earrings or a ring."

When Jerry decided to get Mick's attention, she employed the tried-and-true tactic used by Marianne and Bianca before her. His name was Robert Sangster, a pudgy forty-six-year-old British multi-millionaire and racehorse enthusiast with his own prize-winning stable of three hundred animals.

Jerry had met him back in the mid-seventies with Ferry at the Aga Khan's vacation home on Sardinia and later at the Royal Ascot Races. "I remember that he was always making eyes at me and being real polite," she says. At the time Jerry caught his eye, Sangster was married and in the midst of building a sixty-million-dollar mansion for his wife overlooking Sydney Harbor. By late September 1982 he and Jerry were frequently seen together and Sangster was even rumored to have proposed marriage.

Buttonholed by reporters at the Keenland Yearling Horse Sales in Kentucky, Jerry was asked if the split with Mick was for real and for good. "Robert could buy Mick ten times over" was her reply.

Mick's response was to undertake a high-visibility social schedule, during which he was seen in the company of a number of beautiful and well-bred young women. In October of 1982 he appeared at New York nitery Regine's with socialite Cornelia Guest on his arm. Later he turned up at Xenon, where he huddled in photo-op intimacy with actress Valerie Perrine. In November Venezuelan model Victoria Vicuna flew to Paris to meet Mick, who was in the midst of recording *Undercover.*

In the end he found that while he could fool most of the people most of the time, he could no longer fool himself. "Mick started calling," Jerry recounts. "He was really upset, wanting me to come back. He proposed marriage, said he was going to be good, he wanted to have children. He said that he realized he was being selfish wanting to go out with everyone the way he had. He was in tears, but I was in tears too."

The two met again in mid-November, even as Ms. Vicuna cooled her heels in a hotel suite. It was not all hugs and kisses. "Far from the meeting being joyful," reported gossip great Nigel Dempster in the *Daily Mail*, "Mick started at Jerry as soon as he met her at the airport. She really can't take his abuse any longer and has split. She does not want to see him again."

"Mick isn't going to stand for being humiliated by her going off," predicted a friend close to the storm center. "He just won't ever forgive her."

But Mick was no longer a young stud who could afford to casually toss off a loving, caring, and long-suffering woman like Jerry. Six months from his fortieth birthday, he began calling again. "Come home," he told Jerry. "Everything will be okay."

"So I went back," says Jerry, "and he was really, really sweet and we made up. Then we went back to the château and had a really nice time and everything came together just so wonderfully."

Or at least as wonderfully as it could be in the bewildering realm of Mick Jagger. Although he quickly reneged on his proposal of marriage, he made good on his familial vows. On March 2, 1984, Jerry bore him a daughter, Elizabeth Scarlett, at Lenox Hill Hospital in New York. Mick was present for the delivery.

"Mick was looking completely astonished," Jerry remembers. "I'd never quite seen him like that."

A year later, on August 28, he was handed his first son, James Leroy Augustin. He was now the father, or at least the father figure, for a family of four. Somehow, in spite of all the odds, he had fulfilled a dream as old as Denver Street, Dartford, County Kent.

Which is not to suggest that he's exactly settled down. Mick and Jerry would roam freely with their family, spontaneously pulling up stakes and plopping down at any one of their far-flung homes, including a Texas ranch Mick eventually bought, where Jerry indulged her own horse-raising fancy.

It was, by most accounts, an idyllic life, full of sumptuous, exorbitant pleasures and the time, at last, to enjoy them. Jerry would have still another child, Georgia May Ayeesha, born January 12, 1992, and the extended family co-exists with the monied ease and genteel decadence that is rock aristocracy's reward.

"In France," reported a friend to writer Stephen Schiff in *Vanity Fair*, "you'd have tea and there'd be a big trestle table under the trees, with children and everyone mucking in, grown-ups sharing joints maybe and Mick out in the garden."

"Everyone loves it," another frequent guest concurs. "You're staying with Mick and Jerry in France and everyone comes to the dinner table in drag and it's just huge fun. Masses of people running in and out of each other's bedroom, applying makeup to the boys. . . . It's wild upper-class house party behavior. It's nothing kinky or sexual. And Jerry has very much cottoned to this."

She has indeed. "I still want to marry Mick," she sighs, "but I'm not nagging him about it. All I really care about is our happiness."

But for Mick Jagger, happiness is still a relative proposition. His sexual appetites may have slackened, but the taste for forbidden fruit still gives him the occasional pang, as in his 1992 affair with the twenty-two-year-old heir to the Pirelli tire fortune, Carla Bruni, who would later make a play for billionaire real estate developer Donald Trump.

But it's more than the vanities of waning middle age that haunt him. There is still the tormenting need to be at the center of it all, the icon for an adoring generation of eternally young, infinitely malleable devotees, who want only to be him, to have him, to swallow him whole with their love.

Like the dreams and delusions of the sixties—forever the golden age of the rock-'n'-roll gods—such conquests would hang tantalizingly outside his grasp. He would return to films in 1992, appearing in a cheesy, instantly forgotten sci-fi potboiler called *Free Jack*. And he would return to the studio in 1993 for another solo album, this time employing the cutting edge talents of Rick Rubin, the hottest producer on the scene, who had guided such groups as the Red Hot Chili Peppers and the Black Crowes—both of whom owed an enormous stylistic debt to the Stones—to multiplatinum success.

The album, *Wandering Spirit*, while more intense and energized than its predecessors, pointed up once again the painful passage of Mick's magic. Despite considerable hype, the album struggled briefly into the Top Ten before disappearing into the white noise din of modern music.

Yet there was, on a simple, gospel-inflected track titled "Out of Focus," an intriguing clue as to Mick's own estimation of his life and times. It is, Mick confesses in the chorus, "All out of focus, it's all, baby, so unclear . . ."

In the life of Mick Jagger, the focus, it can be fairly said, is and was always on himself, his extraordinary talent, his crippling contradictions, his unwinnable battle between passion and pragmatism.

And if, in the end, the tragedy of his life is that he loved no one better than himself, it is perhaps because there are so many millions who love him for who he is.

Sources

There are many whose insight, interviews, and inspiration have made this book possible. Among them:

Jessica McPhail, whose generosity served as a foundation for all that followed.

A. E. Hotchner, for his pioneering exploration of the sixties' darkest corners.

Philip Norman, for his elegant insights.

Jerry Hall, for her unfailing charm.

Carey Schofield, for her clarity.

Massimo Bonanno, for his thoroughness.

Ian Stewart, for his honesty.

Hillel Black, for his patience.

Mel Berger, for his patience, too.

The author would also like to acknowledge: Mandy Aftel, Barbara Charone, Marianne Faithful, Georgio Gomelsky, Gered Mankowitz, Andrew Loog Oldham, Anita Pallenberg, Keith Richards, Tony Sanchez, Chrissie Shrimpton, Derek Taylor, and Bill Wyman.

BOOKS

Aftel, Mandy. *Death of a Rolling Stone: The Brian Jones Story*. London: Delilah Books, 1982.

Aldridge, John. *Satisfaction: The Story of Mick Jagger*. Rockport, Mass: Proteus Books, 1984.

Anderson, Christopher. *Jagger Unauthorized*. New York: Delacorte Press, 1993.

Benson, Joe. *Uncle Joe's Record Guide: The Rolling Stones*. Glendale, Cal.: J. Benson Unlimited, 1986.

Blake, John. *His Satanic Majesty Mick Jagger*. New York: Henry Holt, 1985.

Bockris, Victor. *Keith Richards: The Biography*. New York: Poseidon Press, 1992.

Bonanno, Massimo. *The Rolling Stones Chronicle*. New York: Henry Holt, 1990.

Booth, Stanley. *The True Adventures of the Rolling Stones*. London: Sphere Books, 1985.

Charone, Barbara. *Keith Richards*. Mount Kisco, N.Y.: Futura Publication, 1979.

Dalton, David, ed. *The Rolling Stones: The First Twenty Years*. New York: Knopf, 1981.

————, and Farren, Mick, comp. *Rolling Stones in Their Own Words*. London: Quick Fox, 1980.

Dowley, Tim. *The Rolling Stones*. New York: Hippocrene, 1983.

Ehrlich, Cindy. *The Rolling Stones*. San Francisco: Straight Arrow, 1975.

Eisen, Jonathan, ed. *Altamont*. New York: Avon, 1970.

Elliot, Martin. *The Rolling Stones: The Complete Recording Sessions*. London: Blanford, 1990.

Fitzgerald, Nicholas. *Brian Jones The Inside Story of the Original Rolling Stones*. New York: Putnam's, 1985.

Flippo, Chet, *On the Road With the Rolling Stones: Twenty Years of Lipstick, Handcuffs and Chemicals*. Garden City, N.Y.: Doubleday, 1985.

Fricke, David, and Sandall, Robert. *Rolling Stones Images of the World Tour 1989–1990*. New York: Simon & Schuster, 1990.

Goodman, Pete. *Our Own Story by the Rolling Stones*. New York: Bantam, 1970.

Greenfield, Robert. *S.T.P.: A Journey Through America With the Rolling Stones*. New York: Dutton, 1974.

Hackett, Pat. *The Andy Warhol Diaries*. New York: Warner, 1989.

Hall, Jerry, and Hemphill, Christopher. *Jerry Hall's Tall Tales*. New York: Pocket Books, 1985.

Hoffman, Dezo. *The Rolling Stones*. London: Vermillion, 1984.

Hotchner, A. E. *Blown Away*. New York: Simon & Schuster, 1990.

Hughes, William, and Cammell, Donald. *Performance*. New York: Award Books, 1970.

Jasper, Tony. *The Rolling Stones*. New York: Octopus, 1976.

Mankowitz, Gered. *Satisfaction*. New York: St. Martin's, 1984.

Marks, J. *Mick Jagger*. London: Abacus, 1973.

Miles, comp. *Mick Jagger in His Own Words*. Omnibus Press, 1982.

Moritz, Charles, ed. *Current Biography Yearbook*. Bronx, N.Y.: H. W. Wilson, 1972.

Norman, Philip. *Symphony for the Devil: The Rolling Stones Story*. New York: Simon & Schuster, 1984.

Palmer, Robert. *The Rolling Stones*. San Francisco: Rolling Stone Press, 1983.

Platt, John. *London's Rock Routes*. London: Fourth Estate, 1985.

Sanchez, Tony. *Up and Down With the Rolling Stones*. New York: William Morrow, 1979.

Scaduto, Tony. *Mick Jagger, Everybody's Lucifer*. New York: David McKay, 1974.

Schofield, Carey. *Jagger*. London: Methuen, 1983.

Southern, Terry; Leibovitz, Annie; and Sykes, Christopher. *The Rolling Stones on Tour*. London: Dragon Dream's, 1978.

Stewart, Alan, and Sanford, Cathy. *Time Is on My Side: The Rolling Stones Day-By-Day 1962–1984*. New York: Perian Press, 1984.

Weiner, Sue, and Howard, Lisa. *The Rolling Stones A to Z*. New York: Grove Press, 1983.

Wyman, Bill, with Coleman, Ray. *Stone Alone*. New York: Signet, 1990.

Index

255